Film and the
German Left in
the Weimar Republic

Film
and the German Left in the Weimar Republic

From *Caligari* to *Kuhle Wampe*

by
Bruce Murray

UNIVERSITY OF TEXAS PRESS, AUSTIN

Copyright © 1990 by the University of Texas Press
All rights reserved
Printed in the United States of America

First Edition, 1990

Requests for permission to reproduce material from this work should
be sent to Permissions, University of Texas Press, Box 7819, Austin,
Texas 78713-7819.

The publication of this book was assisted by a grant from the
Andrew W. Mellon Foundation.

♾ The paper used in this publication meets the minimum requirements
of American National Standard for Information Sciences—Permanence
of Paper for Printed Library Materials, ANSI Z39.48-1984.

Library of Congress Cataloging-in-Publication Data
Murray, Bruce Arthur.
   Film and the German left in the Weimar Republic : from Caligari to
Kuhle Wampe / by Bruce Murray,—1st ed.
     p.   cm.
   Includes bibliographical references.
   ISBN 0-292-72464-0 (alk. paper).—ISBN 0-292-72465-9 (pbk. :
alk. paper)
     1. Motion pictures—Germany—History.   2. Motion pictures—
Political aspects—Germany.   I. Title.
PN1993.5.G3M87   1990
791.43'0943—dc20
                                                   89-48354
                                                      CIP

CONTENTS

ACRONYMS AND ABBREVIATIONS

The following acronyms and abbreviations appear frequently in the text.

AIH	Aufbau, Industrie und Handels A.G.
AIZ	*Arbeiter-Illustrierte-Zeitung*
BPRS	Bund proletarisch-revolutionärer Schriftsteller
Bufa	Bild- und Filmamt
BVP	Bayrische Volkspartei
Comintern	Communist International
DDP	Deutsche Demokratische Partei
Derussa	Deutsch-Russische Film-Allianz A.G.
DNVP	Deutsch-Nationale Volkspartei
DVP	Deutsch Volkspartei
FuL	Film und Lichtbilddienst
IAH	Internationale Arbeiterhilfe
IfA	Interessengemeinschaft für Arbeiterkultur
IKD	Internationale Kommunisten Deutschlands
KPD	Kommunistische Partei Deutschlands
L.B.B.	*Lichtbild-Bühne*
MSPD	Mehrheitliche Sozialistische Partei Deutschlands
NSDAP	Nationalsozialistische Deutsche Arbeiterpartei
Prometheus	Prometheus Film-Verleih und Vertriebs-GmbH

SPD	Sozialdemokratische Partei Deutschlands
SPIO	Spitzenorganisation der Deutschen Filmindustrie
Ufa	Universum Film A.G.
VFV	Volksfilmverband
Weltfilm	Film-Kartell "Welt-Film" GmbH

ACKNOWLEDGMENTS

I would like to thank the United States Fulbright Commission, the International Research and Exchanges Board, and the Harold Leonard Memorial Film Studies Fund at the University of Minnesota for supporting my research for this book in libraries and archives in the Federal Republic of Germany, the German Democratic Republic, and Switzerland. I also would like to thank the many people at the Stiftung Deutsche Kinemathek (SDK), the Technische Universität (TU), and the Landesbildstelle in West Berlin; the Bundesarchiv in Koblenz, the Medienzentrum in Hamburg, the Deutsches Institut für Filmkunde in Wiesbaden, the Südwestfunk in Baden-Baden, the Bayrischer Rundfunk in Munich; the Staatliches Filmarchiv der DDR (SFA), the Staatsbibliothek, the Stadtbibliothek, and the Universitätsbibliothek of the Alexander von Humboldt Universität in Berlin, GDR; the Deutsche Bücherei in Leipzig, and the Stiftung Studienbibliothek zur Geschichte der Arbeiterbewegung in Zürich for their invaluable assistance in identifying and locating sources of information for my project. I especially would like to thank Werner Sudendorf and Gero Gandert at the SDK, Prof. Dr. Friedrich Knilli and Siegfried Zielinski at the TU, Prof. Dr. Gerd Röscher at the Kunsthochschule in Hamburg, Wolfgang Klaue, Manfred Lichtenstein, Gerd Meier, Gertraude Kühn, and Helmut Morsbach at the SFA, and Theo Pinkus in Zürich.

When I think back to the beginning of my work on this book, I realize that a number of other people have helped me greatly in completing it. I would like to thank Thomas Plummer, Frank Hirschbach, and Jochen Schulte-Sasse for their guidance at the University of Minnesota. I also would like to thank the colleagues who have encouraged me as I have revised the manuscript. I thank the editors at the University of Texas Press for their assistance in putting the final manuscript together. And I especially thank my wife, Gail Newman, whose continuing patience never ceases to amaze me.

I wish to dedicate the book to Gerhard Bienert, Erna Meseke/Beier, and Ilse Trautschold, three of the many individuals who possessed that indefinable something which enabled them to take risks and experiment during the Weimar era in ways that should inspire us all.

INTRODUCTION

THE FORGOTTEN STORY

At the end of 1925 a small film company emerged in Berlin to distribute a Soviet film that had failed to attract widespread acclaim in the Soviet Union. When German censors decided to forbid public screenings of the film early in 1926, a major controversy erupted, and interest in the film increased. The government finally acquiesced in the face of mass opposition to its decision, and the film premiered in Berlin's Apollo Theater on 29 April 1926. The executives of the film's fledgling distributor convinced two internationally famous film stars to attend the premiere, they and the critics raved about the film, and it ultimately became one of the best-known films in the history of cinema.

The film was Sergei Eisenstein's *Battleship Potemkin,* and the visiting film stars were Mary Pickford and Douglas Fairbanks—but who remembers the names of the film company or its executives? Why did the company work so hard to distribute a film that had failed to win acclaim in its domestic market? And what other projects did the company undertake following its unprecedented success with *Potemkin*?

Later in 1926, the same film company began the production of what it hoped would be a second commercial blockbuster. The script was based on a selection of short stories by Anton Chekov. Another Russian, Alexander Rasumny, agreed to direct the film. The company also engaged a number of stars to appear in major roles. They included, among others, Heinrich George, Werner Krauss, and Fritz Kampers. The film premiered in one of Berlin's largest movie houses, the Capitol Theater, on 2 Novem-

Battleship Potemkin: Douglas Fairbanks and Mary Pickford praise the film in the *Film-Kurier,* 7 May 1926. (Staatliches Filmarchiv der DDR)

ber 1926. Its production values should have attracted national, if not international, attention—but who can recall the film? Was this second film as successful as the first? How did the company then proceed?

The film's title was *Überflüssige Menschen* (literally, *Superfluous People*), and it was the first of many films that the tiny Prometheus Film-Verleih und Vertriebs-GmbH (Prometheus) produced and distributed commercially in Germany between 1926 and 1931. The initial Prometheus film failed to excite critics and audiences, but subsequent films did attract substantial critical acclaim. They included *Eins + Eins = Drei* (*One + One = Three,* 1927), *Schinderhannes, der Rebell vom Rhein* (*Schinderhannes, the Rebel of the Rhine,* 1927–28), *Der lebende Leichnam* (*The Living Corpse,* 1928), *Jenseits der Straße* (*Beyond the Street,* 1929), *Mutter Krausens Fahrt ins Glück* (*Mother Krause's Jour-*

ney to Happiness, 1929), and *Kuhle Wampe oder Wem gehört die Welt?* (*Kuhle Wampe or to Whom Does the World Belong?* 1931–32).

Willi Münzenberg, the leader of the Internationale Arbeiterhilfe (International Workers' Relief, IAH) and an extremely talented media man, played a central role in bringing *Potemkin* to Berlin and in organizing Prometheus. He and his associates worked fervently throughout the Weimar era to create an alternative to the dominant sources of news and entertainment, to inform Germans about the cultural changes in the Soviet Union, and to nurture the development of a proletarian culture in Germany. With Prometheus, Münzenberg hoped to challenge what he perceived as the conservative to reactionary ideological influence of mainstream commercial cinema. The German Communist party, as well as a large number of well-known intellectuals and artists, supported him. The list of individuals who contributed to Prometheus endeavors included Béla Balázs, Kurt Bernhardt, Bertolt Brecht, Slatan Dudow, Hanns Eisler, Käthe Kollwitz, Vsevolod Pudovkin, and Carl Zuckmayer.

Among the ranks of Prometheus co-workers were filmmakers who also figured prominently in the production of what have become German film classics. The director of *One + One = Three*, Béla Balázs, was one of the scriptwriters for *The Threepenny Opera* (1931). The scriptwriter for *Schinderhannes*, Carl Zuckmayer, was also a scriptwriter for *The Blue Angel* (1930). Phil Jutzi directed both *Mother Krause's Journey to Happiness* and *Berlin Alexanderplatz* (1931). Prometheus actors, cameramen, and set designers also joined the production teams of these and many other well-known German films.

In addition to Prometheus and its filmmakers, other leftist organizations and individuals contributed measurably to the development of German cinema during the second half of the 1920s. While the German Communists supported the production of Prometheus and created the Film-Kartell "Welt-Film" GmbH (Weltfilm) to coordinate film events for Communist party meetings, membership drives, and campaign programs, the Social Democratic party (SPD) supported the production of a few commercial films and operated its own Film und Lichtbilddienst (FuL) to coordinate SPD film activities. At about the same time, a nonpartisan national consumers' organization, the Volksfilmverband (VFV), emerged with prominent board members, including Leonhard Frank, Leo Lania, G. W. Pabst, and Erwin Piscator; its president was Heinrich Mann.

The VFV, too, set out to create an independent alternative to mainstream commercial cinema, complete with its own production, distribution, and screening network. The organization contributed to the production of one independent feature film and a number of documentaries. It also published a journal, *Film und Volk,* conducted public seminars on the status and potential of cinema, and developed a national system of film clubs that coordinated their own noncommercial film events. Other independent leftists imitated the efforts of the VFV. They published impressive critiques in newspapers, journals, and books, formulated manifestos for new movements in cinema, and worked within the developing institution of cinema to influence its contours.

Although various leftist individuals and groups influenced significantly the development of German cinema in the Weimar Republic, their story has for the most part been forgotten. Popular accounts of German film history, especially those of West German film historians, have included numerous retrospectives of the "Golden Years" of Weimar's mainstream cinema and imply that postwar Germany should strive to regain the glamour and glory of those years.[1] Those that do include information about the film activity of the German left refer only tangentially to films such as *Mother Krause's Journey to Happiness* and *Kuhle Wampe,* characterizing them more as curious anomalies.[2] Rarely do the films of the left appear as expressions of campaigns to compete commercially and ideologically with mainstream cinema.

POSTWAR ACCOUNTS OF WEIMAR CINEMA

The attempt to explain the lack of attention to this chapter in German film history begins in the immediate post–World War II period. After the fall of the Third Reich, the German people began the tedious process of reconstruction. For most, the primary tasks during the first years were to find adequate shelter, guarantee an ample supply of food, and begin clearing away the mountains of rubble. There was little time and perhaps even less energy available for a critical review of the cultural heritage.

When in the 1950s Germans did find the time and energy for fulfilling additional needs, the desire for commercial entertainment in the West and the exigencies of Stalinist rule in the East set the standards for film production and reception. In the Federal Republic of Germany (FRG) most filmmakers followed the Ufa tradition and competed with Hollywood for control of the West German market.[3] In the German Democratic Republic (GDR) many filmmakers who had learned their trade in Nazi Germany combined that experience with the guidelines of socialist realism to produce their films.[4] The film activity of the German left during the Weimar Republic had little influence on filmmaking in the immediate postwar era. Evidence of that activity either disappeared or gathered dust on the shelves of archives.

As reconstruction progressed, historians and sociologists began sifting through the vast intellectual rubble of the German past in search of what could be used to build and sustain a new democratic Germany. For film historians the project included a review of German cinema, from its birth to its development as an institution and its transformation into a medium for promoting and reinforcing National Socialist ideology. Some of the earliest studies became standard works of German film history, but the investigation has continued to the present.

The most frequently cited work of Siegfried Kracauer emphasized the commercial and collective quality of cinema in the Weimar Republic.[5] Kracauer argued that the dominant characteristics of Weimar cinema motivated filmmakers to appeal to the interests of Germany's largest social group, the petty bourgeoisie, and, in the process, to reflect that group's psychological composition. According to his perspective, the analysis of Weimar cinema could reveal important insights about the shared psychological dispositions that nurtured National Socialism. Consequently, he scrutinized what he considered the most significant commercial German films with great care and tended to deemphasize all other films, including those of the German left.

In their effort to demonstrate continuity between the capitalist cinema of the Weimar era, the cinema of the Third Reich, and postwar West German cinema, film historians of the GDR generally have employed Lenin's theory of two cultures to portray the history of Weimar cinema.[6] They often divide Weimar film production into corresponding categories: films of the bourgeois "dream factory," which serve a capitalist elite in its campaign to pacify a dissatisfied working class, and films of an emerging proletarian culture.[7] To be sure, East German scholars have paid some attention to the experiments of the German left during the Weimar era, but their studies often suggest a too simplistic image of powerful conservative and reactionary filmmakers who schemed to influence public opinion while stifling the German left's efforts to offer an alternative.[8] Their accounts of the overwhelming power of the largest commercial producers and the praiseworthy attempts of the Communist left to challenge mainstream cinema generally have paid inadequate attention both to the emerging institutional factors that inhibited experimentation and the mistakes of the German left.

Some of the younger West German film historians of the 1970s, similar to those in the GDR, perceived film as a medium that could be used by opposing interest groups to influence public opinion.[9] In contrast to all other historians of Weimar film, they concentrated almost exclusively on various aspects of the German left's activity in the Weimar Republic. In the majority of cases their intention was to learn from the past what would be necessary to develop a radically new approach to the film medium as an ideologically progressive alternative to the dominant "culture industry" of the West and the relatively orthodox Marxist models of the East. Although some of their studies provided more critical and differentiated accounts of the German left's film activity in the Weimar Republic, their interest waned as the student movement dissolved, and the story has remained incomplete.

FILM AS COMMODITY AND THE MARGINALITY OF LEFTIST EXPERIMENTS

Attempts to explain the lack of attention to the film activity of the German left in the Weimar Republic also require acknowledgment of its marginality. Despite the fact that talented and well-known personalities contributed to the work of Prometheus, the FuL, the VFV, and other projects, they never mounted a serious challenge to mainstream cinema. Kracauer is correct when he claims that it was Hollywood and Ufa's Babelsberg that attracted the interest of the German public in the 1920s. Their films filled the theaters and their advertisements occupied the front pages of the leading trade magazines. But is it also correct that either the psychological dispositions of the petty bourgeoisie or the "scheming" of capitalist producers in mainstream cinema alone squelched the opportunity for a leftist alternative?

As the preceding survey indicates, many possibilities remain for continuing, expanding, and further differentiating the search for information about the relationship between cinema and social development in the Weimar Republic. This study contributes to the process. By reviewing the emergence of a cinematic institution in Germany between 1918 and 1933 (focusing above all on German films and film journalism), it attempts to pinpoint the factors that determined commercial cinema's quality. It outlines the relationship between commercial film production and reception and considers the influence of that relationship on the social structures that generate ideological standpoints, as well as ideological content. It also provides a context for the primary topic of investigation: the efforts of various groups within the German left to compete ideologically with mainstream cinema by producing commercial films and establishing non-commercial alternatives.[10]

At approximately the same time Kracauer's work appeared, Swiss sociologist Peter Bächlin completed his study of film's status as a commodity. Bächlin, like Kracauer, asserted the primacy of economic factors for the quality of film production and the relationship between production and reception (11−18). Both argued that the profit motive significantly influences the selection of subjects for production, the manner in which the subjects are treated, and ultimately the quality of interaction between filmmakers, films, and film audiences. But Bächlin outlined the development of mainstream cinema in greater detail than Kracauer and provided a wealth of empirical evidence to support his claims. In contrast to Kracauer, who relied to a large extent on personal experience and the film libraries at the Museum of Modern Art and Library of Congress, Bächlin based his work more on sociological studies and the statistical reports compiled by the film industry.

According to Bächlin, commercial filmmakers produce commodities to create an exchange value. To increase the exchange value of their commodities, they strive to minimize production costs and maximize the use value for the film audience. He suggests that entertainment is the fundamental use value of commercial cinema (162).

The commodity character of commercial cinema has nurtured what Bächlin refers to as the standardization of film production (164). As early as the first decade of the twentieth century, filmmakers in Europe and in the United States realized that one of the easiest and most reliable methods for minimizing production costs and maximizing the probability of box-office success was to measure the commercial strength of earlier films and to imitate them. Producers measured the success of specific plots and subject matter, then determined which actors appealed most, engaged them with large salaries, and marketed them as stars. The result was the establishment of popular film genres and the birth of the star system. The same considerations influenced the selection of literary models, directors, and other crew members.

Bächlin discovered that as filmmakers refined and expanded their techniques for standardizing production, the degree of artistic cooperation and experimentation decreased. More democratic, heterogeneous, and spontaneous elements gave way to autocratic, homogeneous, and extremely well-calculated forms of production. By relying on a relatively small group of established filmmakers, film companies restricted the number of people who could contribute significantly to the production process; independent contributions decreased as the process of standardization continued. In addition to regulating the degree of deviation from proven plotlines and subjects, companies developed libraries of typical scenes that could be edited into a film and constructed interchangeable backdrops to be used and reused. Production managers rigidly adhered to schedules, and this variety of factors made the production process far more autocratic than democratic, further inhibiting experimentation and creativity.

Of greater ideological significance for Bächlin was the commercial film industry's emphasis on cinematic entertainment. He explained that while imitating with only minor deviations the plots of commercially successful films and marketing stars, producers developed additional strategies to ensure the broadest possible appeal for their films. Like Kracauer, he believed that producers concentrated on the entertainment needs of the largest social class—the petty bourgeoisie. He also argued that filmmakers did everything possible to avoid addressing social, political, religious, and other issues that might please one social group and disturb another (189–193). According to Bächlin, the desire of filmmakers to avoid controversy solidified and strengthened conservative social trends. Although he never precisely explained how the process functioned, one might infer that cinema does so simply by distracting attention from social issues, thus inhibiting the process of democratic social change.

It was not until the 1970s that Dieter Prokop, borrowing from the works of Theodor Adorno, Max Horkheimer, Herbert Marcuse, and Wilhelm Reich, outlined in much greater detail the quality of cinematic entertainment and its influence on the generation and maintenance of ideology within a specific sociohistorical context. Prokop proceeds from the premise that societies develop around strategies to fulfill the material and psychological needs of their members and that mass culture (including cinema) contributes to the establishment of the dominant strategies in modern Western societies (2).

Prokop's first major claim about the ideological quality of film production is that it excludes the majority of society's members from participating in the development of such strategies. Like Bächlin, Prokop asserts that economic considerations determine the quality of film production and reception (3). However, while affirming Kracauer's focus on economic factors, Prokop restates and expands Bächlin's challenge to claims about commercial film's reflection of a collective mentality. He suggests that the desire to maximize profit bureaucratizes the process of production, privileging the positions of producers and production managers while minimizing spontaneous and cooperative artistic experimentation. According to Prokop, the number of people who contribute significantly to the process of production decreases further as the number of production companies decreases. His historical outline characterizes the quality of German cinema as monopolistic as early as 1930 (17).

The most provocative insights of Prokop's work describe the relationship between cinematic entertainment and the regressive elements of the petty-bourgeois mentality (11–34). He maintains that although the overwhelming majority of people never participate directly in film production, the potential exists for everyone to participate in generating ideological standpoints as emotionally engaged and intellectually critical recipients of cinematic material. Yet, according to Prokop, existing cinematic institutions inhibit the critical participation of recipients. Like his predecessors, he asserts that the formula for commercial success motivates producers to focus selectively on the entertainment needs of the petty bourgeoisie. He continues, by citing Wilhelm Reich's concept of a schizophrenic human psyche, claiming that individuals constantly vacillate between progressive and regressive positions and that cinematic entertainment reinforces the regressive positions (6, 27–34).

Prokop bases his explanation of cinematic entertainment's quality on a variation of Freudian perceptions. Instead of referring to the id, ego, and superego, he posits an image of human beings as spontaneous producers of material and psychological needs that are modified, redirected, and/or suppressed by the principle of what is realistically achievable and socially acceptable. For the petty bourgeoisie, experiences at the workplace, in the world of commerce, and in other socializing institutions modify and suppress the need for spontaneity, innovation, productivity, and meaningful social interaction, translating these needs into the desire for competitive success, upward social mobility, consumerism, and security. As a result, the individual simultaneously yearns for freedom from the experience of monotony, subservience, and automation, while fearing the consequences of deviating from the norm, thus jeopardizing the opportunity for success and security.

According to Prokop, cinematic entertainment considers the conflict between the unreflected needs of the petty bourgeoisie and their perceived principles of reality and social acceptability. It responds to the regressive needs that emerge from the conflict. He argues that instead of providing spectators with an opportunity to contemplate the cinematic experience collectively in an effort to develop ideological strategies, commercial cinema encourages them, via emotional identification with fictional figures, to artificially satisfy and then reproduce regressive needs without threatening their integration within society (27–28). Whether filmmakers employ narrative techniques of cinematic realism or contrapuntal montage, by adhering to the formula for commercial success, they stimulate the development of autocratic structures for the generation of ideological viewpoints. They discourage individuals from participating cooperatively either in producing films or in considering their significance for the development and maintenance of the strategies they practice for social interaction.

Five fundamental claims about the relationship between film production and the production of ideology in modern Western societies emerge from Bächlin's and Prokop's work:

1. The quality of film production and distribution depends primarily on economic considerations;
2. Film production within monopolistic systems, or in systems with tendencies toward monopolization, stifles spontaneous, productive, and cooperative interaction;
3. Commercial cinematic entertainment responds to and, to a large extent, fosters the abstract, regressive needs of petty-bourgeois film spectators;
4. The aesthetic form of cinematic entertainment minimizes the possibility for critical and cooperative reception;
5. The potential for alternatives to established cinematic institutions remains limited as long as film retains its quality as a commodity.

This study analyzes to what degree these claims accurately describe the quality of the developing cinematic institution in Germany between 1918 and 1933. It attempts to answer the following questions: Did economic factors significantly influence the quality of film production? What other factors influenced production? Was the quality of film production experimental and cooperative or calculated and autocratic? Did commercial cinematic entertainment focus only on satisfying the regressive needs of the petty bourgeoisie? What were the dominant aesthetic forms of cinema, and how did they influence reception? What attempts were made to establish alternatives to mainstream cinema, and what factors determined the relative success and failures of such attempts? And how do the answers to these questions facilitate a better understanding of the film activity of the German left in the Weimar Republic? While presenting information and positing viewpoints, the study encourages further discussion about the relationship between cinema and social development in the Weimar Republic and in other modern Western cultures.

PART ONE

THE BIRTH OF GERMAN CINEMA AND ITS DEVELOPMENT DURING THE POSTWAR CRISIS: 1919–1923

During the last half of the nineteenth century and at the beginning of the twentieth, Germany experienced an industrial revolution and emerged as a world power. German scientists invented the electric dynamo, improved various liquid fuel engines, and contributed to other technical innovations, including those in cinema. By 1895, at about the time the Colonial Union, Pan-German League, and Navy League were conducting imperialist propaganda campaigns, cinematic technology had developed sufficiently so that the Skladanowsky brothers could demonstrate their "Bioscop" in the Berlin Wintergarten.[1]

While commercial cinema slowly established its institutional foundation during the initial decades of the twentieth century, religious, educational, political, and even military organizations recognized film's mass appeal and began using it for ideological purposes. When members of the German left began to formulate their policy toward the medium following World War I, they referred to cinematic practice before 1919. At least initially, they borrowed from that heritage what they could use in building their own film programs.

1896–1918: FROM COUNTRY ROADS TO MAIN STREET AND THE DISCOVERY OF FILM BY POLITICAL INTEREST GROUPS

During the first ten years of its development, German cinema was characterized by the *Wanderkino* (traveling theater).[1] Theater owners purchased films directly from a producer and showed them in tents to small audiences in numerous cities, until the films literally fell apart. The viewing time was about twenty minutes, and the films were little more than a novelty. At first the new medium attracted all social classes. After the initial curiosity subsided, the middle and upper classes generally rejected film, condemning it as artistically inferior to literature and theater. Cinema's early success was due chiefly to the sustained interest of the working class in an inexpensive form of entertainment.

Between 1906 and 1914 German cinema gradually developed a foundation. The desire to maximize profit motivated much of the development, as filmmakers strove to produce more efficiently and increase the medium's appeal. Wealthier entrepreneurs built permanent theaters with larger seating capacities and ornate decor. Instead of selling their films, producers organized distribution companies and rented films for presentation within a limited area and for a limited time. More successful companies became active in production, distribution, and theater ownership. They also began exporting their films.

The most successful companies prospered by producing films with a mass appeal. To sustain the interest of the working class, they made some films focusing on the lives and problems of workers. By producing film versions of popular plays, the industry hoped to attract the skeptical middle and upper classes.[2] In addition to adaptations of plays, film versions of popular novels, legends, and fairy tales also appeared, including *Der Student von Prag (The Student of Prague, 1913)*.

The developing industry reinforced and prolonged artistic and social trends by institutionalizing other changes. Producers began paying large salaries to actors who had already won public acclaim, especially in the theater, and marketed them as film "stars."[3] By nurturing a cinematic elite, film companies enabled a select number of actors to become role models for moviegoers. The wealth and prestige granted to film stars, although at first conceived only as a means to attract larger audiences, motivated spectators to think, act, and even dress like their heroes and heroines did on the screen. Producers also repeated popular themes. In addition to choosing attractive stories from other narrative forms, they quickly learned that by repeating the plots of successful films, with slight variations, they could reduce the risk of commercial failure. Once *The Student of Prague* succeeded, films with a similar thematic orientation, including *Der Golem* (1915) and *Homunculus* (1916), soon followed. The stars could play almost the same role in many such films and thus increased their potential influence on movie audiences.

As the German institution of cinema took shape, so too did the campaign to control its social impact. Between 1896 and 1906 several civic and religious groups tried to boycott film theaters because of what they described as film's damaging effect on moral standards. By 1908 most critics had abandoned attempts to discourage visits to movie theaters. Instead, they organized cinema reform movements and demanded higher moral and artistic standards.[4] The reformers cited religious and aesthetic concepts of morality, focusing on metaphysical ideals of the Good and Beautiful. They argued that films generally portrayed secular themes and, consequently, were unable to communicate anything about metaphysical ideals. Most critics agreed that film would never be an art form. Given the medium's ability to present what they perceived as an accurate image of everyday reality, reformers concluded that film would be best suited for use in the classroom, for example in natural science courses.

In perhaps the most concise summary of cinema's use by public interest groups prior to World War I, Social Democrat Dr. Samuel Drucker suggested that conservative politics often motivated demands for higher moral and artistic standards, as well as attempts to restrict cinema to the classroom. Drucker's article "Das Kinoproblem und unsere politischen Gegner" ("The Cinema Problem and Our Political Opponents") was the first to document the use of film by religious groups, government offices, and other interest groups. He argued convincingly that they all supported (some subtly and others blatantly) the Reich's nationalist and imperialist policies.

Drucker began with comments on the Catholic church's use of the film medium, referring specifically to the association between the Lichtbilderei film company in Mönchen-Gladbach and the Volksverein für das Katholische Deutschland (People's Association for a Catholic Germany). The association, whose purpose was to combat subversion and to defend the Christian order, had used film in its programs for some time. Drucker asserted that although no official ties existed, the association agitated directly for the Catholic Center party. In most cases the Catholic Center defended the political and social status quo and condemned social democracy.

Drucker also noted the Evangelical church's ideologically conservative film activity, highlighting the work of Pastor Walter Conradt. As leader of the Evangelical theater reform movement, Pastor Conradt had revealed his intentions in a book entitled *Kirche und Kinematograph* (*Church and Cinematographer,* 1910). Conradt proposed that cinema serve the Church in its missionary work, while at the same time filling Germans with enthusiasm for their kaiser and fatherland.

Government offices also employed film to strengthen social stability at the beginning of the century. According to Drucker, a commission of representatives from local governments in Westphalia, which convened in Münster to organize its own theater movement in 1912, promoted German nationalism: "It recommends, among other things, the use of movie theaters to serve *national* interests, and if the establishment of such theaters on the local level is impossible, then it recommends that all *patriotic and/or religious* organizations unite to establish them." [5] Drucker also cited the activity of the Magdeburg Teacher's Association and its cinema commission as a clear example of film's exploitation for conservative political purposes. The commission organized celebrations of the Battle of Sedan and the kaiser's birthday, including short films about the army and navy. Drucker explained that the celebrations stressed to students the importance of loyalty to the Reich and the necessity of defending the fatherland against potential foreign aggressors.

The article concluded with information about the use of film by blatantly patriotic and imperialist groups such as the Gesellschaft für die Verbreitung der Volksbildung (Society for the Cultivation of People's Education) and the Navy League. The former, a National Liberal organization, led by Prince Heinrich zu Schönaich-Carolath, developed an extensive program for film production and distribution. It produced texts to accompany its films and distributed them to a wide variety of groups, including 144 military and veterans organizations. In 1912 it also began operating a traveling theater and established a film archive. According to Drucker, the society received financial support indirectly from the kaiser and supported his policies enthusiastically. The Navy League, which was financed by the navy and the weapons industry, primarily Krupp, incorporated films into its propaganda campaign to build up the navy.

The purpose of Drucker's article was to stimulate the SPD's interest in the film medium by demonstrating the widespread film activity of its political opponents. But the Social Democrats remained skeptical. The Berlin SPD newspaper, *Vorwärts,* often echoed the voice of the cinema reformers, complaining that film damaged the spiritual and moral education of the youth. (See *Vorwärts,* 28 September 1910, for example.) It was not until 1912 that the SPD began differentiating its position in its *Winke und Ratschläge* (*Hints and Suggestions*) and advocated the use of film in its educational programs.[6] At the SPD Party Congress in 1913, the Zentralbildungsausschuß (Central Education Committee) restated its intention to use film, but it accomplished almost nothing before the war. In the spring of 1914 Drucker could document only sixty-two film events that had been organized by the SPD in twenty-seven towns.

THE SPD AND CINEMA PRIOR TO WORLD WAR I

The Social Democratic party's slow recognition of film's significance and its initial emphasis on pedagogical applications reflected its approach to culture in general. During the first decades of its existence, the SPD developed an extensive political apparatus while paying relatively little attention to cultural work.[7] Despite its continued emphasis on political work at the end of the century, the SPD did develop a cultural program between 1890 and 1914. The program was to a large extent a response to the exclusion of the working class from the Reich's educational and cultural institutions.[8] The SPD reacted first and foremost by affirming the existing institution of art and striving to guarantee equal access to it for working-class constituents.

The Social Democrats established courses to introduce workers to the philosophical and literary heritage, and the party founded cultural organizations for workers to cultivate their artistic awareness and raise their intellectual level. In other words, much of the SPD's cultural program concentrated on enabling workers to understand the existing institution of art and appreciate its products. It did far less to encourage workers to question aesthetic norms and establish their own.

The educational background of early SPD cultural activists offers one potential explanation for their conservative cultural policy. Most of them, in contrast to rank-and-file Social Democrats, did attend secondary schools. Many continued their studies at universities. Higher education introduced them to the dominant concept of autonomous art, and numerous young Social Democratic students accepted the concept uncritically.[9]

Journalists for *Die Neue Zeit,* such as Eduard Bernstein, Heinrich Stoebel, David Bach, Friedrich Stampfer, and Franz Diderich, together with numerous others who followed the strategy outlined above, relied for the most part on purely aesthetic criteria to evaluate art. They overlooked art's ideological significance. Consequently, they were unable to reveal systematically the ways in which art could function to support the social structures of the Wilhelminian Reich.[10]

With this in mind, the SPD's approach to the film medium becomes understandable. Most SPD journalists merely assimilated the concept of autonomous art and characterized film as artistically inferior to theater and literature. Fritz Eisner, another journalist for *Die Neue Zeit,* exemplified the tendency in "Das Kinodrama" ("The Film Drama," June 1913:460–463). From his perspective, the dramatic illusion of reality was nothing more than a "poor carnival trick" in comparison to the attempt of art to "grasp the spirit of the universe" and give it physical shape. If that were not the case, Eisner suggested, then artists would be helpless to compete with the accomplishments of filmmakers such as Gaumont and Pathé. As it was, he argued, technology threatened to "suffocate" art by willingly fulfilling the public's desire for the illusion of reality.

According to Eisner, the film medium's weakness lay in its inability to do anything more than reproduce movements of everyday reality. To transcend the superficiality of that reality and to lend form to affirmed metaphysical concepts, he asserted, art required words. Cinema was forced to rely on gestures, "a kind of deaf and dumb language that was completely unable to express abstract concepts" (461).

If one accepts Eisner's premise, it follows that workers, who visited movie theaters frequently, were abandoning the attempt to attain more than a superficial understanding of the world around them. According to him, the only way for workers to transcend such superficiality and gain insight into the metaphysical realm was to integrate themselves into the cultural fabric of the existing society: they should reject cinema and embrace the cultural heritage of literature and theater.

Although he rejected the claims of those who ascribed artistic quality to film, Eisner did perceive a significant use for the medium. Like some representatives of the cinema reform movement, he proposed that film be used to increase the human capacity to control nature and society. Precisely because the camera could fix reality in the cinematic image and present it for empirical observation, Eisner suggested that cinema could aid scientists and students in their attempt to understand and influence natural phenomena (462–463).

The Central Education Committee, with its gradual recognition of film's significance, demonstrated that Eisner's belief in instrumental reason and cinema's role in its acquisition was widespread within the SPD. Without questioning dominant standards of education, it considered how cinema could be integrated into the educational program. In addition to aiding workers in learning to appreciate classical drama, film could assist in providing workers with the technical knowledge necessary to find employment in Germany's growing industrial sector. Only after four years of war, fought with the deadly new weapons developed by modern technology, did anyone in the SPD begin to question the zeal with which humanity strove to instrumentalize nature and manipulate social development.

GERMAN CINEMA DURING WORLD WAR I

World War I contributed dramatically to the development of German cinema. At the end of 1914 the popularity of French and English films diminished, and in 1917 the Allied blockade cut U.S. access to the German market. At the same time, the war's burden on soldiers and civilians increased their need for entertainment. Film studios sprang up everywhere. Initially the industry emphasized the production of patriotic films to capitalize on the sentiment created by the various propaganda campaigns and by the government's explanation of the war effort as national defense. Until 1915, such films experienced great success. Once the trenches were dug and the reality of attrition warfare struck home, patriotic films quickly gave way to others—chiefly, detective and criminal films.

During the final years of World War I, economic and political forces became involved directly with the German film industry. Industrial and government leaders created new film organizations to influence public opinion. The activity began in 1916 when the director of Krupp Industries, Alfred Hugenberg, and shipping magnate Ludwig Klitzsch organized Deulig (Deutsche Lichtbildgesellschaft, German Motion Picture Company). They intended to promote Germany's economy, culture, and tourist industry, at home and abroad. Deulig's films defended the war effort, while the military made increasing demands on the economy and required even greater sacrifices from the populace. The films simultaneously challenged French and English propaganda by presenting a favorable image of Germany abroad.

At the end of 1916 direct ideological involvement in German cinema increased. As the war dragged on, the German High Command decided to form Bufa (Bild-und-Filmamt, Photo and Film Office). According to the Military Press Agency's pamphlet *Das Bild- und Film-Amt und seine Aufgaben* (*The Film and Photo Office and Its Tasks*), the office's purpose was to serve the national interest, i.e., promote the war effort.[11]

The author of the pamphlet, a Dr. Wagner, attempted to legitimize Bufa's activity by referring to the enemy's film propaganda. Just as conservatives had focused on the threat of foreign aggressors to convince the Germans of the need to enter the war, the pamphlet mentioned neither German film propaganda before the war nor the early commercial patriotic films. Instead, it cited over a dozen cases of foreign film propaganda, arguing that Bufa's goal must be to defend Germany against any damaging effect. The presentation drew the public's attention from Germany's own nationalist and imperialist interests by creating uncritical black-and-white images of the relationship between Germany and its enemies.

The proposed method for influencing public opinion included a new element. Cinema's early critics had almost unanimously condemned its tendency to stimulate emotion because of its potentially negative effect on moral behavior. Although aware of such criticism, the Military Press Agency argued that under the prevailing circumstances the ends justified the means. If the film's emotional impact created an irrational hatred for the enemy and equally irrational loyalty to the fatherland, it deserved praise.

Bufa's activity included the collection and distribution of feature, military, and educational films. It relied on commercial cinema as a source for feature and educational films, but employed seven film crews to work on the front collecting film footage for its own military films. It also established an office to monitor foreign propaganda and to control German film imports and exports.

The government's involvement with cinema accelerated further in 1917. As the war continued and dissatisfaction increased, the Supreme High Command, under the leadership of Field Marshal Paul von Hindenburg and General Erich Ludendorff, slowly transformed Germany into a military dictatorship. Ludendorff also took steps to gain control of the film industry. In a letter to the Imperial War Ministry dated 4 July 1917, Ludendorff argued that Germany must act to influence public opinion at home and to diminish the effect of its enemies' film propaganda abroad.[12]

Following meetings in October with various government institutions, the Deutsche Bank, and Bufa, the Supreme High Command moved to consolidate the film industry under its control on 18 December 1917. A single large film company emerged, the Universum Film A.G., or Ufa. According to Ludendorff's propaganda and press officer Major Grau, Ufa was to accomplish three goals: to aid the High Command in carrying out its military goals; to be an instrument for political influence abroad; and to provide a defense against the propaganda work of the enemy within Germany.

The military's efforts created Germany's largest, most powerful film conglomerate. Ufa subsumed the leading companies in every branch of the industry, including Nordisk, the Messter conglomerate, and Davidson's Produktion A.G. Union. Major investors included the Deutsche Bank and the German Reich. The board of directors was comprised of representatives from the shipping industry, the electronics industry, the banking community, the aristocracy, and the military. Although Ufa was organized too late to influence the outcome of World War I, it brought together leaders of the most conservative circles of German society. The company remained intact as a private enterprise following the war and served as a powerful ideological instrument during the first years of the Weimar Republic.

2

1919–1923: THE "GOLDEN YEARS"

On 9 November 1918 Prince Max von Baden announced the kaiser's abdication and gave the Majority Social Democrats (MSPD) an opportunity to organize their own government.[1] The party accepted the challenge. However, instead of initiating the revolutionary change that had been the focus of Social Democratic platforms throughout the second half of the nineteenth century, MSPD leaders worked closely with the existing social institutions to maintain order and legitimize their rule. Their decisions to cooperate with the monarchist military and civil service facilitated the political reaction that characterized the next four years. While the Social Democrats and representatives of other bourgeois parties crafted a constitution that minimized political and economic change, reactionary military leaders felt free to organize Freikorps units. Conservative judges imposed light sentences on right-wing murderers but extremely harsh sentences for lesser crimes on leftist revolutionaries. Many educators promoted nationalist ideals and gave special treatment to students from conservative backgrounds. While these measures were thwarting revolutionary change, industrialists rebuilt and expanded their spheres of influence.

Within this context the commercial film industry continued to grow. Capitalist competition, conservative and reactionary political perspectives, neoromanticism, and expressionism contributed significantly to the emerging cinematic institution. Methods of production, distribution, and reception that had been initiated between 1906 and 1918 now became standards and provided a framework for further development.

Between 1919 and 1923, while the German economy faltered, the commercial film industry flourished. Germany's weakening currency enabled German companies to produce films inexpensively and to market them at low prices abroad. The profit they created by accumulating strong foreign currency was much greater than that of companies in industries that relied primarily on the German market with its weak currency. Established filmmakers accelerated the production of exportable films, and new companies emerged with the same intentions.

Despite favorable export conditions, all branches of the industry struggled to remain competitive at home.[2] A decisive factor in the process was the transition to feature-length entertainment films. The trend toward adapting theater productions and literature had resulted in an increase in the length of films to between one and two hours. Other contributing factors included the developing star system and the popularity of historical pageants with extravagant sets and costumes. Longer films, growing salaries, and the price of developing more elaborate studios greatly increased production costs. Consequently, producers demanded higher prices for film rights from distributors, and distributors passed on the cost to theater owners. The increased film length also restricted the number of daily showings and the potential daily profit. To offset the effect, theater owners increased ticket prices and began constructing palatial theaters: the largest could seat over a thousand.

Another effect of rising production costs was a change in contract negotiations for film rights. Distributors and theater owners traditionally waited to measure the initial success of a film before purchasing the right to show it. Producers now forced theater owners to sign contracts for groups of films before or during production. This made possible production that was otherwise too costly and guaranteed distribution. For distributors and theater owners the problem resulting from a shortage of feature films was eliminated, but they were forced to commit themselves to films for which there was no guarantee of commercial success. As costs continued to rise, competition intensified, and smaller companies perished. Competition also led to mergers within and between various branches of the industry.[3]

In addition to mergers, the increasing association between film companies and investors from the banking world, heavy industry, the publishing industry, and, finally, from the state characterized the cinema of the early Weimar years. Of the leading companies, Ufa was associated with the Deutsche Bank, Dresdner Bank, A.E.G., Hapag Lloyd, and representatives of the military; Deulig was the creation of Hugenberg and

Klitzsch; Terra had connections with the influential Ullstein Publishing House; and Phöbus was temporarily financed by a secret fund of the German War Ministry.[4]

While capitalist competition led to concentration and enabled a relatively small number of individuals and groups to occupy influential positions in the film industry, republican forces struggled to rebuild Germany's economy. The wartime government's fiscal irresponsibility and the overwhelming demands imposed on the German economy by the Versailles Treaty made it extremely difficult for the first postwar governments to pay Germany's debts and rebuild the economy. Between 1919 and 1924 the government responded to growing inflation by printing more and more currency, and inflation rose to astronomical levels. Inflation, widespread unemployment, and reparations payments made it impossible for German citizens to satisfy their material needs. Citizens who watched the purchasing power of their salaries dwindle and those who had no paychecks at all found little consolation in their newly acquired democratic rights. Many of them longed for the relative prosperity of Wilhelminian Germany and associated that prosperity with the old form of government.

As the economy weakened, antirepublican groups grew. Simultaneously, some within the film industry developed a new model for expressing political attitudes. Men such as Rudolf Pabst encouraged producers to follow the example of foreign filmmakers who already had begun integrating ideology and entertainment consciously. In an article published in January 1920, Pabst outlined the potentially subtle influence of feature films. He posited action, suspense, and subtlety as the essential components of cinematic propaganda.[5] At least some commercial filmmakers seemed to follow Pabst's line of thinking and gave preferential treatment to conservative and sometimes reactionary themes. The industry characteristically neglected the ideology of the political left.

Fridericus Rex provides a good example. The film was typical of historical pageants, which, under the guise of historical realism, provided metaphors for contemporary crises and valorized conservative or reactionary solutions. Ufa produced *Fridericus Rex* in 1922, at a time when, in addition to its ties to the banking world and industry, military officers still served on the board of directors. The film portrayed the Prussian monarch Friedrich II as a military genius and patriarchal hero who might have been more successful in the Seven Years' War if his supporters had not abandoned him. The film was set in eighteenth-century Prussia, but parallels to twentieth-century Germany and Wilhelm II were clear. *Fri-*

Fridericus Rex: the monarch as military genius and patriarchal hero. (Staatliches Filmarchiv der DDR)

dericus Rex alluded to the German public's abandonment of the kaiser in World War I, suggesting that the Germans would have been victorious and might have avoided their postwar problems had they remained loyal to the monarchy.

Films with an expressionist style, too, could be perceived to promote a conservative perspective.[6] *Das Cabinet des Dr. Caligari* (*The Cabinet of Dr. Caligari*), produced by Decla Bioscop in 1919, paved the way. The film is significant for three reasons. It illustrates the autocratic quality of mainstream film production, the conservative orientation of executives, and the potential influence of commercial films on public opinion. As has been cited frequently, the producer and director exerted their authority to alter the script (Kracauer, 64–67). They feared that the unsympathetic portrayal of its central figure would disturb spectators and jeopardize the film's success. In contrast to the original script, which portrayed Caligari as the tyrannical head of a mental institution, the film portrayed him as a benevolent authority to whom the healing of a mad and chaotic society could be entrusted. The juxtaposition of order and

chaos in *The Cabinet of Dr. Caligari* almost certainly motivated associations with the struggle between republican and antirepublican forces in the immediate postwar period and privileged the antirepublican position by valorizing authority.[7]

The success of *The Cabinet of Dr. Caligari* motivated other film companies to produce similar films. Instead of stimulating critical thought and encouraging audiences to contemplate democratic forms of social interaction, expressionist-style films drew attention away from everyday reality, focused it on psychological phenomena, and promoted an irrational, conservative, and sometimes even apocalyptic world view. Some advocated obedience to a strong authoritarian figure (*The Cabinet of Dr. Caligari*). Others offered a mystical ray of hope for better times to come (*Nosferatu*, 1922). Still others identified revolutionary activity with chaos and tyranny: *Vanina* (1922) and *Dr. Mabuse, der Spieler* (*Dr. Mabuse, the Gambler*, 1922).

Although many other film genres emerged between 1919 and 1924, the so-called *Aufklärungsfilme* (allegedly educational films about sexuality that producers marketed as personal hygiene films, i.e., to combat venereal disease, etc.) had an especially profound effect on German cinema's subsequent development. Even before the Weimar Republic emerged in 1919, the Council of People's Representatives took steps to abolish the monarchy's censorship laws. Commercial filmmakers moved quickly to exploit their new freedom by producing *Aufklärungsfilme* with the claim that sexual enlightenment should now enter the public sphere. In most cases the plots of the films centered around prostitution.

Aufklärungsfilme functioned indirectly to support the moral and political status quo. Films with titles like *Brautnacht im Walde* (*Wedding Night in the Woods*), *Liebe, die sich frei verschenkt* (literally, *Love That Gives Itself for Free*), and *Das Mädchen und die Männer* (*The Maiden and the Men*) attracted large audiences because they appealed to the sexual fantasies created by the constraints of conventional morality.[8] Such films did little to call into question the values of the traditional patriarchal and Christian moral system or to initiate discussions about the need for social change. In most cases, they contributed to the ongoing repression of material and emotional needs among spectators who accepted conventional moral norms. They did so by inviting them to sympathize with fictional characters who engaged in socially unacceptable forms of sexual activity and were punished for it.

While diverting attention from social change, the *Aufklärungsfilme* also provided the Weimar government with a pretext for regulating film

The Cabinet of Dr. Caligari: Caligari—mad scientist or benevolent authority? (Stiftung Deutsche Kinemathek)

Nosferatu: submission to authority with a mystical ray of hope. (Stiftung Deutsche Kinemathek)

production. In May 1920 the National Assembly reintroduced censorship by passing the Motion Picture Law. In addition to prohibiting pornographic films, the law called for the censorship of films that endangered public order, Germany's reputation, or its relations with foreign countries. These broadly formulated guidelines enabled censors to mask political judgments as aesthetic judgments. Due to the generally conservative makeup of most Weimar censorship boards, the revolutionary left faced stiffer censorship than the radical right.[9] Commercial films with subtle—and sometimes not so subtle—conservative and reactionary ideological orientation were overlooked. Some even enjoyed special tax exemption.

3

THE SPD AND FILM: FROM CALLS FOR REFORM TO AFFIRMATION OF CINEMATIC ENTERTAINMENT AND EDIFICATION

Reactions to the *Aufklärungsfilme* and other films published in *Vorwärts* and *Die Neue Zeit* reveal that the Social Democratic approach to the film medium had changed little during the war years. While government and military leaders had begun to use cinema in support of Germany's war effort, the SPD neglected such cultural activity. Between 1919 and 1924, the party resumed its prewar cultural policy and reaffirmed its allegiance to autonomous art with few exceptions.

"Ein verfilmtes Buch" ("A Filmed Book," *Vorwärts,* 16 January 1920), for example, bemoaned the adaptation of a book: "The book had become a genre film for adults only. Nothing remained of the spiritual depth, nothing of the lofty goals, nothing of the music of the future, only grimaces and brutal action in the visual medium, only sensual teasing." The references to "lofty goals" of literature and the "sensual teasing" of cinema succinctly express the SPD's continuing affirmation of a bourgeois idealism that disdained any connection between art and everyday life.

While most SPD journalists advocated the separation of art and everyday life, they did perceive a connection between aesthetics and morality. *Vorwärts* articles with titles such as "Gegen den Kinoschund" ("In Opposition to Cinematic Trash," 19 October 1919) argued that the *Aufklärungsfilme* reinforced low cultural and artistic standards. Such articles never questioned the dominant concepts of the patriarchal family and the repressive models for relationships between men and women. Instead, they affirmed conventional morality, promoted various methods of reform, and, consequently, affirmed existing structures of familial and social authority.

One of the proposed methods of reform illustrates well the contradiction between the SPD's revolutionary political heritage and its conservative cultural program. In addition to suggesting community theater programs and new censorship laws to control film quality, some journalists argued that the only way to stop cinema's morally damaging effect was to nationalize the industry. Leading members of the SPD supported this revolutionary idea and submitted two proposals to the National Assembly in May 1920.[1] The effort by some SPD members to nationalize the film industry was motivated by an uncritical affirmation of conventional morality, but their arguments *were* based on a new critical perception.

For the first time, individuals within the party began to draw a connection between *Schundfilme* (trashy films) and the interests of private capital. Shortly before the Motion Picture Law was passed, an article appeared in *Vorwärts* entitled "Die Veredelung des Films" ("The Refinement of Film," 7 February 1920). The article expressed some of the same ideas Dr. Samuel Drucker had formulated about the quality of films in 1913. Both argued that the dramatic film satisfied the entertainment needs of workers who had neither the energy nor the inclination to read a book or see a play after a long day on the job. They also agreed that entertainment films had a negative influence on social morality. However, the author of "The Refinement of Film" went on to suggest not that films were by nature morally damaging but that the profit motive determined film quality.

Once the Weimar government moved to censor undesirable *Aufklärungsfilme,* efforts to nationalize the film industry ceased, and the number of articles on film in the SPD press dropped significantly. During the next four years, long periods passed without any significant contributions on cinema. In *Die Neue Zeit* only three essays on film appeared between 1919 and 1923.[2] Even in Berlin, the film capital of Germany, the SPD *Vorwärts* devoted most of its *feuilleton* section to discussions of recent theater premieres and popular novels. The newspaper had initiated a *Filmschau* for reviews late in 1919, but contributions were for the most part descriptive and superficial. Most reviewers expressed their judgments in vague and purely subjective aesthetic terms. They rarely differentiated ideologically at all.

Articles like "The Refinement of Film," which criticized the influence of cinematic entertainment on receptive, working-class audiences by referring to commercial interests, remained infrequent exceptions. *Vorwärts* journalists surprisingly often accepted the "dream factory" quality of commercial cinema and criticized filmmakers for marketing films with only a minimal entertainment value. A review of *Das Haus zum Monde* (*The House on the Moon*) on 30 January 1921, for example, criticized what we would call science-fiction films from this perspective. The reviewer remained skeptical about cinema's ability to free moviegoers from the monotony of everyday reality but seemed to applaud the effort. The reviewer merely noted that the methods employed in this case had failed and that trivial commercial films would never succeed.

In subsequent articles the critical distance to cinematic entertainment continued to decrease. One of the few articles on cinema published in April 1921, "Der amerikanische Sensationsfilm" ("The American Film Spectacle," 15 April) illustrates the tendency well. While comparing the artistic achievements of cinema in other countries with those in Germany, the author noted that a few German films were successful. Like so many other SPD journalists, the author separated the "artistic" from politics but drew a connection between aesthetics and morality. The article criticized cinema's low moral standards but affirmed its ability to amuse masses of weary workers. The ideological significance of such amusement received no attention.

The majority of articles on film in the SPD press during the early Weimar years followed the same pattern. They began by admitting that it had become impossible to ignore or reject film. Then they analyzed cinema's artistic potential, claiming more often than not that the medium was not and perhaps never would be an art form. If cinema could no longer be ignored or rejected, yet failed to qualify as an art form, then it should be employed for educational purposes. Such a message appeared in numerous *Vorwärts* articles, including "Das Lichtbild im Dienste der Bildungspflege" ("The Moving Picture in the Service of Education," 5 July 1919) and "Technische Wunder des Films" ("Technical Wonders of Film," 27 January 1920).

Characteristic of such articles was their uncritical enthusiasm for technological progress generally and film as one product of technology that could be used to achieve still further scientific and technological advances. In "Technical Wonders of Film" Ernst Trebius cited film's ability to present realistic moving images of past events. He emphasized that the cinematic reproduction helped human beings to break the natural constraints on their perception, and he encouraged its use for scientific enlightenment. Others noted the possibility with film projection to control the speed at which recorded images moved and to stop movement altogether for close scientific observation. Still others focused on the possibility of introducing exotic animals, landscapes, and cultures to German citizens.

The perception of the film medium's scientific and educational value led SPD leaders to suggest that the government coordinate efforts to develop new programs for the use of film (e.g., Hans Goslar, "Film, Staat und Volk"—"Film, State and People," *Vorwärts*, 7 July 1921). By April 1922 interest within the SPD had grown sufficiently to motivate the Central Education Committee to announce its intention to develop a program for the educational use of film. The proposed program varied only in scope from that formulated in 1913 (Schumann, 79). It concentrated on monitoring commercial film quality and on building a network of local theaters for educational events.

The Central Education Committee did nothing to develop its program until 1925. In the meantime, a number of union groups in Berlin formed the Volksfilmbühne in 1922, with principles similar to those the SPD had in mind when it organized the Volksbühne in the 1890s. According to its program, the organization should "present to working people films that correspond to their standards for *refined entertainment, true edification, and freedom*" (cited in Schumann, 79). The emphasis on *"refined entertainment"* and *"true edification"* suggests that the Volksfilmbühne strove to counteract the undesirable influence of "nonartistic" commercial films and acquaint workers with the absolute values of Beauty and Truth. Perhaps the emphasis on the idealist concept of culture contributed to the Volksfilmbühne's failure. Between 1922 and 1924 most workers were forced to concentrate almost exclusively on fulfilling material needs. The Volksfilmbühne was unable to attract large audiences and ceased to exist in 1924.

The Social Democrats maintained their reformist attitude toward film throughout the crisis years with a few exceptions. In addition to articles by Joseph Frank, Hans Goslar, and anonymous authors who criticized the use of film by capitalist entrepreneurs, isolated articles accused commercial filmmakers of producing films with reactionary political content. On 23 March 1922 an article appeared in *Vorwärts* entitled "Potsdamer Kino-Offensive" ("Potsdam Cinema Offensive"). It referred to *Fridericus Rex* and encouraged a political protest: "The film *Fridericus Rex* is an obvious attack against the Republic, an audacious provocation against the Republican populace. . . . Since the otherwise overly sensitive censors have failed, here only a boycott can help." Although the perception of a connection between film and politics represented a significant breakthrough, an advertisement for *Todesreigen* (*Dance of Death*), a reactionary portrayal of the October Revolution in Russia (*Vorwärts*, 30 March 1922), which appeared a few days later, demonstrated the limited scope of such perceptions. Two final *Vorwärts* articles indicate that the critical perceptions of SPD journalists were limited in other ways as well.

In the first article, "Volks-Film-Bühne" ("People's Film Theater," 1 August 1922), Pidder am Steen (pseudonym?) praised the initiators for founding an alternative film organization with a republican orientation. The article legitimized the endeavor by focusing on undesirable tendencies in mainstream cinema and proposing an alternative. While accusing some filmmakers of producing films with politically conservative or reactionary content, the article advocated a narrative style that allowed cinema to function as a socially stabilizing force. The thrust was that filmmakers should create fictional heroes with whom spectators could identify. Film should enable tired workers artificially to satisfy the needs that had been cultivated but left unfulfilled by everyday life. Pidder am Steen affirmed commercial cinema's ability to facilitate artificial satisfaction for workers, reproduce the strength they needed to return to work the next day, and lessen their desire to seek authentic ways to identify and fulfill their own physical and psychological needs.

In the second article, "Filmdrama oder Filmlustspiel" ("Film Drama or Film Comedy," 6 January 1923), Gustav von Koczian cited a decreasing interest in cinema and claimed that Germany's economic weakness was only one of many contributing factors. He argued that the public was growing weary of dramatic films and longed for more humorous subjects. Referring to the popularity of Charlie Chaplin, he explained: "This kind of comedy succeeds foremost because it in no way demands that the audience think." Koczian overlooked the subversive potential of satire in Chaplin's films, concentrated on the entertainment value of cinematic humor, and argued that the success of humorous films depended on their ability to promote uncritical forms of reception.

The Social Democratic approach to film between 1919 and 1923 differed insignificantly from the approach taken by what allegedly were more conservative institutions in the Weimar Republic. In 1920 most agreed that the commercial film industry produced few works of art. In making that claim, the Social Democrats and members of more conservative circles relied on standards derived from the concept of autonomous art. The few SPD journalists who began perceiving a connection between film and politics made inconsistent judgments and for the most part affirmed the socially stabilizing techniques of existing cinema.

When *Vorwärts* journalists criticized mainstream film, the[y] echoed the critiques of traditional social institutions. They co[ndemned] morally degrading films, using the criteria of patriarchal Chri[stian mo]rality. Their only deviation from conventional attitudes concerned the method for regulating the production of undesirable films—and even here not all agreed to deviate. Some Social Democrats advocated nationalization, but others sided with more conservative political leaders who could accept censorship far more easily than the jeopardizing of private ownership. In the end, censorship became especially valuable because it could be organized in a way that would allow the SPD and the political right to hinder the activity of their common enemy, the revolutionary German left.

Finally, the SPD agreed with more conservative politicians about employing film for scientific and educational purposes. Widespread fascination with the products of modern technology and the deep-seated belief in "progress" made support for scientific enlightenment virtually unanimous. Uncritical trust in instrumental reason seemed to influence SPD views even more than prior to World War I. Despite four decades of technological progress that accelerated the development of capitalism, and despite the experience of World War I, the SPD continued its promotion of scientific enlightenment. The party now sought to appropriate film for that purpose.

4

FILM AND THE COMMUNIST LEFT: LEFTIST RADICALISM VERSUS DEMOCRATIC CENTRALISM AND THE CONSEQUENCES FOR A COMMUNIST FILM PROGRAM

While the SPD and its coalition partners worked with varying degrees of enthusiasm to build a parliamentary democracy within a capitalist economic system, the revolutionary German left looked for opportunities to transform Germany into a soviet republic with a socialist economy.[1] While most Social Democrats continued to assimilate dominant concepts of culture, the revolutionary left scrutinized Germany's cultural heritage and considered the possibility of establishing a proletarian alternative.[2] It is important to note that as long as inflation, unemployment, and political reaction threatened Weimar's stability, the revolutionary left concentrated on political and military campaigns to overthrow the republican government. For most revolutionary leftists, cultural work played a secondary role between 1919 and 1924.

At the end of December 1918 the Spartacus Union (composed to a large extent of former SPD members who had left the party during the war) met with a recently consolidated group of leftist radical organizations called the Internationale Kommunisten Deutschlands (International Communists of Germany, IKD). Their purpose was to found a new party that would strive for changes in German society more fundamental than those being suggested by either the SPD or the Independent Socialists.[3] Although the Spartacists and the International Communists agreed to unite within a single organization, their tactical and strategic approaches differed from the beginning. At what turned out to be the founding convention of the Kommunistische Partei Deutschlands (German Communist party, KPD), the International Communist and Spartacus delegates disagreed on questions concerning party organization and policy toward existing unions. An especially heated debate erupted over participation in the National Assembly. The proposals expressed in the debate represented the basic choices for the KPD's ideological development over the next four years. Although it focused on political issues, the debate also influenced the discussion of cultural activity, including the potential use of film.

Spartacus leaders such as Paul Levi, Rosa Luxemburg, and Karl Liebknecht conceded that cooperation in the National Assembly would result in undesirable compromises. But, they argued, the German people were unprepared for more radical change. The three-class voting system had just been abolished in Prussia, women had been granted voting rights, and large segments of the population struggled to accept parliamentary democracy. According to the Spartacists, the KPD's first task was to broaden its base of support. They argued that the party could accomplish that task only by participating in the National Assembly and exposing the counterrevolutionary tactics of the SPD and others. The Spartacist delegates proposed the creation of a centrally organized party, a party hierarchy, and a strong program to influence the political awareness of the working class.

The IKD's opposition to the Spartacist approach corresponded to its political platform. The IKD consisted of antibureaucratic, antiparliamentarian, and (to some extent) anti-Bolshevist groups primarily from northwest Germany.[4] The oldest and most influential of the groups was from Bremen. The Bremen group emerged around 1910 in stiff opposition to the SPD's increasing reliance on parliamentary politics. Its leaders, including the Dutch intellectual Dr. Anton Pannekoek, Paul Fröhlich, and Karl Radek, noted that parliamentarianism minimized the active participation of workers in the democratic process. It encouraged them to delegate most political responsibility to a few party representatives, who often compromised the interest of their constituents for personal gain. As Pannekoek explained in *Weltrevolution und Kommunistische Taktik* (*World Revolution and Communist Tactics*):

> While parliamentarianism on the one hand strengthens the superiority of the leaders over the masses, thus exerting a counterrevolutionary influence, on the other hand it has the tendency to corrupt these leaders. When personal skills must replace what is lacking in the strength of the masses, a petty diplomacy emerges. The party, whether it began with other intentions or not, must strive to acquire a legal foundation, a parliamentary predominance. In the end the rela-

tionship between the ends and the means becomes reversed, and the parliament does not serve communism, rather communism functions as a slogan in the service of parliamentary politics. (138)

Between 1919 and 1924 the strength of the radical left in the KPD and in the entire communist movement significantly influenced the relationship between the revolutionary left and the Weimar government. During the period, the policies of the SPD and its coalition partners, the activity of reactionary political and military groups, and economic hardships associated in part with the Versailles Treaty reinforced the leftist radical opposition to parliamentary democracy. Members of the radical left repeatedly discouraged most forms of cooperation with the SPD, and in crisis situations they initiated violent campaigns to overthrow the republican government. They hoped that large segments of the German working class would rise up and join the fight once such campaigns were under way.

The defeat of Communist uprisings in 1919–1920 and the merging of the left wing of the Independent Socialists with the KPD in December 1920 strengthened the position of the more cautious Spartacist minority.[5] The minority accused the leftist radicals of adventurism and argued again that the party would have to develop a strong, centrally organized vanguard of the most class-conscious workers who would be able to work within the existing system to raise the political awareness of German workers. According to their point of view, the KPD could win the support necessary to defeat the republican alliance only in this way. It was one of the greatest shortcomings of the revolutionary German left during the crisis years that the leftist radicals, who were justifiably skeptical of central party organization, and the Spartacist minority, which accurately assessed the balance of power in the Weimar Republic, were unable to unite to build a grass-roots movement strong enough to challenge the reformist and reactionary Weimar alliance.

In addition to the counterproductive competition between opposing factions, the relationship between the German communist movement and the Russian Bolshevists greatly affected the KPD's development. The KPD's submission to Bolshevik leadership began at the founding convention of the Kommunistische Internationale (Communist International, Comintern) in March 1919. The party followed Bolshevik instructions for revolutionary activity at key points throughout the initial period of crisis, a practice that alienated many of those Germans who were concerned about national sovereignty.[6]

CULTURAL DEVELOPMENTS WITHIN
THE COMMUNIST LEFT

The influence of the Soviet Union and opposition between leftist radicals and more moderate members of the German communist movement also characterized the cultural development of the revolutionary left during the postwar crisis years.[7] Among the first news to reach Germany about the changes in Russian society following the October Revolution in 1917 were reports that new proletarian cultural, or *Proletkult,* organizations were emerging everywhere. Leftist intellectuals and artists in Germany exhibited so much interest in the phenomenon that by 1919 almost all left-oriented literary journals included writings by *Proletkult* theoreticians and reports about the practical achievements of *Proletkult* organizations. Works such as *Die Kunst und das Proletariat* (*Art and the Proletariat*) by Alexander Bogdanov, the leading theoretician of the *Proletkult* movement, appeared in German translation in 1919. Bogdanov's ideas provided new impulses for those who sought radical alternatives to the SPD's political reformism and cultural conservatism.

Bogdanov's concept of culture derived from his view of modern society's division of labor. He asserted that the separation of mental labor from manual labor, or organizers from those who carry out orders, created a relationship of power that discouraged laborers from participating in the process of social organization. He claimed further that art figured prominently in that process as a medium for the ideological organization of everyday experience.

Bogdanov also believed that the artist's allegiance to a specific social group determined the character of the artist's production. He perceived proletarian art as the effort of workers or artists with a working-class perspective to organize their specifically proletarian experience. He emphasized that the character of proletarian art, in contrast to feudal art's authoritarian spirit and bourgeois society's individualism, could be described in terms of collectivity. Proletarian collectivity, he suggested, was created by urban living conditions and mass industrial production.

Bogdanov's concept of proletarian culture included two important insights for radical intellectuals and artists in Germany. It defined proletarian culture as unique, justifying an absolute rejection of the cultural heritage. It also outlined the conditions for the development of proletarian culture in capitalistic societies, negating claims that proletarian culture could emerge only after a dictatorship of the proletariat had established a socialist economic system.

Bogdanov's theory almost immediately stimulated a wide variety of experiments in Germany. In the fall of 1919 a group of writers, painters, and architects, including Max Barthel, Arthur Holitscher, Hans Baluschek, and Bruno Taut, joined workers at the Siemens plant in Berlin to found the Bund für proletarische Kultur (Alliance for Proletarian Culture).[8] They also established their own theater to motivate the working masses to foment revolution. The experiment, which was directed by Rudolf Leonhard and Karlheinz Martin, proved too radical for most Berlin workers and soon failed. However, it did provide the impetus for a second attempt, the Proletarisches Theater–Bühne der revolutionären Arbeiter Groß-Berlins (Proletarian Theater–Stage of the Revolutionary Workers of Greater Berlin), organized by Erwin Piscator and Hermann Schüller in the fall of 1920.[9]

Piscator and Schüller had studied Bogdanov's writings and Platon M. Kerschenzev's views in *Das schöpferische Theater* (*The Creative Theater*). In contrast to Leonhard and Martin, who restricted "collectivity" to the interaction between players and imposed their revolutionary perceptions on the audience, Piscator and Schüller developed collective forms of production, reception, and administration. From October 1920 until April 1921, when Berlin's SPD chief of police closed it, the Proletarian Theater performed over fifty times and attracted over five thousand working-class members.

At the same time, radical literary critics and authors discussed *Proletkult* concepts and attempted to write proletarian literature. Among the most active and influential participants in the literary debates was Franz Jung.[10] Jung believed that the interaction of human beings, especially in working situations, created a sensation of pleasure and that a positive concept of collectivity emerged from the association between human interaction and pleasure. He argued that modern industrial society rejected collectivity in favor of individualism and competition. However, he also stressed that uncertainty about workers' chances of succeeding in competition with those who occupied higher positions in the social hierarchy rendered them only cautious supporters of individualism. According to Jung, proletarian literature should thematize the struggle of exploited workers in a way that would encourage already receptive workers to reactivate their latent sense of collectivity.

Jung sought to intensify the experience of collectivity by sharing the text's production with readers: "I wish to tell the reader in advance what I want to accomplish and what technical problems I will experience. While reading, the reader is supposed to help in solving the problems and in producing the text, to check for disruptions in the narration and in that way to establish a real connection between author and reader."[11] Jung's theoretical writings and his stories, novels, and dramas gained widespread attention between 1919 and 1924. Some of his ideas also surfaced in the KPD's discussion of proletarian alternatives to mainstream cinema.

There were many debates about the nature of proletarian culture, but most radical intellectuals and artists agreed that it would have little in common with what they perceived as an outdated bourgeois culture and that they should begin to work on it immediately. Most *Proletkult* advocates aligned themselves politically with the Kommunistische Arbeiterpartei Deutschlands (KAPD), the party whose antiparliamentarian position coincided most closely with their cultural collectivity. The KAPD was also attractive because it emphasized cultural activity. The party's leaders argued that although the material conditions for revolutionary change were present, the German working class was spellbound by the conservative ideology of the existing cultural institutions. In *Vom Werden der neuen Gesellschaft (On the Emergence of a New Society)*, Karl Schröder, one of the KAPD's leading functionaries, summarized the party's program with the following comments:

The essence of the new order, its absolute opposition to the bourgeois-capitalist world . . . necessitates that among the tasks of a proletarian party . . . is the task of becoming a leader in the struggle for a proletarian world view. Everything that corresponds to the task, above all the *Proletkult* (as it is conceived in Russia), is not a luxury, for which there now is no time; rather it is now, in this moment when the economic conditions for upheaval prevail, precisely the *decisive* factor for the acceleration of the social revolution. The problem of the German revolution is the problem of *developing the class-consciousness of the German proletariat.* (15)

While radical intellectuals and artists enthusiastically assimilated *Proletkult* concepts, initiated *Proletkult* experiments, and aligned themselves with the KAPD, influential voices within the KPD remained skeptical. Gertrud Alexander, for example, who was the first editor of the *feuilleton* for *Die Rote Fahne,* strongly criticized the *Proletkult*. She used the arguments of her mentor, Franz Mehring, to assert that revolutionary changes in the economic base must precede revolutionary changes in the ideological superstructure.[12] For her the experiments of such activists as Piscator and Schüller were frivolous and irresponsible. She condemned their attempts to facilitate a radical change in working-class conscious-ness with a proletarian theater while true revolutionaries were fighting in the streets and in parliament to create the economic and political foun-dation for a proletarian culture.

Until 1922 the KPD had no official cultural program. During that pe-riod, the KPD's cultural policy was determined foremost by older mem-bers who had matured with the SPD. These included individuals such as Alexander, August Thalheimer, and Edwin Hoernle who regularly pub-lished statements in the *feuilleton* of *Die Rote Fahne*. Although they of-ten criticized the cultural views of the Social Democratic press, their in-sistence on the primacy of the economic base suggests that, at least initially, most of the KPD's cultural activists still supported cultural con-cepts they had acquired while working with Mehring and others for *Die Neue Zeit* and *Vorwärts*. The attempt within the KPD to overcome bour-geois cultural concepts was a long, slow process. It was marked by nu-merous debates in which younger members who sympathized more with the radical intellectuals and artists struggled to win support for their con-cepts and programs.

FILM AND THE COMMUNIST LEFT

Until 1921–1922 leading members of the KPD considered film to be a distraction to the revolutionary working class.[13] At that point the KPD abandoned its *Offensivtheorie* and established a policy of united fronts with progressive political and union organizations. Cultural work, too, began to play a more significant role. Edwin Hoernle campaigned for an official cultural program, the KPD held its first Reichskonferenz der Bil-dungsobleute und Kurslehrer (Reich Conference of Educational Chair-men and Teachers), and cultural activists began publishing articles about film in *Die Rote Fahne*. Instead of referring directly to the need for a new approach to cultural activity in general, the articles described the pow-erful influence of cinema on the working class and suggested that the KPD must do something to counteract it. Unlike the cinema reformers and SPD journalists who had rejected commercial film because of its per-ceived negative influence on morality, the KPD journalists expressed their opposition almost exclusively in political terms.

The screening of *Fridericus Rex* motivated the KPD's first substan-tial criticism. In its review entitled "Kinokönige. 'Es war ein König in Thule'" ("Cinema Kings: 'There Was a King in Thule,'" 19 March

1922), *Die Rote Fahne* condemned *Fridericus Rex* as a capitalist instrument for the ideological indoctrination of the economically and politically oppressed. The review focused on *Fridericus Rex* but asserted that the entire industry promoted a conservative to reactionary ideology, supporting the claim with a discussion of the treatment of specific subjects in the films of popular genres: "society films" (*Gesellschaftsfilme*) and historical pageants. According to the article, society films portrayed the lives of the social elite as enviable and suggested that upward social mobility was inevitable for the talented. Historical pageants such as *Fridericus Rex* glorified the national heroes of the past and promoted a return to a monarchical system. In substantiating these claims, the review never transcended the level of content analysis. Although it was among the first reviews in *Die Rote Fahne* to discover a direct relationship between film and politics, it did little to explain how commercial films communicated an ideological point of view, and it offered no suggestions for alternatives.

The next major article on film appeared anonymously with a title reminiscent of Bogdanov's *Art and the Proletariat*. However, the perspective of "Kino und Proletariat" ("Cinema and Proletariat," 11 June 1922) differed significantly from Bogdanov's perspective. The article outlined the German film industry's development by referring to competition between young film companies and the powerful theater institution before World War I. It argued that the financial interests of theater owners, investors, and others had motivated the critique of film as artistically inferior. It stressed that the critique did more than protect the theater institution's monopoly on entertainment before World War I. It alleged that by promoting pedagogical uses for film, cinema's critics helped political and religious organizations to recognize the medium's potential ideological impact. Although its supposition about the powerful influence of a few individuals on cultural development was difficult to document, the article accurately cited the activity of the Navy League, the Catholic church, the Supreme High Command, and similar organizations abroad.

The article repeated the earlier criticism leveled against historical films and society films that had appeared in the review of *Fridericus Rex:* "Both film types, more clearly than all others, have transparent plot characteristics that render them instruments for class oppression and enable them to exert ideological pressure without inhibition on proletarian spectators. One can speak of a film ideology today that portrays seductively the 'upward mobility of the talented,'—the economic carrot—in the society film while it glorifies a reactionary model of the state—the political stick—in historical films." The assessment suggests that KPD journalists had developed a more advanced understanding of film content than had their counterparts in the SPD who uncritically affirmed as recreational cinema's fictional portrayals of past and present. At the same time, they lagged behind more radical intellectuals and artists who began to question the existing institutions of artistic production and reception. "Cinema and Proletariat" did mention factors that influenced film production and reception: the dependence on the interests of investors, the employment of full-time screenwriters, the cinematic adaptation of literature, and the construction of palatial movie theaters. But its criticism and suggestions for alternatives ignored such factors and concentrated on film content.

It is here that the article's perspective differed from that of *Art and the Proletariat.* In contrast to Bogdanov, who emphasized collective forms of aesthetic production as an integral element in the process of social change, "Cinema and Proletariat" referred simply to the tasks of a socialist *Arbeitermacht,* to a postrevolutionary workers' regime. Instead of discussing the necessity of developing alternative forms of film production and reception within the existing system, it focused on the content of films that might be produced under socialist conditions.

When and how would this transpire? The reference to a socialist *Arbeitermacht* implied that work could begin on a proletarian culture only after the working class had established a socialist system. Could socialist conditions be created within the existing system? What were those conditions? What should the role of film be in the present situation? What would the role of film be under socialism? Would a proletarian film be defined merely by its subject matter? Would it suffice to replace bourgeois enlightenment with socialist enlightenment in pedagogical films? "Cinema and Proletariat" offered no answers to these questions. Nevertheless, it initiated a discussion about the ideological quality of mainstream cinema and about proletarian alternatives, a dialogue that continued throughout the Weimar era.

In *Die Rote Fahne* Axel Eggebrecht contributed to the discussion by focusing on the allegedly damaging influence of commercial films on working-class audiences. Eggebrecht began his "Die bürgerliche Kinogefahr" ("The Danger of Bourgeois Cinema," 14 June 1922) with a description of cinematography. For him it was a purely mechanical process that could be employed to control the speed of any filmed event. Film's value lay in its ability to aid human beings in mastering nature. Although his understanding of the film medium's technical capacity was extremely limited, Eggebrecht's comments were significant for two reasons. First, in contrast to "Cinema and Proletariat," which only mentioned the danger of ideologically conservative film content, Eggebrecht opened the discussion to questions of form and its effect on reception. Second, he expressed an attitude that appeared again and again in the KPD's documents on film: no matter how much KPD cultural theoreticians rejected the bourgeois cultural heritage, they joined the SPD in uncritically affirming instrumental reason. Proletarian films would provide a scientific Marxist understanding of natural and social phenomena that would allow workers to discover the reasons for oppression and enable them to control their destinies.

Following his thoughts on film's potential, Eggebrecht turned his attention to its development in capitalist society. Using Mehring's theory of decadence, he asserted that members of the dominant but decaying bourgeoisie who controlled the film industry were incapable of producing films that would fulfill the medium's technical potential. Instead, he argued, film producers used film to promote conservative ideology. Eggebrecht characterized films that compensated artificially for the unfulfilled needs of workers as ideological weapons in the service of Weimar's reactionary forces. He also warned against seemingly neutral scientific and educational films, focusing specifically on Ufa's cultural film department and implying that its films, too, advocated a conservative viewpoint.

At this point, the KPD's response to commercial cinema concentrated on exposing the industry's ideological orientation. Eggebrecht, for example, encouraged class-conscious workers to combat the influence of entertainment and pedagogical films by discussing them with their families and friends. He and the other cultural activists of the KPD made no proposals for alternative film production. Their orientation changed when the Volksfilmbühne was founded in Berlin. The emergence of a concrete, union-based alternative to commercial cinema stimulated new discussion: the KPD now considered more seriously the nature of proletarian film activity, including production under the existing economic and political conditions.

A representative from the Kommunistische Jugend (Communist Youth, KJ) named Stephan (pseudonym?) reported on the union movement's efforts with his "Volks-Film-Bühne" ("People's Film Theater") in *Die Rote Fahne* on 3 October 1922. Stephan reiterated the statements of previous critics, claiming that the forces of capitalism had appropriated the film medium to manipulate public opinion and distract workers from revolutionary struggles. Like earlier critics, he offered very little detailed evidence to support that claim. Instead, Stephan praised the efforts of the Volksfilmbühne to counteract the conservative influence of films on workers. His suggestion for production illustrated that he also rejected fictional portrayals that distorted everyday reality. Stephan called for films that would expose the contradictions of capitalism and present strategies to resolve them. He criticized the Volksfilmbühne for selecting a sentimental film about an individual family and asserted that proletarian films must demonstrate the *class character* of social contradictions, as well as suggest strategies to dissolve them.

As had been the case in "Cinema and Proletariat," the perspective here differed significantly from that of cultural activists who had promoted *Proletkult* concepts. On the surface, Stephan's remarks seem similar to those of Franz Jung. Like Jung, Stephan believed that under the existing circumstances revolutionary artists should strive to increase the perception among workers that their experiences were shared and that they were engaged collectively in a struggle against other social classes. But Stephan's suggestion for the cultivation of proletarian collectivity centered almost exclusively on film content. Although he encouraged KJ members to participate energetically in monitoring the quality of Volksfilmbühne films, Stephan seemed interested primarily in creating a medium for the most class-conscious members of the KPD to enlighten workers, from a position of superior insight and authority.

His article reinforced that impression by describing what would transpire if the Volksfilmbühne followed his directions for film production: "Then it will become a powerful tool of the proletariat to arouse the feeble and halfhearted, to . . . steel the workers for new battles." Whereas Piscator, Schüller, Jung, and others developed forms of collective production and reception that would help workers to organize their experiences cooperatively and increase their sense of solidarity, Stephan preserved the narrative authority. He relied on the filmmaker's ability to use film content in a way that would raise the class consciousness of workers. Just how the filmmaker would accomplish that task remained unclear.

In "Der revolutionäre Film" ("The Revolutionary Film"), which appeared in *Die Rote Fahne* exactly one week after Stephan's article, Béla Balázs responded directly to Stephan's proposals and explained how film content could influence audiences.[14] Belázs supported Stephan's appraisal of mainstream cinema, suggesting that absolutely no product of the existing industry could be of use to the revolutionary working class. Like those before him, Balázs detected a conscious effort among conservative capitalists to use film as an ideological weapon. He criticized the portrayal of specific subjects, noting, for example, that revolutionaries appeared in many films as corrupt and villainous figures. Balázs proclaimed that the only alternative for the KPD was to move quickly to begin producing its own films.

He shared Stephan's vision of proletarian film as a tool to be used in raising class consciousness and increasing the desire to fight. However, his proposal demonstrated that Balázs understood more deeply than his predecessors how commercial films influenced their audience. The films evoked emotional responses, exciting and inspiring exhausted workers who longed for entertainment. Balázs rejected the conservative ideology of commercial films, but he accepted and even promoted the prevailing forms of cinematic expression. He perceived proletarian filmmakers to be in competition with influential film companies for the attention of working-class filmgoers. Balázs asserted that the KPD should establish film studios and produce films that would be just as exciting and inspiring as the ostentatious bourgeois films.

Only the subject matter had to change. Balázs called for films about revolutionary events with revolutionary heroes to replace the detective films, royal dramas, Indian hunts, and Oriental fables that dominated the market. Instead of investigating how standard aesthetic forms might reinforce authoritarian structures, promote uncritical reception, and reproduce the need for entertainment, Balázs encouraged proletarian filmmakers to use the dominant forms in their films, also suggesting that such an endeavor could succeed financially.

"Das proletarische Kino" ("The Proletarian Cinema," 11 November 1922) temporarily concluded the discussion of the film medium in *Die Rote Fahne* with a reply to Balázs. The article's author, Barthel-Baßler (pseudonym?), began with the typical critique of commercial cinema's conservative ideological orientation and the need to counteract the industry's influence. However, this article questioned the possibility of making proletarian films in what it characterized as a bourgeois-capitalist society. Barthel-Baßler argued that many of the civil servants who enforced film censorship laws remained loyal to the Prussian monarchy. They tolerated the new republican society but were more likely to allow films such as *Fridericus Rex* than those with a progressive orientation. Barthel-Baßler used the argument to support the claim that economic and political change would have to precede revolutionary cultural change. The article cited the birth of proletarian film in Soviet Russia as a model. By 1922 the Aufbau, Industrie und Handels A.G. (Construction, Industry, and Trade Inc., AIH), an organization of the IAH, had begun to distribute Soviet films in Germany. Barthel-Baßler had seen some of the films but made no mention of possible cooperation between the Soviet Union and the KPD in making and distributing films. Such films only demonstrated to German workers what they could have as soon as they succeeded in their struggle for revolutionary economic and political change.

Although articles on film appeared with relative frequency in *Die Rote Fahne* in 1922, the KPD's discussion of film remained unsystematic. As the deterioration of Germany's economy accelerated in 1923, the party once again focused on political struggles. The increase of hunger seemed to spur interest in those activities perceived as more likely to bring about rapid social change. The Communist press only occasionally published articles on film, and plans for the production of proletarian films gained little support.

According to the existing research, before renewed revolutionary fervor could postpone work on a proletarian cinema, the defeat of Communist uprisings and the cultural heritage of the SPD had fostered skepticism.[15] The defeat of uprisings, culminating with that of March 1921, allegedly had rendered the Communist left insecure and relatively submissive to Weimar authority. It seems likely that similar attitudes influenced Communists like Barthel-Baßler who considered it inappropriate to advocate the production of revolutionary films that conservative Weimar censors easily could reject. Those who asserted the primacy of the material base and argued that revolutionary economic and political change was necessary to create the foundation for proletarian film production based their judgments to a large extent on what they had learned from Franz Mehring, Karl Kautsky, and others.

The continuing discussion of film in the Communist press suggests that at least one other factor limited the party's interest in film production before 1924. In "Der proletarische Film" ("The Proletarian Film," *Internationale Presse-Korrespondenz*, 7 April 1923), Edwin Hoernle, the KPD's leading cultural advocate, expressed his skepticism by referring to the strength of the film industry. Hoernle agreed with Eggebrecht, Stephan, and others who asserted that dominant capitalist forces had utilized film consciously to promote a conservative and often reactionary ideology. He also believed that the only way to counteract the influence of mainstream cinema was to challenge it with an alternative cinema. According to Hoernle, proletarian filmmakers should produce dramatic films with just as much suggestive power as commercial films, but with a revolutionary perspective. They should produce humorous films, satirizing and ironically portraying the dominant social forces. They also should produce newsreels and pedagogical films, exposing the accounts of natural and social phenomena in commercial films as superficial and slanted.

But Hoernle was less optimistic than Balázs about the possibility of competing successfully with the film industry under the existing conditions. In contrast to Barthel-Baßler, who cited the constraints of censorship, Hoernle emphasized economic constraints. It was difficult for him to imagine how the young and relatively weak German Communist party could compete with the industry's impressive studio system, extensive theater network, and experience in making films, which were attracting over one million customers daily.

Although Hoernle questioned the KPD's ability to compete prior to a proletarian revolution, like Balázs he was unable to do anything but develop plans within the context of direct commercial and ideological competition with the existing industry. They felt compelled to counteract the powerful influence of commercial film, but at least initially, their only model for such an endeavor was that of the existing cinema. As a result, they borrowed from it what they thought would help them in competing with it. Hoernle and Balázs were far ahead of their counterparts in the SPD insofar as they began to investigate the relationship between film and politics. However, their understanding of the film industry and the ways in which it communicated and reinforced an ideological point of view remained fairly superficial.

All of the participants in the KPD's discussion of film perceived the influence of politically conservative individuals in film companies and suggested that such individuals determined the subject matter and the portrayal of specific character types. They criticized filmmakers who preferred historical films that glorified the Prussian monarchy and idolized its political and military leaders. Some of them also recognized the tendency of commercial films to appeal to the unsatisfied desires of workers and to suggest that talented people would be rewarded with upward social mobility. But no one articulated that, in addition to political orientation, capitalist competition and the profit motive influenced the choices of decision makers in the film industry. There was no discussion of the fact that one commercially successful film about the Prussian monarchy would motivate the production of similar films relatively independent of ideological considerations. Furthermore, no one mentioned the efforts of producers to market films using stereotypical stars, sensational publicity, and palatial theaters. Questions about the ideological impact of standardized production and about the degree to which competing proletarian filmmakers would be forced to use similar methods remained unanswered.

Most KPD critics of mainstream cinema concentrated on film content, arguing that proletarian filmmakers should replace conservative subject matter with revolutionary subject matter: proletarian films should portray the October Revolution, the life of Karl Marx, and the concepts of dialectical materialism, not the Seven Years' War, the life of Frederick the Great, and concepts of metaphysics or positivism. Eggebrecht, Stephan, and others seemed less concerned with the organizational structure that enabled individuals to determine subject matter than with the decisions made by such individuals. Their critiques also ignored aesthetic factors and their effect on reception. Even Hoernle and Balázs, who discussed film's suggestive power, were vague about the aesthetic techniques that produced the effect. Moreover, they encouraged proletarian filmmakers to strive for a similar effect. Their proposals opened the door for the uncritical appropriation of forms of production and reception that reproduced authoritarian relationships among filmmakers, as well as between films (as the authoritative and suggestively appealing portrayals of natural and social phenomena) and uncritically responding, misinformed, and uninformed audiences.

Only Hoernle considered an alternative. Instead of restricting his discussion to film content and tacitly affirming conventional forms of production and reception, Hoernle advocated the establishment of a *Proletkino* in which revolutionary workers would make suggestions about subject matter and critically evaluate the final product. According to him, though, the *Proletkino* would become a reality only under socialism. It was another five years before the KPD participated in building an organization similar to Hoernle's *Proletkino* to facilitate social change within Weimar's capitalistic economic system. (See the discussion of the Volksfilmverband in Chapter 11.)

In the meantime, the moderate factions in the communist movement gradually suppressed political and cultural forms of leftist radicalism. Their growing strength increased the likelihood that proletarian filmmakers would reject Hoernle's concept of a *Proletkino* in favor of a cinema that employed conventional forms of production and reception. The last article on film to appear in *Die Rote Fahne* during the postwar crisis years, P. M. Kerschenzev's "Aufgaben des staatlichen Kinos" ("Tasks of the State Cinema," 4 February 1923), offers a good example. Kerschenzev, who had been a leading proponent of *Proletkult* ideas in the Soviet Union and who in 1920–1921 had provided Piscator and

Schüller with important impulses for their experiments, proposed an approach to socialist cinema that differed remarkably from the *Proletkult* approach to culture. The change in Kerschenzev's perspective was a result of the confrontation between the Bolshevik party leadership and the *Proletkult* movement.

In 1920 an adversary relationship developed between the Russian Communist party (Bolshevik) and the *Proletkult* movement. To a large extent it resembled the political and cultural disputes between more moderate KPD members and leftist radicals in Germany.[16] Lenin accused the *Proletkult* leaders of expecting too much change too soon. When, by the end of 1920, the *Proletkult* organizations had attracted over five hundred thousand members, the Bolsheviks moved to weaken their influence. The measures succeeded. By 1922 the *Proletkult* movement had submitted to party rule, and its leading theoretician, Bogdanov, had been discredited. The *Proletkult* slowly disappeared.[17]

The *Proletkult*'s submission to party control and the effect of that submission on cultural development in the Soviet Union is apparent in Kerschenzev's comments on film. (The appearance of his article in *Die Rote Fahne* also demonstrated the growing unity between the Bolsheviks and the KPD on cultural issues.) As the title suggests, Kerschenzev subjected film production to the control of central state authority. Nowhere in the article did he mention the potential value or even the possibility of collective production and reception at the grass-roots level. On the contrary, Kerschenzev's proposals imply an authoritarian relationship between the state's filmmakers and uneducated, uninformed audiences. Film would function as a medium with which filmmakers could teach workers and peasants about the class struggles of the past and present.

Kerschenzev criticized the treatment of history in commercial films, but he expressed none of the *Proletkult*'s skepticism about the value of history for contemporary struggles. He advocated the production of historical films in which individual participants in past struggles would appear as heroic leaders. He made no reference to the possibility that such films might reinforce a trust in authoritarian personalities and hinder the development of democratic proletarian collectivity.

Kerschenzev made a similar suggestion for a film chronicle. Here, too, he mentioned nothing about the advantages of allowing workers and peasants to collect their own information and organize their own experiences into an ideological viewpoint. The state's film chronicle would assume responsibility for informing about and explaining current events. According to Kerschenzev, the film chronicle would be most effective if it posited simple binary oppositions. Instead of presenting the complex contradictions inherent in all social phenomena and challenging spectators to produce an ideological view in dialogue with the film, the film chronicle should juxtapose czarist conditions with socialist conditions or compare conditions in the capitalist West with those in the Soviet Union. It should portray czarism and capitalism as evil and the socialist system of the Soviet Union as good.[18] He also suggested that Soviet films could be very important in spreading socialist ideals and news about the Soviet Union to foreign countries. He was affirming the type of activity the IAH had initiated in cooperation with Soviet filmmakers beginning in 1921.

THE FILM ACTIVITY OF THE IAH: 1921–1924

In the fall of 1921 the executive committee of the Comintern organized the IAH to coordinate efforts to aid Russians suffering because of a severe drought in the agriculturally vital Volga River region.[19] The IAH almost immediately commissioned Soviet filmmakers to produce short documentaries on the effect of the drought on living conditions in Russia. By October 1921, when Max Barthel traveled to several German cities to seek donations for the IAH, his presentation included screenings of the first Soviet documentary films to reach Germany. As early as 1922 the IAH had begun to schedule major film events. On 26 March 1922 *Hunger in Sowjetrußland* (*Hunger in Soviet Russia*) premiered in Berlin, and *Die Wolga hinunter* (*Downstream on the Volga*) followed a short time later. In the summer of that year, the IAH organized the AIH to administer the distribution of Soviet films in Germany and in the other countries where the IAH was active. The AIH developed contractual agreements with the Proletkult collective and the state-controlled Goskino in Moscow. It also was involved directly in the film production of the Rus film collective.

Until 1923 the IAH concentrated exclusively on the distribution of informative documentary films about everyday life in the Soviet Union, which illustrated the early achievements of the Bolsheviks and paid tribute to Soviet leaders. The films were so successful that the AIH decided to expand its program to include featured films and to open its own theater. The first Russian entertainment films shown in Germany were *Polikuschka*, produced by the Rus collective in 1919, and *Das Wunder des Soldaten Iwan* (*The Miracle of Ivan, the Soldier*), the work of another collective of young Russian artists. Both films portrayed life in czarist Russia in the nineteenth century.

Polikuschka, based on a story by Leo Tolstoy, juxtaposed the hopeless living conditions of the servant Polikuschka and his family with the luxurious life of his master. The plot was simple: Polikuschka's master sends him to the city for money; Polikuschka loses the money while returning from the city and hangs himself. According to Gertrud Alexander, who affirmed the film's ability to evoke sympathy for Polikuschka, its value lay in Ivan Moskvin's portrayal of the servant (*"Polikuschka* im Ufa-Palast," *Die Rote Fahne,* 7 March 1923).

The Miracle of Ivan, the Soldier, a humorous film about a young farmer's son who is forced into the army, exposed the hypocrisy of czarist society. While Ivan is away, his parents suffer from a bad harvest, and the landowner harasses Ivan's girlfriend. In the army he sees the treasures of the court and realizes that just a fraction of that wealth would suffice to restore the happiness of his family and girlfriend. He steals a jewel from a religious idol, which his regiment has received as a gift, and claims that the Holy Virgin gave it to him. His officers and the priests refuse to believe Ivan, but the superstitious masses accept his story. In the end, the czarist authorities choose to release Ivan, instead of discrediting their own authority by questioning the popular belief in religious miracles.

Both films portrayed czarist Russia superficially. The world of Polikuschka and Ivan was good, and the world of the landowners and the court was bad. The first Soviet feature films screened in Germany encouraged audiences to sympathize with the exploited and to condemn the ruling classes of czarist Russia as wasteful and hypocritical. They did little to stimulate workers to develop their own critical skills.

The surprising success of the IAH's film program, including the first documentaries and features from the Soviet Union, contributed to the changing attitude about film in Communist circles, as did both the victory of moderate factions in their struggle with the leftist radicals and, not least of all, the strength of the commercial film industry, itself. Communists gradually developed long-term political and cultural strategies that included a proletarian film program.

PART TWO

THE YEARS OF RELATIVE STABILITY: 1924–1928

Until the middle of 1923, the owners of production plants and other substantial properties seemed content with inflation.[1] The decreasing value of currency strengthened their investments. It lowered the cost of production, reduced the real value of tax payments, and stimulated export. Manufacturers easily undercut the prices of competitors on foreign markets and attracted customers who paid in currencies that were much more valuable than the German reichsmark. Inflation also enabled speculators to obtain credit, purchase floundering businesses, and build more stable conglomerates. Among the most powerful speculators was Hugo Stinnes, who had organized a concern of 1,535 companies and 2,888 production plants, before he died in 1924.[2] Alfred Hugenberg, another influential businessman, began investing heavily in the film industry during this period, a strategy that led to the purchase of a controlling interest in Ufa in 1927 and culminated in the formation of his ideologically reactionary monopoly of the film industry by 1933.

As long as the populace tolerated inflation, Weimar governments seemed unable to control it. Toleration weakened at the end of 1922 when the Cuno cabinet, consisting primarily of business executives, assumed power. Cuno and his ministers hesitated with reparations payments, providing the French an excuse to occupy the Ruhr in January 1923. The already struggling economy faltered while currency presses operated around the clock. Between January and August the exchange rate rose from 10,000 to 4.6 million reichsmarks for one U.S. dollar. In November a copy of the SPD newspaper, *Vorwärts*, sold for 130 billion reichsmarks! As the process continued, the number of demonstrations in the Ruhr and in other industrial centers increased, the likelihood of revolutionary uprisings grew, and German farmers threatened to withhold their harvest from the open market.

Finally, in November 1923 Gustav Stresemann replaced Cuno, organized a new cabinet, and introduced the rentenmark. At the same time, leading government officials and bankers in the United States recognized that by offering financial assistance to Germany, they could benefit themselves. A healthy economy would allow the Germans to pay reparations to the French and English, who then could absolve their war debts to the United States. Substantial loans would increase German dependence on U.S. credit, and when the economy recovered, investments would pay high dividends. In addition, financial assistance would help to balance what the United States perceived as a threat to its economic interests in Europe, represented by the growing influence of the Soviet Union. In a sense the competition between the United States and the Soviet Union for influence in Europe began in Germany, albeit modestly, during this period.

In January 1924 the U.S. government appointed C. G. Dawes to chair an international committee on reparations in Europe, and at the end of August a German delegation joined the Allies in signing the Dawes Plan. Germany began receiving substantial loans, paying reparations in its own currency, and accepting attractive offers from foreign investors. In the following months the German government also moved to integrate itself into the League of Nations, and consequently, the Soviet Union began to question Germany's relationship to its eastern ally. Stresemann responded in April 1926 by negotiating the Treaty of Berlin with the Soviets. Healthy trade continued, including the Soviet sale of weapons to the Reichswehr. Soviet and German film companies also began to cooperate. The position of Germany seemed fairly well balanced between the United States and the Soviet Union.

Despite their expressed gratitude for U.S. support and for favorable trade agreements with the Soviet Union, many Germans became increasingly sensitive about foreign influence in their affairs.[3] The Allied role in shaping post–World War I Germany had nurtured their sensitivity. Between 1924 and 1929 it was primarily foreign economic investment that intensified anxiety and eventually fostered hostility. The film industry especially struggled as the influence of Hollywood and Soviet companies increased.

5

HOLLYWOOD, MOSCOW, AND THE CRISIS OF GERMAN FILM

For the greater portion of the stable years, the governing coalition of the Weimar Republic, the *Bürgerblock,* consisted of the Deutsche Zentrumspartei (Catholic Center party), the Deutsche Volkspartei (German People's party, DVP), the Deutschnationale Volkspartei (German National People's party, DNVP), and a number of smaller splinter parties. The coalition members tolerated the republic, some more willingly than others, as long as their leading constituents, ranging from middle-class Catholic merchants to wealthy landowners and the industrial elite, could sustain their political influence and prosper as they had during the crisis. Such was the case until 1929.

The influx of loans and investments stimulated speculation and industrial concentration at a rate parallel to that prior to 1924. In the electronics, chemical, and steel industries, huge conglomerates such as Siemens, A.E.G., I. G. Farben, and the Vereinigte Stahlwerke acquired smaller companies and joined international cartels to guarantee higher and more stable prices for their products at home and abroad. For a minority of the most powerful and wealthy, the Weimar government once again nurtured conditions under which substantial wealth could be accumulated. To a much lesser extent, even the working masses prospered. The system seemed to be functioning smoothly.

In reality, the German economy grew dependent on continual support from foreign governments and banks. Approximately one half of the annual gross national product during the years of relative stability was expended to cover short-term loans (Rosenberg, 164). If the source of credit vanished, the economy would collapse and once again threaten the nation's stability. Between 1924 and 1929 German political and economic leaders spent, invested, and allocated funds with little apparent regard for the inherent danger. At least until 1929, it worked to the great satisfaction of those at the top of the social hierarchy and with sufficient prosperity for the rest to avoid significant political conflict.

The potential for political conflict existed in part because, although the Dawes Plan stimulated employment and wage increases, less attractive working conditions became more and more prevalent. To maximize profit German industrialists accelerated efforts to streamline production. Smaller factories gave way to larger production plants where anonymity, mechanization, and alienation prevailed. The workers' interest in their jobs and the workplace decreased. The same process now spread into the realms of business and government. Streamlining here was especially significant because the number of white-collar workers grew almost three times faster than the number of blue-collar workers during the period.[1] The armies of new clerical workers and bureaucrats joined the ranks of the lower-middle-class and working-class Germans who feared further descent in the social hierarchy and coped with poor working conditions by hoping for upward social mobility.

Improving material conditions and increasing political independence from the Western Allies strengthened the position of those who supported the republic and fostered the tolerance of the *Bürgerblock*. However, the struggle between republican and antirepublican; democratic and autocratic; communist, socialist, and capitalist ideologies persisted. As illustrated by Hindenburg's election in 1925 and the plebiscite to disinherit the German aristocracy in 1926, public opinion more often than not marginally favored an ideological orientation associated with the relative prosperity and security of the Second Reich.[2] Nevertheless, the ideological war continued. During the years of relative stability, mass media—the printed media, radio, and cinema—played an increasingly significant role in the process. For various reasons mainstream cinema continued to exert a conservative to reactionary influence on public opinion.

The Dawes Plan contributed to a further concentration of power among a few very wealthy and very conservative men in the film industry. The stronger currency made it impossible for exporters to compete as successfully as they had between 1919 and 1923. Many young companies went out of business; others were acquired. Larger companies survived, but even the largest experienced difficulty as U.S. and European firms began showing more interest in the German market.

Hollywood film companies posed the greatest threat. By 1927 they owned German theaters, operated distribution offices, and purchased stock in German production companies. In 1923 National Film began distributing Paramount films, and David Selznick negotiated an agreement with Trianon. Even the largest German film conglomerate, Ufa, found it necessary to accept a partnership with Universal, Paramount, and MGM in 1926.[3] Similar interest groups developed between Terra and Universal in 1925 and between Phöbus and MGM in 1927.

At the same time, Hollywood producers enticed German film talent to work in the United States. By 1926 Hollywood had engaged Ernst Lubitsch, Friedrich Murnau, E. A. Dupont, Conrad Veidt, Emil Jannings, Pola Negri, and others. Some returned, but the exodus of Germany's best directors, actors, and technicians continued throughout the stable years and beyond.

In contrast to the less visible U.S. involvement with German companies in the new international chemical, electronics, and steel industry cartels, Hollywood's very visible influence on the film industry stimulated a heated debate in the media. Most journalists emphasized Germany's gratitude for U.S. assistance but bemoaned the consequences for the film industry. On 9 January 1926, for example, Germany's leading film journal, the liberal *Lichtbild-Bühne* (*L.B.B.*), featured a headline editorial, "Amerikanisierung der Ufa?" ("Americanization of Ufa?").

The journal's editors attempted to dispel rumors that Ufa had fallen under Hollywood's control. Far from quieting the fear of readers who perceived Ufa's development as a barometer for the future of the entire industry, their comments indicated just how difficult it would be for Ufa to avoid requesting further credit, a move that would necessitate additional concessions. According to the article, U.S. newspapers, including the *Sun* and the *Chicago Tribune,* claimed that U.S. film companies had gained control of the German market. The newspapers used terms such as "rivals," "victor's prize," "conquer," and "domination" in their description of the initial competition among the U.S. companies and their ultimate joint agreement with Ufa. The *L.B.B.* discounted the reports of conquest, acknowledged fierce competition, and asserted that Ufa would remain sovereign. It argued that the Deutsche Bank, the principal Ufa stockholder, would provide enough credit so that Ufa could continue and expand its production without more foreign assistance. If that failed, the

German government would intervene to protect Ufa's integrity. Why? The article noted: "In the end, not only individuals have an interest in the German Ufa, rather the entire population and the government that represents and carries out its wishes."

The *L.B.B.* editors, despite their liberal tendencies, certainly felt some obligation to support Ufa. Their income depended in part on payments from Ufa for advertising in the journal. There were other reasons for the journal's point of view. The residual impact of prewar propaganda, the fresh memory of warring nations, the insecurity, hunger, and violence that conservative and reactionary interest groups associated with the constraints of the Versailles Treaty, and the reality of intense competition at the national and international levels contributed to the perception of Hollywood's influence as a potential threat to Germany's national well-being. For the same reasons many insecure Germans preferred to retreat to older concepts of security and accept explanations for crises that linked individual identity to industrial interests and the interest of the nation. In addition, mainstream cinema's capacity to satisfy unfulfilled needs artificially by encouraging spectators to identify with popular heroes and heroines, including patriarchal and authoritarian figures such as Friedrich II, Königin Luise, Bismarck, and Wilhelm II, stimulated among large segments of the German population an interest in the fate of a particularly German film industry.

Within this context film quality became a secondary factor. Although some journalists continued to argue that the industry could survive and prosper only by producing high-quality films, many others argued that every effort should be made to assist German producers in their competition with Hollywood companies. In fact, the German government had attempted just that by introducing an import contingency law.[4]

The law very precisely stated the desired ratio of imported to domestic films but offered no clear guidelines for enforcement. Film companies traded and sold their contingency certificates, foreign companies induced their German partners to produce inexpensive, low-quality films, or they produced them in Germany themselves so that they could import blockbusters. Joint productions made it difficult to distinguish foreign from domestic films, and the government allowed two companies, Ufa and Phöbus, to transfer contingency certificates directly to their Hollywood associates. With the development of international cartels, national economic interests became less easy to identify and protect.

As the crisis continued, film companies began soliciting domestic investments to remain competitive. Terra Film, which had a close association with the liberal Ullstein Publishing House, received investment assistance from the far less liberal I. G. Farben group,[5] and the chemical concern's Dr. Friedländer joined Terra's board of directors. Seen in this light, the Dawes Plan both accelerated the cartelization that enabled industrial giants to diversify their growing assets and created conditions that forced the film industry to solicit such investments. Terra Film was no exception. In the majority of cases new investments came from conservative to reactionary circles.[6]

Ufa also faced pressing financial difficulties in 1927. Following the negotiation of the Parufamet agreement in 1926, the Deutsche Bank and the German government were either unwilling or unable to undertake what the *L.B.B.* had prescribed for Ufa. By 1927 bankruptcy once again threatened Germany's largest film conglomerate.[7] Mismanagement and Hollywood competition forced Ufa to renew its search for investors late in 1926.[8]

The I. G. Farben group expressed interest and eventually invested, but Alfred Hugenberg's group, the Wirtschaftsvereinigung zur Förderung der geistigen Wiederaufbaukräfte (Economic Association for the Promotion of the Intellectual Forces of Reconstruction), assumed control. When the Deutsche Bank abandoned its position as major Ufa stockholder in 1927, the Economic Association invested sufficiently to gain a 75 percent share of Ufa, and eleven men who either sympathized with or were members of the Hugenberg group joined Ufa's board of directors.[9] To take control of Ufa, *Die Rote Fahne* estimated that the Hugenberg group invested thirty-five million marks.[10] That was an extremely large sum of money in 1927, but well within the means of an association whose members included some of Germany's wealthiest men.[11]

For more than a decade the association, composed to a large extent of western coaling magnates, had used money from their vast trust fund to invest in all forms of mass media. Under Hugenberg's leadership the association strove to influence public opinion in opposition to Social Democracy. At the time of its investment in Ufa, its media concern ran the Telegrafen-Union, a news wire office that serviced over sixteen hundred German newspapers. It controlled one of the nation's largest publishing houses, the August Scherl Verlag. It also operated fourteen regional newspapers, including Scherl's *Berliner Lokal-Anzeiger*, and the *Kinematograph*, an influential conservative film journal that counterbalanced the mildly liberal *L.B.B.*

While building their media empire, Hugenberg and his followers sustained and even intensified their political conservatism.[12] The success of the October Revolution in 1917, the transfer of power from the Hohenzollern monarchy to the Social Democrats in 1918, and the birth of the German Communist party at the end of 1918 had increased their insecurity. The founding of the Weimar Republic made them even more determined to stop the shift to the left in Germany. Hugenberg detested the Weimar Republic and opposed all efforts to strengthen its democratic foundations. He and a small but powerful right wing of the DNVP even struggled against their own very conservative political party when they perceived it to be cooperating with republican forces.

Under Hugenberg's leadership the right wing of the DNVP hoped to abolish the Weimar constitution and establish a national dictatorship or restore the Hohenzollern monarchy. They strove at all costs to eradicate German socialism, a fairly undifferentiated concept for them that described the activity of Social Democrats, Communists, trade unionists, Jews, and almost anyone who supported the republic. By October 1928 the right wing of the DNVP had grown sufficiently so that Hugenberg could assume leadership of the entire party.

With the acquisition of Ufa in 1927, Hugenberg greatly expanded the sphere in which he and his associates could foment public opposition to the Weimar Republic. The Ufa conglomerate consisted of 140 companies. It included film distribution offices all over Europe and in the United States.[13] Ufa also controlled 116 theaters, including the largest and most attractive palaces in most major urban centers in Germany.

Weimar film historians have claimed that the Hugenberg Concern initially only sought commercial success.[14] As long as the republic remained stable, they have asserted, Ufa remained neutral. That seems questionable considering Hugenberg's adamant opposition to his own party's tolerance of the republic. Upon closer scrutiny, it becomes clear that Hugenberg's ideological orientation affected Ufa policy immediately. Shortly after the Economic Association took control of Ufa, one of Hugenberg's associates, Dr. Ludwig Bernhard, published *Der Hugenberg-Konzern. Psychologie und Technik einer Großorganisation der Presse* (*The Hugenberg-Concern: Psychology and Technique of a Mass Press Organization*). In the brochure, Bernhard asserted that the Hugenberg group had very clear political motivations for its investment in Ufa. Bernhard noted that the group's major concern was not that Hollywood would subsume Ufa and conquer the German film market. Much more threatening was the possibility that the "communist propaganda center" would take possession (92).

Almost immediately after Hugenberg's old partner Ludwig Klitzsch became Ufa's general director, and a host of Hugenberg associates assumed leading roles in its executive committee,[15] Ufa quietly developed new policies. Just two days after the executive committee had been formed, it acted to remove intertitles from *Metropolis* that committee members judged to have communist connotations (R109, 1026a, 7 April 1927). From the outset the new executives refused to screen any Soviet film that in their estimation promoted "bolshevism." In one particular case on 21 September 1927 the committee discussed the possibility of rejecting *Südfilm* distribution of the Soviet film *Bett und Sofa* (*Bed and Sofa*, R109, 1026a, 21 September 1927). Apparently, even a relatively innocuous love story represented too great a threat.

In 1928 Ufa increased efforts to restrict access to the German film market for distributors of Soviet films. When Soviet exporters experienced difficulty in procuring contingency certificates at the beginning of that year, the executive committee suggested that the Soviets be allowed to import only one film for every three German films they allowed to be imported into the Soviet Union (R109, 1027a, 3 January 1928:1). Later that year Ufa's executive committee excluded all Soviet-German coproductions of the Derussa company from its theaters (R109a, 5 July 1928:1). Ufa initiated a similar proposal in the Spitzenorganisation der deutschen Filmindustrie (SPIO), an organization that developed policies for the entire industry and whose chairman was Ludwig Klitzsch.

Although the ideological orientation of the Hugenberg Concern significantly influenced Ufa's production and distribution decisions, it is accurate to assume that Ufa strove for commercial success. Economic considerations, as well, moved Ufa and, to some extent, the entire film industry to pressure the Soviet film industry. When the Germans and Soviets signed the Berlin Treaty in April 1926, many German film journalists speculated about possible advantages for German companies.[16] In 1925 the Soviet Union had purchased 35 percent of German raw film exports. Soviet law also allowed German distributors to export films to the Soviet Union in large quantities. However, Soviet officials refused and perhaps were unable to pay enough for screening rights to satisfy German distributors. In light of the ever-increasing financial difficulties that resulted from competition with Hollywood film companies, the German industry hoped to maintain its advantage in trade agreements with the Soviet Union and, if possible, dominate the Soviet market to compensate for Hollywood's domination of the German market.

In 1926 the Germans intensified pressure on the Soviet film industry. Following the amazing commercial success of *Battleship Potemkin,* Soviet companies moved quickly to export films to Germany. The *Film-Kurier* predicted a threat to the German industry in February in "Russisches Monopol—Deutsches Kontingent" ("Russian Monopoly— German Contingency," 16 February 1926). To avoid an "assault" and to increase profit in the Soviet market, the industry together with a cooperative German government used contingency restrictions as a lever. Soviet access to German theaters depended on Soviet willingness to allow German distributors greater access to the Soviet market. When Ufa suggested an exchange ratio of three German export films for every one Soviet film imported into Germany in 1928, its motivation was ideological and economic. The desired effect was the same: Soviet access to the German market was restricted while German access to the Soviet market was maximized.

6

THE DEVELOPING RELATIONSHIP BETWEEN POLITICS, ECONOMICS, AND COMMERCIAL FILM AESTHETICS

The economic pressures imposed by competition with Hollywood concerned leaders in the German film industry as much as the potential ideological influence of Soviet films. In September 1927, for example, Ufa's Consul Marx spoke to representatives of the Hungarian film industry in Budapest and publicly declared his desire to organize a Pan-European coalition to combat Hollywood's "invasion" of European film markets.[1] Ufa's general director reprimanded him. At the next meeting of Ufa's executive committee, Ludwig Klitzsch asked its members to resolve not to discuss Ufa's business policies publicly, referring specifically to receptions attended by Ufa delegates as potentially dangerous situations (R109, 1026a, 16 September 1927).

Ufa and other companies nurtured their partnerships with Hollywood companies publicly, although they privately contemplated strategies to overcome the burdens associated with Dawes Plan prosperity. The industry's preferred strategy, as outlined above, was to tolerate the influence of U.S. companies and exploit the Soviet market. If successful, the industry would serve simultaneously the ideological and economic needs of its most conservative members. It would use partnerships with Hollywood companies to remain competitive and limit Soviet access to the German market while increasing German access to the Soviet market. In the process, it would increase its profits and ideological impact while decreasing those of the Soviet industry. As Consul Marx's comments indicated, ideally Ufa would achieve similar goals in its competition with American companies.

In addition to his desire to maintain favorable relations with foreign companies, it seems likely that concern about Ufa's image at home motivated Klitzsch's resolution against publicly discussing policy. It is unlikely that conservative interest groups and their representatives in the film industry could have influenced public opinion as they wished, if they had blatantly opposed Hollywood credit that many German producers needed to survive. Such opposition also might annoy those Germans who uncritically accepted Dawes Plan assistance and those who were fascinated with American society, especially with Hollywood images of it. On the other hand, to openly criticize the Soviet film industry might annoy a growing number of Germans who, almost regardless of their political orientation, praised the achievements of young Soviet directors such as Sergei Eisenstein and Vsevolod Pudovkin. It would certainly annoy those German workers who found attractive what they read, heard, or saw regarding the new Soviet society. It is also unlikely that conservative and reactionary filmmakers could have persuaded most Germans to accept a national dictatorship or the restoration of the Hohenzollern monarchy if they had proclaimed their intention to do so, and thereby benefit a small minority of the wealthy at the expense of most Germans.

THE RELATIONSHIP BETWEEN FILM AND POLITICS

The assertion that film and politics should remain separate effectively masked the political intentions of men such as Ludwig Klitzsch. In this vein, some film company executives and their allies in the print media condemned most, if not all, Soviet films, characterizing them as *Hetzfilme* (film that agitate politically), while defending their own films or films they wished to promote as artistically valuable. Ufa executives employed the strategy frequently to legitimize their rejection of Soviet films. For example, when a theater owner appealed to the SPIO to act against blatantly political Soviet films in April 1928, executive committee members discussed the issue and formulated the following response: "It is resolved that we refer to the decision of the SPIO which has opposed the screening of all political films" (R109, 1027, 10 April 1928). The SPIO consisted of nine members in 1928. Three, including the chairman, also served as Ufa executives. In this case, Ufa was able to cite the decision of an allegedly higher authority, suggesting that all theater owners and distributors follow the established policy. By referring indirectly to a concept of autonomous art, it could reject Soviet films and imply that its own films were apolitical and therefore above reproach.

The German government, too, often opposed Soviet and other ideologically undesirable films through censorship and contingency laws, but also under the pretext of aesthetic judgments. The Lampe Committee, organized by the ministry of the interior and named after its chairman Felix Lampe, worked with national censorship boards and decided whether films were *künstlerisch* (artistic), *volksbildend* (generally contributing to public edification), or *Lehrfilm* (educational film).[2] Films that qualified were granted partial exemption from the *Lustbarkeitssteuer,* the entertainment tax levied on box-office receipts.[3] During the years of relative stability, the Lampe Committee increased its preference for Fridericus and World War I films, characterizing them as artistic and educational, while withholding its approval and any tax privileges from those who made, distributed, and screened Soviet and other "leftist" films.[4] Although the committee used aesthetic and intellectual labels, its decisions belied ideological preferences. The newspapers and journals of the German left protested the government's decisions but with little success.

A majority of leading German film journals joined the opposition to "political" films. Scherl's *Kinematograph* was the most conservative in its assessment. Early in 1926, for example, the *Kinematograph* explained its lack of attention to *Battleship Potemkin,* noting that the film certainly functioned as an ideological tool of the Soviet government and that film and politics should have nothing in common (*"Potemkin* him, *Potemkin* her"—*"Potemkin,* Back and Forth," 5 November 1926).

Such explanations appeared to explain why the journal criticized Soviet films, but they demonstrated something entirely different in light of the close association between the *Kinematograph* and Ufa, especially after Hugenberg's acquisition of Ufa in 1927. The *Kinematograph* only pretended to support the separation of film and politics. In reality it followed the strategy of Ufa and others in condemning films it perceived as threatening while praising ideologically acceptable films, particularly Ufa films, from a supposedly nonideological position.

The *Film-Kurier* also opposed the political use of cinema, but at least acknowledged that groups from every point on the political spectrum engaged actively in cinematic propaganda. According to a cartoon (*Film-Kurier,* 11 August 1926), all major political parties competed for influence in cinema, while cunning theater owners offered a wide variety of films to please an ideologically heterogeneous audience. More often than not, though, theater owners accepted the guidelines of the SPIO, preferred to screen films with a partial tax exemption, and generally limited access for distributors of Soviet films and the films of the German left.

Beginning in 1926, and coinciding roughly with a controversy surrounding the censorship of *Battleship Potemkin,* the *L.B.B.* periodically called for the separation of film and politics. Like the *Film-Kurier,* the *L.B.B.* noted that the political right as well as the political left had used the film media for political purposes. "Hetzfilme" ("Agitational Films," *L.B.B.,* 22 February 1926) reported that the DNVP had challenged the government to modify censorship laws to forbid "political propaganda" films such as *Freies Volk (Liberated People),* an SPD-affiliated film, and *Sein Mahnruf (His Warning),* a Soviet film. According to the DNVP, these films threatened social stability by promoting class struggle and encouraging German workers to join the world revolution. The article asserted: "It is somewhat curious that such 'protective measures' are being proposed today precisely by the parties of the *right,* who have employed film propaganda themselves, and who only call for police assistance when left-orientated films begin to make them uncomfortable." The *L.B.B.* worked diligently to expose the political right's attempt to conceal the ideological nature of conservative and reactionary films and to condemn as propaganda the films of the German left and the Soviet Union. The journal took the same position in the debate about the censorship of *Battleship Potemkin,* arguing that the political right had no reservations about the monarchical *Fridericus Rex* in 1922 and should therefore have none about *Battleship Potemkin.*

Although the *L.B.B.* rejected any combination of film and politics, it did advocate social functions for cinema. The author of "Agitational Films" exclaimed: "*Ban political films from the movie theater! . . .* They poison cinema's atmosphere of pure entertainment." For him and many others cinema's function was entertainment. The distinction between political and entertainment films surfaced frequently in *L.B.B.* articles. Dr. Hans Wollenberg, the editor of the *L.B.B.* during much of the Weimar Era, emphasized the same distinction in his article "Grundgedanken zu dem Referat 'Film und öffentliche Meinung'" ("Fundamental Consideration Concerning the Lecture 'Film and Public Opinion,'" 26 June 1926).

According to Wollenberg, cinema should establish a direct connection to the everyday world in the realm of education and science. There, "objective" forms of discourse and perception made it impossible for any one interest group to gain political advantage over another. Educators and scientists could employ film to influence public opinion, i.e., aid in the effort to acquire and communicate a better understanding of natural and historical processes so that humanity could master them and construct a better world.

However, Wollenberg asserted, in the movie theater there should be no connection between film and the everyday world, no connection between film and politics. Wollenberg's comments indicate that he had abandoned the project of philosophical idealists who promoted autonomous art to mediate between the world of superficial appearances and metaphysical essences. Similar to some of the SPD journalists cited in Chapter 3, Wollenberg hoped that autonomous films would entertain audiences. The only constructive influence film should have on public opinion—and in this regard Wollenberg *does* invoke an idealist notion of autonomous art—should be aesthetic.

Instead of highlighting the contradictions, struggles, and injustices of the everyday world to stimulate critical perceptions and motivate change, films should portray the world in all its "beauty and adventurousness," entertaining audiences in a form that "unconsciously cultivates" their aesthetic taste. For what purpose? Wollenberg's cinema would diffuse the potentially revolutionary energy created by dissatisfaction in the everyday world. It would help spectators regain the strength necessary to cope with unsatisfactory conditions by focusing their attention on abstract notions of beauty. Wollenberg's cinema would function as a socially stabilizing medium, not as a medium for social change. Wollenberg's comments are significant because they represented the views of the *L.B.B.*, but even more so because they reflected and reinforced mainstream perceptions of cinema's function in German society in the 1920s. A majority of German film journalists and citizens, positioned at various points between the antirepublican right and Communist left, opposed what they perceived as blatantly political films. They separated acceptable cinema into two categories: educational cinema and cinematic entertainment. From their perspective, documentary, educational, and scientific films offered empirically accurate, apolitical reflections of natural and social phenomena and contributed to public education. Commercial theaters that included documentaries, primarily newsreels, were contributing to this end. The commercial theater's perceived primary function, though, was to entertain.

Nevertheless, as the reference to documentaries and newsreels suggests, the public's perception of what the commercial theater should provide was slowly changing. While public opinion generally insisted on the separation of film and politics, film and everyday life, it accepted documentaries and newsreels and began to accept a connection between film and the "real" world in features. The Lampe Committee nurtured the change by asserting that entertainment films could teach moviegoers something about the world in which they lived. Many German educators acknowledged the possibility and began organizing field trips to film theaters that, according to the Lampe Committee, screened educational films.[5] Good candidates for the distinction were historical films, including World War I films, films about contemporary social problems, and those that introduced audiences to exotic cultures. In all of the cited categories, antirepublicans in the film industry took advantage of the new possibilities to present a clearer ideological standpoint on controversial issues.

THE POLITICS OF UNIVERSAL APPEAL

As mentioned above, both ideological and economic concerns influenced commercial film production in Weimar Germany. As competition increased and production costs steadily rose, producers redoubled their efforts to minimize risks. For smaller producers, who depended to a large extent on the income from one film to produce the next, a single commercially weak film could mean financial ruin. Producers could calculate the cost of film production but experienced difficulty in calculating in advance the commercial value of their films. As a result, they concentrated more intensely on devising techniques to ensure the appeal of their products.

The risk of failure on the one hand and the potential for profit on the other motivated producers to attempt to make films with universal appeal. To approximate the ideal, they calculated the basic elements of the dominant intellectual and emotional needs of the German public and worked to address those needs with their products. Between 1924 and 1929 such calculations required close attention to the needs of a growing lower-middle class. Its ranks were filled with people who looked back with feelings of insecurity to the political unrest and threat of proletarianization in the early Weimar years. They also looked forward to the possibility of moving upward in the social hierarchy, enjoying greater material wealth, and increasing leisure time under the Dawes Plan economy. Although commercial cinema could offer no real guarantee to individuals who had lost their sense of social stability and hoped to work less but earn more, it could provide inexpensive fictional alternatives.

The basic formula for commercial success in German film continued to shift more and more away from the formulas of earlier phases in German film history. Whereas filmmakers could appeal to the public's fascination with novelty between 1896 and 1906 and strove to demonstrate the artistic quality of cinema to attract skeptical middle- and upper-class audiences between 1906 and 1914, they now increased their emphasis on cinematic entertainment. Producers did make a small number of films with the intention of focusing on the needs of marginal social groups. For example, they produced expensive "prestige" films to address the interests of an intellectual and economic elite, but primarily to legitimize their concentration on film production that appealed to what that elite condemned as low or trivial art.

To maximize the accuracy of calculations about the appeal of films and to control production costs, companies continued efforts to standardize film production. To control production costs they developed libraries of standard sequences. Footage of mountain blizzards, waves crashing on the rocks, and congested urban traffic functioned as transition material, or as the visual signifiers of a protagonist's emotional condition, or as some expression of the narrative standpoint. Filmmakers also created filmed backgrounds that could be inserted repeatedly when characters drove through a city, soldiers rode through the countryside, etc. These and numerous other techniques minimized production costs. But they also minimized the possibilities for directors, camera crews, and other technicians to participate creatively in film production. Standardization in the form of productive efficiency privileged the administrator's and bookkeeper's position in the decision-making process.

Filmmakers refined other techniques of standardization to increase the use value of the final product for potential audiences. As mentioned in Chapter 1, even before World War I, producers began to develop attractive stars and to identify film types that had been commercially successful in the past. Film marketing, too, became a significant factor in the early years of the republic, beginning with Erich Pommer's sensational promotion of *The Cabinet of Dr. Caligari.*

During the middle years of the Weimar Republic, film companies practiced such techniques in established as well as innovative ways. Ufa, for example, required its stars to make public appearances at film premieres and generally to participate more actively in the company's marketing program (R109, 1026b, 24 February 1928). By making appearances at provincial and at large urban theaters, film stars did more than increase box-office receipts. When film celebrities appeared in public, they demonstrated that real individuals could move to higher positions in the social hierarchy, just as the fictional characters they portrayed in films often did.[6]

In addition to expanding the star system, the largest producers also exerted pressure on the press to ensure favorable publicity for their films. Ufa's activity demonstrates this clearly. Beginning in the summer of 1927 the executive committee waged a battle with the *L.B.B.* as well as other trade journals and newspapers that, in its opinion, had attacked Ufa with their reports. The *L.B.B.* had expressed reservations about the Hugenberg Concern's takeover of Ufa as early as February 1927, warning that Ufa might become an instrument in the service of the DNVP ("Scherl soll die Ufa finanzieren!"—"Scherl to Finance Ufa!" *L.B.B.,* 21 February 1927). It followed ensuing developments with caution, reporting on incidents such as director Karl Grune's complaint that Ufa had altered the ideological and aesthetic components of his *Am Rande der Welt* (*On the Edge of the World,* see "Fabrikant und Regisseur"—"Producer and Director," *L.B.B.,* 24 September 1927). It also published a review of Ludwig Bernhard's brochure, revealing Ufa's desire to limit communist influence in the German film industry and criticizing the Hugenberg Concern with a note of sarcasm for exaggerating the communist threat ("Hugenberg und Ufa," *L.B.B.,* 2 June 1928).

While the *L.B.B.* filed these and other reports, Ufa's executives contemplated methods to control the publication of potentially damaging information about its policies. In July 1927 the executive committee decided to temporarily cease advertising in the *L.B.B.* (R109, 1026a, 20 July 1927). By August 1928 it resolved to permanently withhold advertising contracts from the journal, to cancel its subscription, and to forbid Ufa executives to establish contact with *L.B.B.* employees (R109, 1027a, 3 July 1928, 9 July 1928, 26 July 1928, and 27 August 1928). Ufa acted similarly to punish the Mosse publishing house's *8-Uhr Abendblatt* and ultimately decided to use advertising contracts generally as a lever to influence what newspapers and trade journals printed about the company and its films (R109, 1027a, 18 April 1929).

Ufa also created positive publicity in newspapers and journals belonging to the Hugenberg Concern. It could rely on positive reviews and reports from Scherl's *Kinematograph* and major newspapers such as the *Berliner Lokal-Anzeiger,* but Ufa moved to increase its influence by publishing the *Ufa-Wochenmagazin*. In the weekly trade journal, which was filled with "objective" accounts of recent developments in the film industry, ample space was available for Ufa film advertisements and flattering reports about the conglomerate's activities. Like its Hollywood competitors, Ufa also operated a news service, supplying both foreign and domestic newspapers and trade journals with articles about film production and its most popular stars. In Germany alone, approximately fifteen hundred newspapers provided Ufa with what amounted to free publicity.[7] The Hugenberg Concern created images of critical acclaim for Ufa's films and friendly attitudes toward the conglomerate, though acclaim and friendship were in fact bound to ideological and economic interests (R109, 1026a, 12 October 1927; and R109, 1027a, 18 April 1929).

While improving their marketing techniques, producers also paid special attention to film types that entertained profitably. Film companies searched even more intensely for potentially popular film subjects in literature and drama, including *Faust* (1926), *Die Liebe der Jeanne Ney* (*The Love of Jeanne Ney*, 1927),[8] and *Frühlings Erwachen* (*Spring Awakening*, 1929). They varied the plots of commercially successful films such as *Die Straße* (*The Street*, 1923), *Dirnentragödie* (*Tragedy of a Prostitute*, 1927), and *Asphalt* (1928). They developed film series like *Der alte Fritz* (*Old Fritz*, 1927, in two parts). And they began to remake successful films from the past: *The Student of Prague* (1913, 1926), *Bismarck* (1913, 1925–26), and *Königin Luise* (*Queen Luise*, 1912, 1927).

Creativity decreased as producers concentrated on entertainment. Weimar film historians suggest that the aesthetic quality of films declined markedly during the period of relative stability. To explain the decline, Siegfried Kracauer invoked his theory of the collective mind and its reflection in film. He claimed that the masses were authoritarian-minded when they entered the stabilized period and that the republican regime prevented those tendencies from finding an outlet. Allegedly too persistent to yield, authoritarian dispositions fell into a state of paralysis, and the decline of the German screen was a reflection of the paralysis (Kracauer, *From Caligari to Hitler*, 54).

Certainly the German people struggled to adjust after the hardships they experienced between 1919 (or even 1914) and 1923. There also can be no doubt that support for the republic diminished in favor of authoritarian models based on recollections of the past. However, as political events such as the presidential election in 1925 and the plebiscite about the aristocracy in 1926 indicated, the German public was, to follow the metaphor, schizophrenically split between republican and antirepublican, democratic and authoritarian, ideologies. The film industry responded to the desires of investors as well as to economic pressures and it privileged an antirepublican, authoritarian orientation. Cinema reflected mass desires only insofar as its ideological orientation addressed the fears and hopes of Germany's lower-middle class. Many films of mainstream cinema recommended submission to authority and the myth of upward social mobility as solutions to social insecurity and the fear of proletarianization. As the German left's critique of such films demonstrated, that was only one of the potential ideological responses to the social reality of Weimar Germany.

7

THE PAST AS METAPHOR FOR THE PRESENT AND *DER ALTE FRITZ (OLD FRITZ)* AS AN EXAMPLE

One of the most popular film subjects during the Weimar era was the Hohenzollern monarchy. Although films about the monarchy had surfaced before World War I, beginning with *Old Fritz* in 1896,[1] over half of all such films produced in Germany appeared between 1918 and 1933. The tremendous commercial success of *Fridericus Rex* prompted Ufa to distribute the planned third segment and to accept a fourth segment in 1922–23.[2] Between 1924 and 1929 German filmmakers produced the following films: *Bismarck I und II* (1925), *Die elf Schillschen Offiziere* (*The Eleven Schillian Officers*, 1926), *Des Königs Befehl* (*The King's Command*, 1926), *Zopf und Schwert* (*Pig Tail and Sword*, 1926), *Die Mühle von Sanssouci* (*The Mill of Sanssouci*, 1926), *Der Emden* (*The Emden*, 1926), *Weltkrieg* (*World War*, 1927, in three parts), *U-9 Weddigen* (1927), *Königin Luise* (*Queen Luise*, 1927–28), and a remake of *Old Fritz* (1927–28, in two parts).

Films about the Hohenzollern monarchy typically focused on the story of Friedrich II between 1756 and 1763, Queen Luise between 1806 and 1815, and Wilhelm II between 1914 and 1918 (Schoenberner, 11). The monarchy in crisis, defending itself against foreign aggressors, received the greatest attention, whereas Friedrich's wars of conquest, the reactionary period of police repression following 1815, and the rise of German imperialism prior to World War I were forgotten.[3] At a time when many Germans contemplated various political models and committed themselves to none, the films mentioned above glorified the monarchical system and motivated audiences to draw parallels to their own social contexts.

Old Fritz: Otto Gebühr in the role of the aging monarch. (Staatliches Filmarchiv der DDR)

Old Fritz is an excellent example. Although it deviated from the norm by portraying the life of Friedrich II from 1762 until his death in 1786, it posited an image of Prussian crisis that was particularly relevant for German moviegoers in 1927. It also offered an impressive protagonist to remedy the situation.

The film featured Otto Gebühr in the role of the aging monarch. Gebühr had begun his career playing the Prussian king in *Fridericus Rex.* The success of that four-part series prompted producers to typecast Gebühr. In his role as king, Gebühr became known as an excellent military strategist, a cunning diplomat, a conscientious and hardworking public servant, and the peasants' guardian against the injustices of the wealthy. He was a patriarch who remained cold and calculating but fair with cosmopolitan intellectuals and bureaucrats in the public sphere. In the private sphere he demonstrated warmheartedness, love, and preference for simple, old-fashioned values.

Gebühr became so closely associated with the role that people often identified him as Friedrich II when he appeared in public.[4] By developing Otto Gebühr into one of the best-known figures in German cinema, the film industry reinforced the attraction to authoritarian strategies for solving the problems of the underdog, that is, the white-collar and blue-collar workers with a lower-middle-class mentality. The content and narrative style of *Old Fritz* reveal that, although the story unfolds in the period between 1762 and 1786, spectators could easily distinguish its antirepublican orientation and apply its message to their situation in 1927.

The film begins with the end of the Seven Years' War. The crisis is twofold: Prussia struggles with postwar reconstruction and with problems related to the eventual change of leadership. As soon as Friedrich II has negotiated peace with the Austrians, he returns to Berlin and begins the task of economic and industrial reconstruction. The plot develops around scenes that demonstrate the aging monarch's conviction and ability to complete the task. He converts Prussia's wartime industries into peacetime industries. He founds banks to administer credit to faltering businesses and new enterprises. He introduces the taxes necessary to finance Prussia's reconstruction and develops a foreign policy to protect the kingdom against potential threats from Russia and Austria. When Austria threatens to annex Bavaria, the old king musters his troops, commanding their respect and proving his unwavering capacity to rule as both administrator and soldier. To audiences in 1927 the film suggested that monarchs or other authoritarian figures might have negotiated a better treaty at the end of World War I, avoided the chaos of the crisis, and guided the economy to an orderly recovery with minimal sacrifices for the masses and with control over speculation and profiteering.

The narrative style of *Old Fritz* reinforces its ideological standpoint by motivating sympathy for the king and stimulating spectators to perceive the film's relevance for them. A very restricted production budget limited the film's director, Gerhard Lamprecht, to a relatively simplistic narration.[5] Nevertheless, he managed to communicate a specific point of view with intertitles and montage. Intertitles allowed Lamprecht to suggest an omniscient narrator with the ability to document the authenticity of the fiction.[6] Before the audience sees any pictorial images, a text appears with the message: "The year 1762 comes to an end." Such statements purport that what the spectator is about to see is what actually transpired in 1762. Once Lamprecht has posited the omniscient narrator, he uses the device to convey more detailed information and allows his characters to speak with the same degree of authority.

Lamprecht amplified sympathy for Friedrich II by intermingling scenes that depict the king, his subjects, and the crown prince. Numerous scenes portray popular anecdotes about the "benevolent" Friedrich II that had acquired a mythical validity in German folklore and heightened his appeal to the little man.[7] Other scenes reveal that his subjects reject his efforts to rebuild the economy, fail to understand his increasing asceticism, and almost gleefully await his death. Still others depict a crown prince who complicates his father's efforts to rebuild Prussia's economy; he flirts with women, commits adultery after his marriage, giving every indication of his inadequacy as successor to the throne.

Lamprecht concluded each part of *Old Fritz* with scenes that invite the audience to reflect further on the juxtaposition of an extremely competent king and his incompetent successor, a dedicated public servant and his ungrateful subjects—and to transpose those juxtapositions into the present. At the end of part one, the monarch renews Prussia's alliance with Russia, visits Joseph II in Austria, gives his last flute concert in Sanssouci, and finally retires to his office where he composes his testament. The sequence of events reminds spectators that Friedrich conducted foreign policy to Prussia's advantage by negotiating a workable peace treaty with Austria. He deserved their admiration and sympathy for ruling the kingdom masterfully, despite his weakening physical condition. In the dark solitude of his office, Friedrich writes: "My wishes in that moment when I breathe my last will be for the happiness of my realm. May it be governed with justice, wisdom, and vigor, may it through the mildness of its laws be the happiest, may it with respect to finances be the best administered, may it through an army which strives for honor and noble glory be the most gallantly defended state; O may it continue to prosper until the end of time."

The text summarizes Friedrich's reign and encourages the audience to contemplate Prussia's future after the monarch's death, as well as Germany's condition following the demise of the Hohenzollern monarchy. The portrayal of the crown prince suggests a bleak future. The final scene of part two confirms the negative appraisal: Friedrich has died, twenty years have passed, and Napoleon stands with his generals before the great monarch's grave. A final text expresses the conqueror's and the narrator's judgment: "Hats off Messieurs! If he still lived, then we would not be standing here today!"

Old Fritz communicated a very clear and relevant message to German moviegoers who had questioned the negotiation of the Versailles Treaty, protested the French occupation of the Ruhr, criticized the speculation of wealthy investors, suffered under inflation and unemployment, and contemplated the political right's caricature of the Soviets as "Bolshevik terrorists." The film asserted that just as the Prussians rejected their aging monarch while he continued to serve them, so also the German people had abandoned their kaiser prematurely. If the Germans had maintained their allegiance to their monarch, he would have served them as Friedrich II served his people following the Seven Years' War. By stimulating the spectator's respect, admiration, and sympathy for the monarch and creating a negative image of the Russian people and Friedrich's successor, the film had the potential to intensify their regret about the loss of the Hohenzollern monarchy and their skepticism about the successors to the throne.

Under the guise of historical realism, *Old Fritz* claimed to educate the German public about its past, while it contributed to the ideological campaign of political reactionaries such as Alfred Hugenberg and his growing faction of antirepublicans in the DNVP. Although it is relatively easy to decipher the ideological message of films like *Old Fritz* and to associate it with the political platform of, for example, the DNVP's right wing, many critics and spectators perceived the films as nothing more than informative and entertaining narratives. By claiming to present an historically authentic and politically neutral account of Germany's past, some filmmakers even succeeded in convincing the Lampe Committee to label their films educational and artistic. In fact, between 1924 and 1929 the overwhelming majority of historical films promoted authoritarian, predominantly monarchical, patriarchal, and militaristic values. Even the World War I films of the period, many of which incorporated documentary footage and relied on the participation of military personnel to substantiate their authenticity and objectivity, concentrated on Germany's military victories, avoided reflection about the imperialist motives for the war, and minimized references to civilian sacrifices—hunger, physical and emotional anguish, death—and revolutionary uprisings.[8]

8

THE QUESTION OF SOCIAL MOBILITY AND A CLOSE LOOK AT *DIE VERRUFENEN (THE NOTORIOUS)*

The narrative suggestion that films such as *Old Fritz* were authentic portrayals of German history helped to legitimize their presentation of antirepublican perspectives. During the years of relative stability, producers employed similar strategies as they gradually introduced contemporary subjects.[1] While public opinion generally remained sensitive to any combination of film and politics and reacted skeptically to realistic films about everyday life in Germany, the film industry experienced increasing success with *Kulturfilme* (documentaries primarily about foreign cultures).

The head of Ufa's cultural film division from the end of World War I until 1928 was Major Ernst Krieger. As early as 1919 Krieger had outlined the goals of his cultural film program in a special report to the government.[2] Krieger summarized the use of documentaries by Germany's opponents during the war and urged the German government to compete energetically in the area of cinematic propaganda. Among other things, Krieger proclaimed: "In Germany, too, we will place film in the service of politics. . . . For colonial propaganda and for other *foreign policy* issues, film will demonstrate its effectiveness" (48). At the end of the report he reiterated the necessity of competing with other industrialized nations and suggested that failure to accept the challenge would allow the Western Allies to gain the same advantage they had enjoyed during the war—an advantage, Krieger implied, that had contributed to Germany's defeat and the postwar crisis (57).

The "authentic" portrayals in Ufa's cultural films followed Krieger's guidelines. Ufa's cultural films, including *Wege zu Kraft und Schönheit*

(*Ways to Strength and Beauty,* 1925) and *Auf Tierfang in Abessinian* (*On Safari in Abyssinia,* 1926), as well as the Cultural Film Society's *Weltgeschichte als Kolonialgeschichte* (*World History as Colonial History,* 1927), affirmed the German nationalism that had moved Germany into the race for colonial acquisitions and culminated in World War I.

The illusion of authenticity played an equally significant role in two other popular film genres of the stable years. Between 1924 and 1929 "street" films and "Zille" films became very popular. The films of both genres *did* portray contemporary life in Germany, and they encouraged audiences to perceive their portrayals as authentic.

The street films, named after Karl Grune's *Die Straße* (*The Street,* 1923), represented a further development of the *Aufklärungsfilme* discussed in Chapter 2.[3] Although the *Aufklärungsfilme* affirmed patriarchal concepts of the family and sexuality, conservative religious and political organizations had argued that they tempted more than they deterred. Protest led to the reintroduction of censorship laws and to increased attempts to control sexual attitudes. However, the commercial success of the *Aufklärungsfilme* influenced production more than did censorship. Filmmakers continued making films about socially unacceptable forms of sexuality, but they devised less provocative titles and emphasized more the dangers of sexual deviance. The result was the development of the street film genre, including G. W. Pabst's *Freudlose Gasse* (*Joyless Street,* 1925), Bruno Rahn's *Dirnentragödie* (*Tragedy of a Prostitute,* 1927), and Joe May's *Asphalt* (1928).

Like the historical films of the period, the street films employed various cinematic techniques to suggest authenticity. Karl Grune, for example, began his film *The Street* with an omniscient narrative text that connected the cinematic fiction and everyday reality: "There comes a time in the life of nearly every man, be he good or bad, when, appalled by the monotony and drabness of his daily life, his soul yearns for something different—he longs for the unknown, for the glamour and excitement he imagines to be the lot of the other man, the man in the street." Joe May began *Asphalt* similarly: "Asphalt—pavements—the pounding of muscle and sweat and iron to make a path for man: a smooth path—an asphalt path—feet—wheels—the rumble and roar, the hiss and shriek, the clangor and clamor of a city—moving—endlessly flowing—like life itself." In addition to positing an omniscient narrator with texts, many of the street films integrated footage of real urban street scenes with fictional studio street scenes to increase the suggestion of authenticity.

While developing their claim to authenticity, street films portrayed urban environments as inherently dangerous, evil places, dominated by prostitutes, pimps, criminals, and alcoholics.⁴ They juxtaposed the evil public sphere of the street with a virtuous private sphere of lower-middle- to middle-class families and developed their plots around dissatisfied daughters, sons, and sometimes husbands. These characters abandoned domestic security, suffered misfortune in the street, and returned to their families cleansed of discontent.

This film genre encouraged the large numbers of lower-middle-class and working-class Germans to exercise caution. If they were dissatisfied with their standard of living and contemplated the type of radically democratic change that was generally associated with the urban working-class environment, disaster awaited. To venture into the street and associate with its inhabitants meant to succumb to the potential destruction of what was an inherently evil public sphere. If filmgoers were dissatisfied, they should content themselves with the relative security they could find or fabricate in the private spheres of their homes and families. The street films presented a powerful image of everyday life that discouraged the social interaction necessary for a flourishing democratic society.

The so-called Zille films promoted a similar ideological orientation with similar techniques. Beginning in 1925 with Gerhard Lamprecht's *The Notorious,* a number of films focused on contemporary problems such as social reintegration for ex-convicts, *The Notorious;* care for illegitimate children, *Die Unehelichen (The Illegitimate,* 1926); and alcoholism, *Die Gesunkenen (The Fallen,* 1926). The producers of such films drew on the success of Heinrich Zille, an extremely popular Berlin artist whose close contact with the working class enhanced the image of his work as the most trustworthy artistic expression of the working-class environment. To attract audiences, producers used various methods to associate their films directly with Zille and to claim a degree of authenticity equal to that of the artist's work. This connection also increased the credibility of the narrative perspectives and maximized their impact on spectators.

Like the street films, Zille films juxtaposed an inherently negative working-class environment with a generally virtuous and especially philanthropic middle- to upper-class environment. Whereas the street films concentrated on the potential downward social mobility of middle-class men and women and emphasized the impossibility of upward social mobility for the inhabitants of the street milieu, the Zille films sustained hope for a fortunate few who maintained high moral standards and resisted the temptations of alcohol, sex, and crime. Those who strove re-

The Notorious: a mainstream Zille film. (Stiftung Deutsche Kinemathek)

lentlessly to improve their standard of living would succeed. Such people, regardless of their class or personal background, found their way out of the quagmire with the help of benevolent individuals and the existing social institutions. While the street films warned middle-class and lower-middle-class spectators about the possibility of downward social mobility and advised them to avoid social interaction with the lower classes, the Zille films offered hope to those who began to question the myth of upward social mobility. *The Notorious* illustrates how Lamprecht established the Zille connection and used it to promote the myth.

A short narrative text introduces the story, claiming that it is based on Heinrich Zille's firsthand experience. The first pictorial images depict Heinrich Zille at work. They are followed by an image of what the artist is sketching: a bar scene. The sketch dissolves as images of "real" characters in a bar appear. The relatively short sequence suffices to associate the cinematic fiction with the work of Zille and invites spectators to accept what they see as authentic. Lamprecht creates the illusion of reality through other techniques, as well. He integrates documentary footage and relies on natural surroundings for staged scenes. And his characters speak colloquially, often in dialect.

In addition to substantiating the claim to authenticity, the opening sequences foreshadow the fundamental tension of the plot. The story focuses on Robert Kramer, who strives to reintegrate himself into middle-class society after serving a prison sentence. At every step along the way, Kramer meets resistance. His middle-class father refuses to accept an ex-convict into his household, his fiancée has abandoned him in favor of a wealthy stockholder, and prospective employers reject his pleas for work. Kramer takes refuge in a sanctuary for the homeless, finds work in a sweatshop, and eventually contemplates suicide. A prostitute, Emma, dissuades him and cares for him.

At that point Kramer has landed in an environment reminiscent of the street film settings. There he meets his former prison mate Gustav and considers whether he should continue to search for honest employment or join Emma and Gustav in a life of crime. Kramer continues his search. He becomes a photographer's assistant and eventually finds work in a factory. In the factory he demonstrates his engineering skill and pleases his employer, who listens to Kramer's story, buys him new clothes, transfers him temporarily to another city, and recalls him to a respectable post when everyone has forgotten the ex-convict's past. At the conclusion of the story, Kramer even develops an intimate relationship with his employer's sister, Regina.

In the end the narrator moves into the foreground again and summarizes the film's ideological perspective: "Poverty and misery, vice and alcohol turn these people into what we call the fifth estate." The image of Robert and Regina with the superimposed image of marching lumpen proletarians replaces the text. Robert has escaped the stream of misery. These images, in turn, are replaced by the final narrative text: "Human beings, who can not escape their destinies. A world in itself, a world one can combat, but can not heal." Now the spectator sees Robert, who kisses Regina's hand, and the film ends.

Except for Robert, the inhabitants of the "street"-like environment are doomed to remain where they are. According to the narrator, poverty, misery, vice, and alcohol are the causes of the lumpen-proletarian existence; there are no causes for these "causes." The audience is left with the assertion that the lumpen-proletarian conditions can be combated but they never disappear. The film discounts the possibility of fundamental social change. The only solution for people who find themselves trapped in the lumpen-proletarian world is to work harder. The film prescribes obedience to the existing social authority and promotes the myth of upward social mobility. Under extenuating circumstances philanthropic individuals intervene on behalf of those who deserve a better life.[5]

The films of the most popular genres during the stable years did little to support a republican perspective. Historical films glorified a monarchical system of government, and cultural films rejuvenated German nationalism. The street films counseled spectators to content themselves and avoid social interaction in an inherently dangerous public sphere, while the Zille films promoted loyalty to, but not active participation in, the existing system of social authority.

The narrative techniques of such films also encouraged authoritarian modes of perception, thought, and communication. Their illusion of reality discouraged audiences from participating in the narrative process and blocked the opportunity for critical reception. Their documentary footage, natural settings, nonprofessional actors, dialect and colloquial language, as well as omniscient narrative texts, suggested to spectators, who merely consumed with little self-initiative in what was already a passive environment, that the filmic point of view was definitive, and not open to question.

During the second half of the 1920s, German filmmakers continued to experiment with camera techniques and montage. Weimar film historians have alternately emphasized the influence of Edwin Porter, D. W. Griffith, Dziga Vertov, Sergei Eisenstein, and Vsevolod Pudovkin.[6] It is extremely difficult to determine who influenced whom, when, and in precisely what way, but one thing is certain: German filmmakers grew increasingly aware of the possibilities for creating new effects with the camera and with the scissors. Often, filmmakers developed techniques to strengthen the illusion of reality and to increase their influence on the audience's perception.

F. W. Murnau, Carl Mayer, and Carl Freund attracted widespread attention and set many new standards in 1924 by employing a fully automatic camera in *Der letzte Mann* (*The Last Laugh*). As Kracauer has noted: "Throughout the film [the camera] pans, travels and tilts up and down with a perseverance which not only results in a pictorial narrative of complete fluidity, but also enables the spectator to follow the course of events from various viewpoints. The roving camera makes him experience the glory of the uniform as well as the misery of the tenement house, metamorphoses him into the hotel porter and imbues him with the author's own feelings" (*Caligari*, 105). Of special significance here is the focus on the camera's ability to associate the spectator's perception with that of fictional characters and the narrative. Kracauer first claims that the camera "enables" the spectator to perceive the action from a plurality of viewpoints, suggesting that there is a choice. He then more accurately describes the camera's power over the spectator. It "makes him experience," "metamorphoses him," "imbues him." In doing so, the camera lends the fictional experience an illusion of reality, that is, the camera makes it more difficult for spectators to distinguish between cinematic fiction and reality—even between fictional characters and themselves.

One of the most powerful examples from *The Last Laugh* is a scene in which the devoted hotel porter drowns his sorrows in alcohol. Instead of restricting the spectator's perception of drunkenness to images of Emil Jannings, pantomiming his condition, the camera assumes his perspective and forces the audience to see and move with/as the porter. For the duration of the segment the spectator no longer merely watches the drunkenness portrayed as cinematic fiction, but experiences it almost as directly as reality.

The effectiveness of such narration depended on a moving camera, but also on montage. Only with well-organized cuts between shots of Jannings drinking, standing, and staggering—and shots of wildly moving scenery (an effect created by moving the camera erratically, as if it were the eyes of the porter)—could the association between the spectator and the protagonist develop. Filmmakers also worked more consciously to develop montage techniques that organized spectators' perceptions into narrative units, motivated them to draw preestablished connections between isolated segments, and guided them to an intended ideological conclusion about the film's material.[7]

The discussion of Gerhard Lamprecht's *Old Fritz* illustrated how the juxtaposition of scenes encouraged spectators to sympathize with the aging monarch (see Chapter 7). In *The Notorious,* Lamprecht intensified his influence on the audience's response by constructing match cuts between segments. Transitional objects, activities, or characters link segments with one another in a way that encourages the audience to compare and contrast and eventually to form conclusions as the narrative develops and finally resolves its conflict. The series of sequences in which Kramer almost commits suicide, accepts Emma's aid, acquaints himself with her environment, and contemplates his situation provides a good example.

After the prostitute, Emma, prevents Kramer's suicide, she takes him to a bar and buys him a meal. There is a cut, and the spectator sees Kramer's former fiancée, Gerda, eating with her stockbroker husband. The consumption of food with the corresponding setting connects the two segments. It also signals a comparison between the lumpenproletarian milieu, in which Kramer now resides, and the middle-class environment, from which he apparently has been excluded.

While Gerda eats, her husband reads a newspaper article. A cut to the text of the article reveals that it is about an unemployed accountant who hanged himself after suffering severe malnutrition. The husband comments: "Lazy bum! If a man really wants to work, he can always find a job." The newspaper article, with its references to unemployment, hunger, and suicide, connects this segment with previous ones in which Kramer diligently seeks work, receives alcohol instead of money as compensation for his work in the sweatshop, and considers suicide. The audience already knows that Kramer is anything but lazy. The newspaper article reminds the spectator to connect this segment with previous segments. It motivates sympathy for and curiosity about Kramer, antipathy toward the stockbroker, and doubt about the promise of success for hardworking individuals. Then there is another cut. The narrative returns to Kramer and Emma, who join a party in the bar with Gustav and other lumpen proletarians. Further cuts juxtapose the scene in the bar, which Kramer observes from a distance, and mental images of parties that Kramer celebrated with Gerda in the past; they also juxtapose images of Kramer with

Emma and images of Kramer with Gerda. While Kramer and the party serve as matching images, the montage distinguishes between Kramer's present and his image of the past.

This organization of sequences encourages spectators to associate with Kramer as he perceives his new surroundings and compares them with his past middle-class surroundings. The montage evokes sympathy for the unjustly disadvantaged Kramer and increases the hope that he will eventually succeed in his quest for upward social mobility. By creating the expectation and by developing tension around it, the film prepares spectators to transform their sympathy for Kramer into an uncritical affirmation of the solution to his problem. The solution invites the audience to have faith in the status quo, to applaud Kramer's efforts to succeed within the system, and to support social philanthropy as a solution to extenuating circumstances.

Between 1924 and 1929 Lamprecht and many other filmmakers employed new cinematic techniques that allowed them to construct tightly knit narrative structures using fewer and fewer intertitles and more and more visual signals. They encouraged spectators to sit quietly and let the film act upon them, stimulating their emotions generally and shaping their reception.[8] Although the industry continued to permit a modicum of experimentation, it preferred well-organized narrative films that entertained audiences. Such films were better financial risks and, in most cases, more in line with the ideological expectations of the industry's decision makers.

9

THE SPD AND FILM: AMBIVALENCE TOWARD MAINSTREAM CINEMA AND THE INITIATION OF AN INDEPENDENT FILM PROGRAM

Between 1924 and 1929 the SPD no longer felt extreme pressure within its ranks to practice radical methods of social change.[1] The proponents of such change had left the party in large numbers during the crisis years. Some found their way back to the SPD after 1924, but most of these now embraced parliamentary democracy. Only a fairly weak left wing of the SPD continued to promote revolutionary class struggle.[2] Its members confronted a party leadership that now denied the existence of a state mechanism for the oppression of subordinate social classes by a ruling elite. Leading Social Democrats, such as Rudolf Hilferding, posited an alternative concept of democratic socialism, claiming that it would permit increased government inducement to economic development and increased worker participation in organizing production; Weimar democracy would, in other words, facilitate an evolutionary transformation from capitalism to socialism.

The theoretical debate between the SPD's leadership and its weaker left wing continued throughout the stable years, but the party's practical work concentrated increasingly on legislative reform. As mentioned earlier, the SPD and KPD cooperated in initiating a plebiscite to disinherit the German aristocracy in 1926. In 1927 and 1928 the party supported a more generous unemployment insurance law, advocated other improvements in social programs, opposed close connections between the German Reichswehr and big business, and waited for the appropriate moment to establish a governing coalition.

The SPD's strategy enabled it to regain leadership in the Great Coalition from 1928 to 1930, but the predicted evolution toward socialism failed to transpire. Instead of developing into a socialist state, the Weimar Republic began its gradual transformation into a totalitarian dictatorship. Hilferding's scenario for progressive evolution toward socialism depended on uninterrupted economic support from Western banks. When Weimar's source of credit vanished, so did any hope for the social change he and the other prophets of democratic socialism had envisioned.

Social Democratic cultural development in some respects paralleled the party's political development between 1924 and 1929. As in the political sphere, a debate between factions of the party mainstream and a weak left wing shaped activity in the cultural sphere; three major trends emerged.[3]

The party's oldest and most influential theoreticians continued to posit concepts of autonomous art. Karl Kautsky's *Die materialistische Geschichtsauffassung* (*The Materialist Concept of History*, 1927) exemplified the trend. Kautsky persisted in abstracting art from everyday life. He ascribed to art an entertainment value, asserting that it could serve working people who strove to escape from and lessen the monotony of their daily routines. From his perspective the SPD's task was to provide the working masses with the same cultural opportunities that the dominant social classes enjoyed (2: 279). Kautsky also implied the conventional juxtaposition between a high culture of the allegedly more intelligent, sophisticated bourgeoisie and a low culture of the less refined working class. To accept his juxtaposition meant to affirm and to assimilate the dominant values of Weimar culture. The majority of SPD cultural leaders did accept it and continued to nurture the process of assimilation.

In contrast to the Kautsky faction, some Social Democratic intellectuals followed Franz Mehring's example and investigated the relationship between artistic production and sociohistorical conditions from a materialist perspective. Alfred Kleinberg with his *Die deutsche Dichtung in ihren sozialen, zeit- und geistesgeschichtlichen Bedingungen* (*German Literature in Its Social, Historical, and Intellectual Contexts*, 1927) provides a good example. Kleinberg rejected the concept of autonomous art, but his conclusions about the relationship between art and everyday life were tenuous. He perceived strict cause-and-effect relationships between artistic expression and the dominant material as well as ideological conditions of each sociohistorical period. To explain differences in the works of various artists in a specific period and to avoid being criticized for reducing art to a mechanical process, Kleinberg held to the notion of an intangible artistic genius. He also paid no attention to the relationship between production and reception. For him books, paintings, films, etc.

were complete and fixed entities. Within the mainstream of the SPD, cultural theoreticians such as Alfred Kleinberg attempted to develop a Marxist approach to literary history, but their projects included a residual tension between idealism and materialism that derived from an inability or unwillingness to grasp the dialectical nature of social and cultural development.

Opposed to the mainstream factions was a smaller, less influential left wing, represented by cultural activists such as Anna Siemsen.[4] Siemsen had come from the Independent Socialists and criticized the popular concept of democratic socialism. She also attacked the cultural orientation of the party. Instead of uncritically accepting concepts of art that emphasized its entertainment or edification value, Siemsen strove to explain the evolution of art, by referring to the division of labor in capitalist society and polemicizing against it. She criticized the development of art as an occupation, the separation of artist from audience, and the exclusion of art's consumers from the process of production. Capitalist modes of production, she argued, had diminished the capacity of humans to express themselves creatively through art.

Siemsen recognized that modern mass media accelerated the trend toward uncritical reception. She suggested to workers that the first step toward regaining the capacity to express themselves creatively through art must be to combat the monopolization of mass media by a social elite. The next step would be to build independent cinema and radiobroadcasting organizations. The final step would be to create new forms of artistic self-expression that would allow workers to interact, emotionally more than rationally, in a way that would promote a sense of solidarity and social responsibility.

Siemsen's concept of art associated her with the Soviet *Proletkult* movement and with German *Proletkult* experiments. Within a party whose leadership generally opposed the tactics of the Communists, there were few opportunities to experiment with the concepts that had provided a significant impulse for the cultural work of the most radical segments of the German communist movement between 1919 and 1921.[5] During the years of relative stability, the SPD's left wing challenged the party's cultural orientation, but it was unable to compete effectively with the influence of theoreticians such as Kautsky and with the party's solidifying educational and cultural institutions.

The Reichsausschuß für sozialistische Bildung (Reich Committee for Socialist Education, a new name for the Central Education Committee), for example, considered it less and less necessary to develop its own mass adult education system, arguing that it could rely on existing public and trade union programs.[6] By relying on such programs, the SPD supported education that for the most part sustained the authoritarian relationship between teachers and students, concentrated uncritically on raising vocational and general intellectual capabilities, and paid little or no attention to political theory and sociology. At the same time, the Reich Committee did organize tutorial courses on political theory, but did so primarily to train its officials. Consequently, the party nurtured the development of a bureaucracy that perceived itself as separate from and superior to the rank and file. Social Democratic educational programs lost contact, at least temporarily, with large numbers of SPD members and voters, while solidifying the bureaucratic structures within the party.[7]

In the cultural sphere, the SPD could boast an extremely broad range of activities, in contrast to the educational sphere, where the number and variety of programs decreased. Its efforts in the Second Reich to establish working-class cultural organizations had been very successful. The Arbeiter-Turn und Sport-Bund (Workers Gymnastics and Sport Federation) and the Arbeitersängerbund (Workers Federation of Singers), for example, had memberships considerably larger than that of the entire SPD by the end of the 1920s. Yet such organizations, which by their very existence had seemed revolutionary within the context of the Wilhelminian monarchy, had a socially stabilizing influence in the Weimar Republic. Following standards promoted prior to World War I, members in Social Democratic cultural organizations to a large extent perceived their involvement as recreational or educational and applauded events that concentrated on "high" culture. The SPD responded affirmatively to demands for "masterpieces" and expressed pride in the high intellectual and cultural standards of the party.[8]

There was some concern about the lack of political intensity in cultural work. However, party bureaucrats, as was the case with the organization of the Sozialistischer Kulturbund (Socialist Federation of Culture) in 1925, usually initiated efforts to rectify the problem from above. Such initiatives failed to influence the rank and file significantly.[9] In some cases the party's programs began to resemble public relation campaigns, designed to increase member and voter allegiance to party leaders. May Day celebrations, for example, had become well-orchestrated ceremonies, held after work and featuring musical and dramatic performances. Such occasions provided an excellent opportunity for party leaders to polish the SPD's image, highlight their achievements in parliament, and solicit the continued support of their constituents. They did little to encourage members and sympathizers to exercise their own initiative in the process of social change.

FILM CRITICISM IN THE SPD PRESS

Between 1924 and 1929 the SPD's *Vorwärts* covered cinema more comprehensively than any other party publication. In addition to publishing regular reports on the status of the film industry and critiques of individual films and film genres, the newspaper occasionally included theoretical articles on the medium as an art form and as a factor in the ideological struggle between opposing political factions. The party's theoretical journal, *Die Gesellschaft* (*Die Neue Zeit* through the end of 1923), published no articles on film between 1924 and 1929. It is likely that party leaders considered it more appropriate to broaden film coverage in the SPD's largest press organ, since cinema had become an important part of everyday life.

From February 1925 until February 1928, the *Vorwärts* Sunday edition included a special one-page section, "Aus der Filmwelt" ("From the World of Film"), with a feature article on a relevant topic from the world of cinema, a variety of film critiques, and a list of what the editors considered to be the week's best films. Articles on film also appeared occasionally during the week under the rubric "Unterhaltung und Wissen" ("Entertainment and Knowledge") but more often than not only when an event such as the Hugenberg Concern's investment in Ufa or national conventions of the film industry's leaders seemed to warrant immediate attention. In February 1928 "From the World of Film" disappeared, and the number of articles on film slowly decreased to the point where months passed with none at all.

There are two plausible explanations. At precisely the time *Vorwärts* editors dropped the "From the World of Film" section, the VFV emerged and began to publish a journal. It is possible that the SPD leadership agreed sufficiently with the VFV's orientation to depend on its program. *Vorwärts* articles on film illustrate that the Social Democratic critique of mainstream cinema at least partially corresponded with that of the VFV. But *Vorwärts* journalists never supported the VFV explicitly, and though Social Democrats worked in the organization, the party never officially cooperated with the VFV. (See Chapter 11 for further information.) In 1929 the SPD began to publish its own monthly journal to report on the activities of the Film und Lichtbilddienst (FuL). It is also possible that its *Monatliche Mitteilungen* had been intended to replace the "From the Film World" section of the *Vorwärts* Sunday edition.

Although it is difficult to determine what exactly motivated the changes in press coverage, one thing is clear: the SPD's interest in film steadily increased during the middle years of the Weimar Republic. It is equally clear that while their interest grew, most Social Democrats more intensely criticized mainstream cinema's influence on ever larger audiences. However, published attitudes toward film in general, the mainstream cinema, and Social Democratic alternatives largely developed within the parameters outlined in chapter 3.

By 1924 the perception that some films were artistic slowly brought an end to the debate among SPD cultural activists about the medium's artistic potential. K. H. Döscher announced that it was time to end the discussion in "Volksbühne und Film" ("People's Theater and Film," *Vorwärts*, 26 May 1924). The Volksbühne, following the example of the Volksfilmbühne of 1922–23, had attempted to expand its sphere of influence by scheduling a film event. Döscher applauded the effort. He referred to the "proven organization" of the Volksbühne and hoped that the party now would concentrate more on practical work and less on theoretical discussion. The Volksbühne, according to Döscher, should identify artistic films, screen them for working-class audiences, and reform German cinema. The films selected for the first Volksbühne event, including excerpts from *Scherben* (*Shattered Fragments*, 1921) and *Der müde Tod* (*Destiny*, 1921), suggest that the organizers still accepted experimentation with expressionism as a legitimate artistic endeavor, regardless of the ideological significance.

Following Döscher's report, interest in the program diminished, but supporters of an autonomous art cinema persevered. At least as late as 1927, some Social Democrats insisted on the separation of film and everyday life as an important criterion in evaluating the artistic quality of films. The argument between opposing factions within the SPD intensified in 1927 over the concept of *Tendenzfilme*. A *Vorwärts* article titled "Tendenzfilme" (13 March 1927) illustrated the intensity by adamantly stating: "Cinema, insofar as it requires our serious attention, has the damned duty and responsibility to reflect with its images the intellectual issues and problems of our times."

Between 1924 and 1929 *Vorwärts* journalists moved slowly to accept feature films about contemporary social problems. The process included retracing intermediate steps taken prior to World War I and again in the postwar period of crisis.[10] Whereas the decisive criterion for accepting a connection between film and everyday reality had been the perceived objectivity of a scientific or educational film, some journalists now began to affirm cinema's power to evoke emotional responses as a positive factor in mass cultural education.

In "Der Film als Kulturproblem" ("Film as Cultural Issue," 7 June 1924), for example, *Vorwärts* published the views of Dr. Erwin Ackerknecht, a leader of the cinema reform movement. Ackerknecht posited film's educational value as the recorder of factual events from the world of reality and as narrator of fictionalized real events. He asserted that educational films were especially effective when they appealed to the human desire for "emotional experience" in a "healthy manner" and managed to dissolve what he perceived as far too much "disharmony between the intellectual and spiritual forces" in contemporary society.

Other articles, too, began to affirm the spectator's desire for emotional experience, but they described only generally how narrative fictional films should satisfy that desire. "Kulturfilm und Publikum" ("Cultural Film and Audience," 3 May 1925), for example, reinforced Ackerknecht's position by advocating that cultural films appeal emotionally without abandoning their intellectual quality. A review of three features (see "Dem Filmpublikum zur Freude"—"For the Pleasure of the Film Audience," 22 February 1925) stated simply: "Uniforms, circus, and charming, unselfconsciously playing children—that is what the film audience enjoys."[11]

The number of articles that overlooked cinema's ideological component decreased significantly during the stable years, and *Vorwärts* criticism of commercial film's conservative to reactionary portrayal of history gradually increased. Hans Lefebre, for example, in "Der Film der Deutsche" ("The Film of the Germans," 17 January 1926) exposed the orientation of the Filmhaus Bruckmann by citing nationalistic phrases from its letter to theater owners about *Bismarck*. Other articles such as an earlier review of *Bismarck* (25 December 1925) described how producers appealed to the need for security among the growing numbers of lower-middle-class Germans with films about strong authority figures. And in "Filmzensur der Reaktion" ("Reactionary Film Censorship," 21 February 1926) *Vorwärts* editors encouraged opposition to the DNVP's proposal for tighter censorship of allegedly leftist films. The article implicated DNVP members in the production of films such as *Fridericus Rex* and *Bismarck,* claiming that they falsified history in order to increase antirepublican sentiment and therefore deserved the close scrutiny of film censors themselves.[12]

Vorwärts contributors also began to analyze commercial films about contemporary social problems. In "Der erste Zille Film" ("The First Zille Film," 30 August 1925) the newspaper praised the makers of *The Notorious* for thematizing pressing social issues. The newspaper responded similarly to the first Soviet films screened in Germany, focusing exclusively on their proletarian subject matter and applauding them for counterbalancing the large number of German films about the Hohenzollern monarchy and members of the social elite (see "Palast und Festung"— "Palace and Fortress," 10 May 1925). *Vorwärts* critics soon transcended their fairly undifferentiated position and began to look more critically at the treatment of contemporary topics. The review of *The Illegitimate* (12 September 1926), for example, criticized the film for developing simple dichotomies: that the inhabitants of the proletarian environment were inherently bad and the rich inherently good people, whose philanthropy represented the only possible salvation for the illegitimate children of the working-class world.

Although most *Vorwärts* critics concentrated on the influence of producers, distributors, and theater owners, or on plot lines, a few also investigated solidifying techniques for maximizing commercial success and their effect on film quality. Three articles, "Deutsche Filmproduktion 1926" (11 July 1926), "Manuskript und Film" (28 February 1927), and "Schema im Film" ("Standardization in Film," 24 December 1929), bemoaned the effect of standardization. The first considered the exploitation of the *Battleship Potemkin* subject in films such as *Hessen, Emden,* and *Die gesunkene Flotte (The Sunken Fleet)*; the second cited use of the Zille concept; and the final article discussed more generally the development of typical narrative structures. All three demonstrated that the Social Democratic understanding of commercial film production continued to deepen, but slowly.

Whereas *Vorwärts* critics now discussed the ideological orientation of filmmakers and the ideological significance of plot, they were either unable or unwilling to criticize existing patterns of production in anything but terms of artistic quality. Instead of condemning narrative standardization for pacifying filmgoers who might otherwise have channeled everyday frustration and dissatisfaction into attempts at social change, they merely bemoaned the lack of artistic experimentation. As Felix Seherret emphasized in "Standardization in Film"; "Every standardization is injurious to art and kills promising innovations. When one sees five average films of German and five of American production, then one knows the themes, characters, structure, and mise-en-scène of modern film."

For the most part *Vorwärts* articles on cinematic form encouraged the emotional impact of film on audiences. Von Pfan (pseudonym?) in "Bühne und Lichtspieldramen" ("Theatrical and Cinematic Dramas," 1 March 1925) argued that films depended on traditional dramatic conventions: "And one may assert without reservation that the film is in its innermost essence *dramatic*. When it loses its dramatic structure, dramatic tension, and resolutions of conflict, it has failed to recognize its goal—at least the goal of being effective in the popular sense."

Between 1924 and 1929 only one article, a review of the Béla Balázs film *K13513—Die Abenteuer eines Zehnmarkscheins* (*K13513—The Adventures of a Ten-Mark Note*), on 31 October 1926, questioned the effect of the traditional dramatic form on spectatorship: "The question is whether such a film, which doubtless is in many aspects more cinematic than most of the usual successful film dramas, engages the audience. For the present the film viewer prefers a closed narrative, and the most powerful films we have are constructed according to that model. Nevertheless, this other approach has a future."

As it became increasingly clear to Social Democrats that cinema not only had become the primary form of entertainment for the working class but also served antirepublican interests, they submitted proposals for alternatives to commercial cinema with greater frequency. Most proposals concentrated on film as another medium to be used by SPD leaders and party organizations to communicate a republican perspective to the working-class constituency. For the most part they made no reference to the authoritarian quality of commercial film production and reception.[13] Three final *Vorwärts* articles illustrate the SPD attitude toward authoritarian models.

In "Erziehung und Film" ("Education and Film," 16 May 1926) Alice Simmel advocated the use of film to counterbalance commercial film's invitation for young people to flee from mechanized reality. Simmel's goal was to motivate young people who had become dissatisfied with life in the mechanized modern world to reject the egotistical individualism associated with commercial films and to accept socialism as a viable alternative. She emphasized the attraction of building a true community from the chaos of contemporary society, but envisioned a cinematic model for communicating her viewpoint that excluded young people from taking initiative. She believed that film should demonstrate, as a teacher would from a position of authority to obediently responding young people, the values of socialism. From Simmel's perspective changes in production and reception were unnecessary. Her comments implied that it would be acceptable to assimilate dominant forms of cinematic narration and encourage spectators to sympathize uncritically with fictional characters and their value systems as long as they were Social Democratic characters with Social Democratic values.

In "Aufgabe der Bildreportage" ("The Goal of Cinematic Reportage," 22 May 1927), Dr. Herbert Feld concentrated on newsreels. Although he recognized that even they had an ideological orientation, Feld also restricted his proposal to questions of content. Newsreel reporters, he argued, should resist the temptation to present the views of any one political party and instead nurture a generally republican perspective. Newsreels should pay more attention to the following items: "Images of important personalities who work for progress; scientists, artists, philanthropists; workshops; tuberculosis; miserable living conditions." Feld concluded: "The weekly newsreels must acquire a social tone, they must facilitate the removal of social inadequacies, demonstrate the effectiveness of social institutions." To a large extent Dr. Feld promoted a public relations approach to newsreel production similar to the growing trend toward ceremonial events in SPD cultural work. They would reinforce authoritarian structures by encouraging trust in the ongoing efforts of government institutions and representatives.

The third article, "Unsere Filmexpedition" ("Our Film Expedition," 10 February 1929) described an SPD film crew's work. It demonstrated that Feld's guidelines for newsreels served as a model for at least some of the party's practical work: "The purpose of a film-shooting trip, which led throughout Germany, was to document the tenacious goal-oriented work of the SPD in the realm of *local politics* and *welfare*." The majority of SPD activity followed the guidelines expressed in the cited articles.

DIE SCHMIEDE (THE FORGE) AND FREIES VOLK (LIBERATED PEOPLE)

After years of talk about an independent film program, SPD leaders finally acted at the beginning of the period of relative stability by joining the ADGB in sponsoring and financing the production of two features, *The Forge* (1924) and *Liberated People* (1925).[14] Martin Berger received the commission to direct both films. It is unclear whether a commercial film company produced *The Forge,* but the Veritas company produced *Liberated People.* Both films have been lost, but press reports provide at least superficial information about their plots.

According to a report in *Die Glocke* (8 November 1924), *The Forge* compares workers who poorly organize a strike and abandon it with other well-organized workers who continue the strike successfully. As the report described: "The strike's young leader has a mother and sister who must scrape out a living by doing piecework for the factory. Nevertheless, they are a little better off than the small-scale artisan's family, for whom unemployment exhausts the last reserves and for whom the organized striker can become a small benefactor. The strikers are promised improvements if they give up the demand for an eight-hour workday. They reject the offer, but during the strike they save the plant from a storm that threatens to flood the area." In the end, dawn breaks and a shoemaker's apprentice, who appears as an idealized flag waver, leads the masses over the hills to the assembled comrades in the factory.

The plot of *Liberated People* is somewhat more complex. The film begins with the story of a house servant named Jenssen who loses his job as the result of financial transactions which ruin his employer. As reported in the *Jungsozialistische Blätter* (3 March 1926):

> He moves to the countryside where he works on a manor. During a wage dispute a fight breaks out, and Jenssen is arrested and imprisoned. The owner of the manor, von Borgsdorff, summons a private army detail to crush the strike. After his release Jenssen becomes the spokesperson for his organization. Then he is fired because he permitted his son to replace his sick mother during the harvest chores. The son is flogged by the headmaster for missing school. The son's teacher, Ronneburg, who had given him permission to be absent, is fired. Borgsdorff had recommended this measure, because Ronneburg had been able to interest Borgsdorff's daughter, Agathe, in his socialist-democratic ideas and had worked in the same way at the village school. The capitalists' oppression in the city and countryside leads to the outbreak of war. The first battles are presented; however, the war ends as the result of the worldwide general strike. The film concludes with an international peace rally at the head of which the couple, Ronneburg and Agathe von Borgsdorff, strides along.

Considering the status of SPD cultural politics and the quality of *Vorwärts* contributions on film at the beginning of the stable period,

Berger's films offer few surprises. The party's lack of experience with production and the SPD approach to cultural work motivated the Social Democrats to borrow more from commercial cinema than they rejected. Their first films were produced commercially for mainstream audiences and made use of standard production techniques.

For example, both relied on plot conventions to soften their subversive potential (Schumann, 80). Instead of requiring a revolution to change society in *The Forge,* a natural catastrophe functions as a deus ex machina to reduce the conflict between striking workers and their employers. At the end of *Liberated People* the class struggle resolves itself in an intimate relationship between Ronneburg and Agathe von Borgsdorff. The representatives of the opposing social classes hold the peace rally in the final scene, symbolizing a reconciliation of class differences and providing a harbinger, if not a model, for the much-criticized utopian ending to *Metropolis* (1926–27).

The Forge and *Liberated People* differed from most commercial films only on the level of content. In contrast to most commercial films, they portrayed a society composed of opposing social classes. And, unlike the popular film genres in which social hierarchy did play an important role, the protagonists are from the lower levels of the hierarchy while the antagonists come from the upper levels. They depicted the struggles of the exploited, suggested the necessity of strikes, and demonstrated the effectiveness of working-class solidarity.

Both films posited relatively undifferentiated images of society and employed traditional dramatic and narrative conventions to influence reception. They supplied easily discernible individual heroes (the flag-waving shoemaker's apprentice in *The Forge;* Jenssen, Ronneburg, and Agathe von Borgsdorff in *Liberated People*) with whom the audience was encouraged to sympathize. According to a *Vorwärts* report on *The Forge* (4 November 1924), the motivation for a sympathetic response increased during the final scene when the orchestra played the "International." The censors report on *Liberated People* suggested that its narration also relied heavily on intertitles.[15] As discussed earlier, commercial filmmakers often employed that technique to ascribe meaning to images.

The Forge and *Liberated People* represented a significant breakthrough in the cultural program of the SPD. For the first time Social Democrats had been able to challenge conservative and reactionary perspectives in mainstream cinema with feature films promoting a republican viewpoint. However, the first two Social Democratic features were far less than revolutionary. They assimilated existing standards of production and reception—and used them to advocate traditional trade unionism, class reconciliation, and working-class dependence on authority. A *Vorwärts* reaction to attacks against *The Forge* in the Hugenberg Concern's *Tag* even admitted that SPD support for commercial film production corresponded to the party's campaign strategy ("Bolschewismus in Film"— "Bolshevism in Film," 21 November 1924). Following unfavorable election results in May 1924, the SPD looked forward to a better showing in the elections scheduled for December. *The Forge,* with its flag-waving shoemaker's apprentice serving as a symbol for effective party leadership, appeared in November 1924.

Neither of the SPD's first films was commercially successful. According to a *Vorwärts* review (4 November 1924), *The Forge* ran in Berlin's commercial theaters but experienced difficulty elsewhere. There was very little press information on *Liberated People,* and none to indicate any degree of commercial success. The Bavarian Ministry of the Interior merely noted: "The press material indicates that its producers intended to oppose nationalistic films such as *Fridericus Rex,* etc., with a major republican film."

THE FILM UND LICHTBILDDIENST

The SPD's endeavor to employ film took another step forward in 1925 with the founding of the Film und Lichtbilddienst (FuL). After a fairly modest beginning in 1926 (only 15 films were distributed), the FuL distributed sixteen times as many film copies in 1927 and continued to expand its operation until 1930, when it distributed 2,645 films and consumed approximately one-third of the Reich Committee budget (Schumann, 83). During the period, local SPD chapters filed optimistic reports about the success of events at which they screened films. The Hamburg SPD scheduled 96 film shows in 1927–28 along with 193 slide shows, attracting a total audience of 70,220 (Guttsman, 196).

The party's educational journal, *Sozialistische Bildung,* reported in 1929 that the Braunschweig SPD has been particularly successful with film events (Schumann, 83). The Braunschweig report indicated that the SPD perceived film as a very effective lure to attract large numbers of otherwise disinterested party members and sympathizers. Between 1926 and 1929 the primary task of the FuL was to select what it considered to be worthwhile films from commercial production and to coordinate their distribution to Social Democratic organizations throughout Germany for precisely that purpose.

In 1927 the FuL, with the help of relatively inexperienced film crews, produced the following films: *Die Kieler rote Woche* (*The Red Week in Kiel*), *Maischau* (*May Day Exhibition*), *Kinderrepublik Seekamp* (*Children's Republic at Seekamp*), *Das Bundestreffen des Reichsbanners in Leipzig* (*The National Meeting of the Reichsbanner in Leipzig*), *Die Heime der Arbeiter Wohlfahrt* (*The Homes for Workers' Welfare*), and *Das Treffen der weltlichen Schulen in Duisberg* (*The Meeting of the Secular Schools in Duisberg*). As the titles suggest, the films informed, solicited support, and encouraged allegiance. To maximize the popularity of film evenings, FuL officials warned the organizers of local events against relying too heavily on political documentaries. Too much political content, they claimed, decreased interest. The following format served as a model: "At the beginning of the event there was an introductory speech of approximately ten minutes. Then we played a record of a male choir. First we screened the short comic animation film, then the Pressa film. After that there was a fifteen-minute intermission. Then came the feature film. In the intermission and at the conclusion we played our agitational songs."[16]

Until 1930 FuL production remained limited for the most part to short comic animation films, documentaries, and election campaign films exclusively for internal use. In 1927 the organization cooperated briefly with the Reich Committee and with other working-class organizations to produce and distribute a *Volkswochenschau* (*People's Weekly Newsreel*) to compete commercially with conservative newsreels such as the *Ufa-Wochenschau* (*Das Jahrbuch der Sozialdemokratie*, Berlin, 1927: 205). The newsreels enjoyed only very limited success, and the initiators responded by contemplating the production of a proletarian newsreel to supplement programs like the SPD film evenings.

IM ANFANG WAR DAS WORT (IN THE BEGINNING WAS THE WORD) AND FREIE FAHRT (FULL SPEED AHEAD)

The two most impressive projects undertaken by the FuL between 1925 and 1930 were the production of *In the Beginning Was the Word* (1928) and *Full Speed Ahead* (1928). Whereas *The Forge* and *Liberated People* extolled the virtues of trade union organization, these films concentrated on the achievements of Social Democracy. *In the Beginning Was the Word* reviewed the eighty years of socialist press from 1848 to 1928, and *Full Speed Ahead* juxtaposed two segments in the development of a Social Democratic family, beginning in 1905 and culminating in 1928. Both films employed the narrative techniques of mainstream historical films that encouraged audiences to perceive their portrayals as authentic and accept their ideological orientation as credible.

Max Barthel, a leader in the German communist movement at the beginning of the Weimar era who eventually found his way to the National Socialists, wrote the manuscript for *In the Beginning Was the Word.* Barthel had proven himself as a journalist and author with works such as *Botschaft und Befehl* (*Message and Command,* 1926). Erno Metzner, who established himself as a set designer in the films of Arnold Fanck and G. W. Pabst, directed the film. Phönix, the company that cooperated in the distribution of the first Prometheus film (*Superfluous People,* 1926) and later participated in the Derussa venture, produced it. Well-known actors such as Fritz Kortner and Elza Temary played the leading roles in the film. In short, although the FuL intended to use the film for the Cologne Press Exhibition in 1928, it made every effort to produce a film that would match the standards of mainstream cinema.

As mentioned above, the film tells the story of the socialist press in Germany. Following expositional shots, depicting the birth of the press in 1848, the first major segment portrays the period of the Anti-Socialist Laws, including the efforts of exiled Social Democrats to print newspapers abroad and smuggle them into Germany. A shorter middle segment outlines the struggles of the press from 1890 until the outbreak of World War I, noting, for example, that between 1890 and 1910 all Social Democrats combined served a total of thirteen hundred years in prison. The final, extensive segment presents statistics, graphs, and other pictorial images indicating the status of the Social Democratic press in 1928. The film concludes with information about the broader cultural and political programs of the party and asserts that spectators must join together to continue the struggle against antirepublican forces.

In the Beginning Was the Word employed a variety of techniques to convince its audience that it presented a trustworthy account of socialist press history and, by implication, offered a credible ideological viewpoint. The process begins with an intertitle associating the film with the Bible, suggesting to spectators that they ascribe the same degree of authority to the film that the Judeo-Christian tradition does to the recorded word of God. Throughout the film, dates appear, implying that what the audience sees is an authentic account of what happened in 1848, 1878, etc. Intertitles regularly interrupt the flow of images to associate them with real historical events and thus strengthen the chronological framework. Juxtapositions of staged scenes, such as the one in which the police notify an SPD newspaper worker (played by Fritz Kortner) that he must leave the city by Christmas, with documentary shots of urban scenes further solidify the illusion of authenticity.

All of these techniques lend *In the Beginning Was the Word* the quality of a dramatic documentary similar both to historical documentaries such as *Bismarck, World War,* etc., and, to a lesser extent, feature films such as the Fridericus films and the Zille films. Like those films, *In the Beginning Was the Word* established an authoritarian relationship with spectators that in no way encouraged their self-initiative in producing an ideological viewpoint.

The second film, *Full Speed Ahead,* was the only feature the FuL produced and distributed independently. Erno Metzner agreed to direct the film, and prominent stage actors, including Alexander Granach and Sybille Schmitz, played the leading roles. *Full Speed Ahead* demonstrated the achievements of the SPD from 1880 to 1928 by following the development of one urban working-class family.

The film begins in 1905 with the story of a railroad fireman, his pregnant wife, and their young daughter, Erna. Although the wife is expecting, she must work under poor conditions at a bookbindery so that there will be enough money to support the growing family. When both father and mother work, the woman next door cares for Erna. A child molester abducts Erna before the neighbor notices what is happening. Upon hearing of her daughter's abduction, the mother collapses and dies. In the meantime, the father has found Erna, but it is too late to save the mother. The first part concludes with a juxtaposition of images portraying the father toiling at his job and others focusing on the sad and lonely face of Erna.

In the next part Erna appears as a young woman in 1928, and the plot now develops around the marriage plans of Erna and her railroad worker friend, Max. Max's brother-in-law, Gustav, explains to Max that he has mortgaged everything that he and his wife own to collect enough money to raise their child. Their belongings will be repossessed shortly unless Max helps them with the money he has saved to marry Erna. Eventually, the state intervenes to remedy Gustav's situation and decrease Max's financial burden. Max's father begins to collect retirement payments, his sister receives daycare support for her child, and Erna's request for a honeymoon vacation is granted. Just when everything seems to be falling into place, Gustav has a severe accident while at work in a foundry. Max is the only one who can offer assistance. He provides the money needed for Gustav's hospital expenses, and the wedding is postponed.

The last part of *Full Speed Ahead* begins with a conversation between a despondent Max and a railroad engineer who is also a long-time member of the SPD. The engineer watches Max discard his application for party membership and begins to tell him about the obstacles the party has overcome since 1888. While he talks, flashback sequences portray the SPD's fights for better working and living standards. The engineer proclaims that it is time for the youth of Germany to join the struggle for further improvements, and Max retrieves his application form.

Again the use of intertitles clearly associates the cinematic fiction with a sociohistorical context, especially the sequence connecting the first and second parts of the film. Following the juxtaposition of shots that depict the toiling father and Erna's sad and lonely face, a sequence of intertitles explains: "Proletarian Fate in 1905," then "Still 1905," followed by a track-in and "Year after year passed. Many things changed. Much improved—through struggle!"

By mentioning the date and claiming that what transpired was realistic and typical for German proletarians at that time, the short sequence reinforces the connection between the cinematic fiction and the sociohistorical context of Wilhelminian Germany. The rest of the sequence shapes the audience's perception of what follows. It sustains the claim to historical authenticity and asserts that struggle, i.e., the struggle of the Social Democratic party, was solely responsible for improvements in proletarian working and living conditions. The information invites the audience to look for improvements in the lives of the fictional characters, perceive them as common aspects of everyday life in Weimar society, and accept them as achievements of the SPD.

Despite the significance of this transition, it is important to note that Metzner relied far less on intertitles as a narrative technique in *Full Speed Ahead* than in his first SPD film. Whereas dates and short passages functioned almost exclusively to establish the historical credibility of *In the Beginning Was the Word*, Metzner depended more on natural environments as settings to increase the credibility of *Full Speed Ahead*. And, in contrast to *In the Beginning Was the Word*, in which short texts regularly interrupted the flow of visual images to guide audience reception, montage operates in *Full Speed Ahead* as the most significant tool for organizing audience perception and evaluation.

At the beginning of the film in fairly rapid succession, the audience sees a night watchman, a streetlight, a clock set at 4:45, a worker's cabinet, and a foundry—all images of an authentic, urban, working-class environment in the early morning hours. When, in the next sequence, a breakfast scene unfolds in a small apartment, the audience already surmises that the participants are members of a real working-class family in a large industrial city. After the breakfast scene, the father walks to work and passes a sign announcing a reward for the child molester. A stream-of-consciousness sequence moves from a medium shot of the father reading the announcement, to a shot of Erna, back to a close-up of the father's face, to a whistle blowing at the railroad yard, to the father again, and to a clock showing 6:00. The montage suggests the father's concern for Erna, introduces the conflict between his concern for her and for his job, and creates suspense about Erna's eventual abduction. Despite his concern for Erna, the father now must run to work.

Additional sequences at the railroad yard and in the bookbindery confirm the financial necessity for leaving Erna with neighbors and demonstrate the parents' good intentions. A parallel montage sequence, juxtaposing Erna's abduction with shots of the mother suffering back pains while toiling at her job, increases sympathy for the mother and suggests social injustices.

Intertitles invite the audience to criticize a ruling class, its institutions, and its representatives for the destitution of the working-class family at the end of the first segment. When the father arrives at work, the foreman waits with a watch. An intertitle proclaims: "If he's not on time, he's fired." As the child molester flees through the streets with Erna, policemen can be seen, guarding over a demonstration. Another intertitle communicates their sentiment: "We have better things to do than to watch out for children." When Erna's father finds her, a text asserts: "Yes, when coincidence doesn't come to the aid of working-class children . . . !" Such passages create an evaluative connection between the workers and members of the social elite and their representatives.

A striking example occurs in the foundry, where Gustav notices a crack in one of the containers full of molten metal. He informs the director who responds: "We can't repair every little thing." The following shot depicts the director, walking to his limousine, discerning some scratches, and ordering his chauffeur: "Take the car to the repair shop immediately." Such montage sequences, combined with intertitles, help to establish oppositions between the good working class and the bad ruling class. They encourage relatively undifferentiated sympathy for the film's Social

Democratic protagonists and equally uncritical condemnation of every-one associated with the dominant social class.

At the end of the film, following a relatively long flashback that por-trays the engineer's recollection of SPD struggles since 1880 (filmed from the perspective of a locomotive), an accelerating montage sequence brings the film's emotional appeal for support to a climax. The engineer finishes his speech, Max retrieves his application, and images of a demonstration appear. Repeated cuts to the accelerating locomotive and the tempo of the marching demonstrators reinforce the escalating tempo of the mon-tage and create a compelling invitation to join the movement with the concluding intertitle "Full Speed Ahead!" [17]

It is appropriate that in *Full Speed Ahead* the fictional characters re-sponsible for presenting the film's ideological viewpoint, Erna's father and the experienced engineer, are traditional figures of authority. The Social Democratic films of the stable period communicated to audiences in much the same way that such authoritarian figures did to Max and Erna. Although they paid lip service to socialism, their concepts and methods, because they were oriented toward the past, betrayed a stagnat-ing satisfaction with occasional legislative reform and an unwillingness to contemplate more radical forms of social organization and change. Such was the quality of Social Democratic cultural policy and film ac-tivity between 1924 and 1929.

10

THE KPD AND FILM: THE DEFEAT OF LEFTIST RADICALISM, THE THEORY OF THE "SCHEMING" CAPITALIST FILM INDUSTRY, AND THE COMMUNIST RESPONSE FROM *PANZERKREUZER POTEMKIN (BATTLESHIP POTEMKIN)* TO PROMETHEUS

Only at the beginning of the period of relative stability could the radical left sustain a significant influence in the KPD.[1] It accused party leaders of failing to recognize Germany's revolutionary potential during the second half of 1923 and argued that the party should fight to regain its momentum. Leftist radicals such as Ruth Fischer, Arkadi Maslow, and Ernst Thälmann proposed abandoning the old *Einheitsfrontpolitik* and in 1925 convinced the party to disregard Comintern instructions to support the SPD's candidate for *Reichspräsident*. The KPD nominated Ernst Thälmann and attracted just enough votes to allow Hindenburg to defeat the more moderate Marx. The leftist policies of the KPD also contributed to a decrease in Communist influence in the established trade unions and in parliament.

At the end of 1925 and in 1926 the Comintern intervened successfully. In its open letter to the KPD in August 1925, the Comintern explicitly criticized the policies of the leftist faction in the Central Committee and called for party leaders to break with Fischer and Maslow. In 1926 Stalinist forces in the Comintern further weakened the KPD's left wing as a part of their campaign to challenge the leadership of Sinoviev and Trotsky. Stalin pressed for recognition that the postwar revolutionary period had ended with a capitalist consolidation of power in western Europe. His followers rejected Trotsky's concepts of permanent revolution and the impossibility of socialism in a single country. They argued, instead, that the Soviet Union must consolidate its power as a defense against foreign aggression and in preparation for the next revolutionary period. The Stalinists were able to focus Comintern attention on the October

Revolution. They asserted that the Bolshevik victory legitimized strict adherence to the principles of democratic centralism among western European communist parties. Those parties should intensify their allegiance to the Soviet Union. Thälmann accepted the Stalinist approach unconditionally and retained his leading position in the Central Committee. Fischer and Maslow, despite their willingness to compromise, were excluded from the Central Committee by the end of 1925 and from the party late in 1926.

As the KPD's alliance with the Soviet Union and the Comintern intensified, the party assumed a more moderate course. Although the KPD remained extremely critical of the SPD, it invited the Social Democratic leadership to engage in united political action such as the plebiscite to disinherit the German aristocracy in 1926. The party also concentrated on attracting members, augmenting its influence in parliament, regaining leadership in the trade unions, and supporting the Soviet Union. The Bolshevist trend toward a stricter organizational hierarchy along with generally improving material conditions in Weimar society actually contributed to a small decrease in party membership. At the same time, the party successfully established and maintained contact with voters, sympathizers, and potential supporters through its expanding press and cultural programs.

Between 1924 and 1929 the attitude toward cultural work within the KPD slowly changed.[2] Contributors to the *feuilleton* of *Die Rote Fahne* and to KPD cultural journals continued to assert the primacy of the economic base and promoted concepts of autonomous art, but the number and influence of such contributions decreased. Articles by Mehring's students appeared only occasionally, and the steady increase in proletarian experiments with art forced the authors of such articles to modify their positions. Gertrud Alexander, for example, in "Arbeiterfilme in Amerika" ("Workers' Films in America," *Die Rote Fahne*, 5 February 1925), noted the progress of IAH film production in the Soviet Union and expressed surprise at the organization's success with distribution in New York, but she focused on the failure of similar attempts in Germany. Success, she argued, still depended on the cooperation of existing social institutions. Censors could ban or change the quality of films, theater owners could exclude films from their programs, and the police could designate alternative screening places unsuitable.

The most substantial theoretical challenge to those who seriously contemplated the possibility of proletarian art came from Leon Trotsky's widely discussed *Literature and Revolution* (1924).[3] Trotsky denied the possibility and even the desirability of proletarian art, basing his argument on the belief that the ultimate goal of human society was to conquer nature.[4] All social practice aimed in that direction was, for him, the defining characteristic of a society's culture.

As the proletariat consolidated its power and eventually abandoned its dictatorship over the old ruling class, a number of factors would dissuade its members from developing their own culture and even render such development undesirable. Before a new culture could flourish, the proletariat would have to lay the foundation for a new economy. As Trotsky explained: "Culture feeds on the sap of economics, and a material surplus is necessary, so that culture may grow, develop and become subtle" (200). He suggested that to reach the point where it could accumulate a material surplus, "the energy of the proletariat itself [would] be spent mainly in conquering power, in retaining and strengthening it, and applying it to the most urgent needs of existence and of further struggle."[5] Once the proletariat had consolidated its power, established a new economic base, and created a material surplus, its purpose would be fulfilled and it would cease to exist. A new classless human culture would emerge. Trotsky argued that, given the proletariat's need to concentrate on "noncultural" tasks and the transitional character of proletarian society, it would be counterproductive to develop a distinctly proletarian culture.

His final argument was that the proletariat had been culturally deprived in bourgeois society. Initially bourgeois art had contributed to cultural progress by elevating humanity's understanding of itself. But the working masses had had no access to bourgeois cultural achievements and were, as a result, culturally backward. Any attempt by the proletariat to develop its own culture would be regressive. Consequently, Trotsky advocated continued military, political, and economic efforts to accelerate movement toward world revolution.

In May and June 1925, *Die Rote Fahne* published a series of articles on proletarian culture by K. A. Wittfogel. Wittfogel criticized Trotsky's analysis, described what he perceived to be an emerging proletarian culture, and attempted to justify its existence.[6] Like Trotsky, Wittfogel affirmed anthropological perceptions of culture as the entire system of material *and* ideological elements that characterize a society at a given point in time. However, in contrast to Trotsky, Wittfogel perceived no absolute distinction between economy and culture and no cause-and-effect relationship between material change and ideological change. For Wittfogel it was possible to discover the seeds of a proletarian culture developing as workers began to perceive themselves as members of a class, became conscious of the material and ideological preconditions for class development, organized their perceptions into a new ideological perspective, and created new proletarian institutions to challenge bourgeois institutions. While Trotsky emphasized the temporary transitional quality of proletarian rule, the primacy of economic change, and the cultural backwardness of the proletariat, Wittfogel argued that a proletarian society would develop, last an entire epoch, and succeed only if the revolutionary working class established new material and ideological standards simultaneously. For Wittfogel, as had been the case for the *Proletkult* activists, the proletarian revolution was a cultural revolution in the broadest sense.[7]

As the Stalinist program of consolidation developed, the KPD formulated cultural policy that affirmed neither Trotsky's devaluation of cultural work nor Wittfogel's concept of a grassroots proletarian culture. The Comintern, recognizing that the consolidation of capitalism in the West had diminished the likelihood of militant revolutionary activity, initiated the process by devoting more attention to ideological work. As early as 1924 the Fifth Congress of the Comintern adopted proposals to establish a system of party education. Because it developed at a time when the Comintern accepted Stalin's leadership and bolshevized the western European parties, the system perpetuated traditional authoritarian structures. The Bolsheviks, whose authority stemmed from their successful revolution in 1917, would instruct the European Communist parties in revolutionary ideology and practice. They, in turn, would impart to the uneducated masses the knowledge necessary to understand and gain control of social development. The KPD accepted the role and, in addition to participating in the Comintern's educational program, founded its own Marxistische Arbeiterschule.

The orientation of Comintern and KPD educational programs indicated that Trotsky's concept of social progress and especially of working-class cultural backwardness was far more prevalent among the Communists than was the *Proletkult* concept of radically democratic cultural activity. Communist party education strove more to convey correct ideology to workers than to encourage them to organize their own everyday experiences into an ideological perspective. Within this context the suggestive power of the press, literature, theater, film, and even radio attracted new interest. Between 1924 and 1927 the Comintern and the KPD adopted various proposals to establish national and international associations for proletarian journalists, authors, actors, etc. In addition, the KPD held a conference for the correspondents of *Die Rote Fahne* in

December 1924 and founded a working committee of Communist authors in the Schutzverband Deutscher Schriftsteller in 1925.[8]

The real breakthrough in the KPD's cultural program came at the Eleventh Party Congress in March 1927. At that time the party, which had observed a rapid increase in working-class cultural activity, including trade union and SPD activity, instructed its members to join existing organizations to build a Red Front in opposition to the dominant cultural institutions in Weimar society.[9] Communists began to play an active role in existing cultural organizations and to contribute significantly to the establishment and/or reorientation of many organizations, including the Bund proletarisch revolutionärer Schriftsteller (The League of Proletarian Revolutionary Writers, BPRS), the Arbeiter-Theater Bund Deutschlands (The Workers' Theater League of Germany), the VFV, etc.

Whereas the KPD had moved slowly to build a solid cultural program, the IAH developed an extensive system of cultural organizations and strove consciously to compete with existing institutions of art and journalism.[10] Although the Comintern controlled the IAH, it nurtured a nonpartisan image. It did so to reach broader segments of the working class and to provide a bridge for workers who sympathized with the Communists but were cautious about party membership. By 1929 its cultural network included the Neuer Deutscher Verlag, the Universum Bücherei, as well as widely distributed journals and newspapers such as *Eulenspiegel, Arbeiter-Illustrierte-Zeitung* (*AIZ*), and *Die Welt am Abend*. Of even greater significance here, the IAH initiated most film activity associated with the German communist movement. Among other things, it founded Prometheus Film-Verleih und Vertriebs-GmbH (Prometheus) in 1925–26 and the Film-Kartell "Welt-Film" GmbH (Weltfilm) in 1927.

As the IAH grew, critics accused its founder and organizational leader, Willi Münzenberg, of building a concern similar to the Hugenberg media concern. Münzenberg's response summarizes the orientation of the IAH cultural program: "We are no utopians. We do not consider it possible to defeat capitalism with economic endeavors. We are revolutionary Marxists and know that we can overcome capitalism only through revolutionary class struggle, armed uprisings, and civil war. But we also believe that it is a punishable crime to allow bourgeois and social-democratic concerns to monopolize the media for influencing public opinion without a struggle. We believe that everything must be done to break this monopoly whether in the daily press, the illustrated journals, or wherever."[11] Münzenberg affirmed the ultimate necessity of violent revolution, but he also recognized that the most powerful media institutions in Weimar society exerted anything but a revolutionary influence on the working class. As a result, he promoted competition with Hugenberg, Scherl, Ullstein, and Mosse as the primary goal of IAH media activity.

The IAH frequently experimented with campaigns to encourage members and readers of its journals and newspapers to participate in production. For example, the publishers of the *Blätter für Alle,* the journal of the Universum Bücherei, solicited, printed, and answered readers' letters, offered prizes for articles about their weekend activities, and invited them to send in stories about their everyday lives. The editors explained: "A newspaper like ours can only act as a catalyst and guide. It can never be a textbook or commentary." [12] This and similar efforts in the *AIZ* and other IAH publications indicate that, while competing with the commercial press, the IAH did attempt to develop new forms of production that allowed readers to participate creatively in molding a working-class perspective.

It must be stressed, however, that IAH journals and newspapers to a large extent assimilated the techniques of production and reception employed by the mainstream press to attract the attention and hold the interest of its readers. The format of most IAH publications resembled that of their commercial counterparts, as did the organizational structures of production and reception. The only significant difference was in content. And whether experiments like the ones initiated by the editors of *Blätter für Alle* also surfaced in the film activity of the IAH remains to be seen.

FILM CRITICISM IN THE COMMUNIST PRESS

Die Rote Fahne continued to function as the KPD's official forum for discussion about film in the second half of the 1920s. Most articles and reviews appeared in the *feuilleton,* where the only consistent heading on film was the *Filmschau (Film Review).* [13] An increasing number of articles made broader judgments about commercial cinema and proletarian alternatives tangentially while evaluating German films, Soviet films, and films associated with the SPD and KPD. A few individuals, including Gertrud Alexander, Alfred Durus, Alfred Kamen, Hilde Kramer, and Otto Steinicke, contributed frequently, but there were also many onetime and anonymous contributors. Only once before 1930 did *Die Rote Fahne* invite readers to submit reviews,[14] and the conclusive tone of its formulations discouraged reader participation in the evaluative process.

Three IAH newspapers, the *AIZ, Die Welt am Abend,* and *Berlin am Morgen,* also published articles on film.[15] The *AIZ* began devoting more space to film following the success of Eisenstein's *Battleship Potemkin* in 1926. Its reports generally compared tendencies in Soviet film production to those of Hollywood and Ufa.[16] The format for the other two papers included a relatively short section of political news, followed by a large *feuilleton* and a sports page. Articles on film often appeared in the *feuilleton* sections of both newspapers. Each also included special film supplements: *Die Welt am Abend* added a "Film und Radio" section on Sunday, and "Theater und Film" accompanied *Berlin am Morgen* sporadically throughout the week.

The coverage of film in the IAH newspapers differed from that of *Die Rote Fahne* in many ways. They, too, focused on reviews, but whereas *Die Rote Fahne* consistently condemned cinematic entertainment, *Die Welt am Abend* and *Berlin am Morgen* occasionally praised entertaining films with no blatant political orientation. Both newspapers also printed the reports of correspondents who had observed the production of Prometheus films. Such reports diminished the mystique associated with filmmaking while simultaneously arousing the reader's curiosity—in essence providing free publicity. *Berlin am Morgen* focused further attention on specific films, among them mainstream entertainment films, by recommending them under the heading, "Filme, die man sehen soll" ("Films That One Should See"). As the practice suggests, the film critics for the IAH newspapers, like those of *Die Rote Fahne,* maintained their claim to authority and limited the invitation for a dialogue with readers.

Die Welt am Abend and *Berlin am Morgen* did encourage readers to perceive a connection between cinematic fiction and everyday reality. The *feuilleton* often focused on literary, theatrical, and cinematic portrayals of contemporary issues that had been covered in the political section. Occasionally the process worked in reverse. The editors of the IAH newspapers also included articles in the news sections that related directly to the subject matter of the novels, dramas, and films discussed in the *feuilleton*. At the end of 1929, for example, *Berlin am Morgen* printed a series of articles on prostitution, "Stätte der Prostitution" ("Places of Prostitution"), following the premiere of *Beyond the Street* and just prior to the release of *Mother Krause's Journey to Happiness* (two Prometheus films in which prostitution figured prominently). The editors, thus, took a step in returning art to everyday life but offered readers no opportunity to create the connection with their own reviews.

All of the claims about film that were expressed before 1924 surfaced again in the Communist press in the second half of the decade. Critics continued to suggest the influence of conservative to reactionary interest groups on film production. For example, kn (Klaus Neukrantz?) reported on monarchist financial support for the production of *Bismarck* (*Die Rote Fahne*, 22 December 1925); Hans Roth wrote about "Die Hugenbergisierung der Ufa" ("The Hugenbergization of Ufa," *Die Welt am Abend*, 28 March 1927); and numerous articles explained the connection between the military and the Phöbus film company in the fall of 1927.

A new object of criticism, but one that only reinforced the perception of scheming behind the scenes, was the cooperation between major film producers and both film journals and commercial newspapers. Articles such as "Kritik der Filmkritik" (*Die Welt am Abend*, 17 August 1927) argued that connections between Ullstein and Terra and between the Scherl Verlag and Ufa increased the ideological manipulation of filmgoers. These articles asserted that the reviews of Terra films in Ullstein newspapers and of Ufa films in Scherl newspapers were nothing more than advertisements in disguise.[17]

The film critics of the Communist press also maintained the focus on the ideological significance of film content that had begun in 1922 with the reaction to *Fridericus Rex*. Between 1924 and 1929 they criticized mainstream historical films for falsifying history, glorifying the lives of legendary figures, and thus promoting monarchism. As was the case before 1924, critics rarely analyzed in any detail how such films persuaded audiences ideologically. For example, instead of discussing the narrative techniques employed by Gerhard Lamprecht in *Old Fritz*, the review in *Die Rote Fahne* (5 January 1928) simply explained: "The direction hobbles more feebly on its crutches than old Fritz from peace settlement with Austria to the composition of his will. A loose stringing together of sometimes historical and sometimes legendary episodes from the life of Frederick 'the Great.' Nevertheless, an excellent example for the bourgeois trivialization of history."[18]

Other critics bemoaned the effects of contingency, tax, and censorship regulations on proletarian film activity. They more frequently recommended mass protest and legislative change to ease restrictions. But a small group of cultural activists persisted in citing such inhibiting factors to demonstrate that proletarian art would flourish only when the proletariat gained economic and political control of German society.

As late as 1929 Edwin Hoernle proclaimed: "There is no place for the workers' struggle for their ideals in the cinema of the capitalist society. The workers have yet to conquer this place in struggle, not against cinema,

but against the capitalist society" ("Kampf—nicht gegen den Film"—
"Struggle—Not Against Cinema," *Film-Kurier,* 1 January 1929). Hoernle
accurately perceived the unwillingness of major companies to produce
subversive films, the financial inability of working-class organizations to
compete with the largest production and distribution companies, and the
difficulties created by government regulations. But he refused to acknowledge the possibility of a proletarian alternative, despite the growing
popularity of Soviet films and the production and distribution programs
of Prometheus, Weltfilm, etc.

As the distribution of Soviet films expanded, more contributors to the
Communist press considered seriously the possibility of an alternative to
mainstream film. At first, *Proletkult* advocates such as Berta Lask discovered the possibility for new collective forms of expression in Soviet films
("Uraufführung des Lenin Films in Berlin"—"Premiere of the Lenin Film
in Berlin," *Die Rote Fahne,* 17 September 1924). Within a short time the
connotations of collectivity in proletarian films shifted from the *Proletkult* notions of radically democratic productivity to a socialist-realist
principle of typicality. As early as 1925, in her review of *Palace und Fortress* (*Die Rote Fahne,* 8 May 1925), Alexander explained: "No actor
moves into the spotlight with outstanding individual performances. Everyone appears to play a scene from their own lives. This film assumes
the collectivity of unreflected experience."

The value of typicality increased in correspondence with the KPD's
growing desire to use film and other mass media to broaden its base of
support. Soviet films served a dual purpose. They represented the most
effective medium for informing large audiences about the Bolshevik revolution and the efforts to build a new socialist society in the Soviet Union.
They also could encourage workers to defend the Soviet Union and to
accept it as a model for social change in Germany.

With this in mind, and given the potential ideological impact of commercial film on German audiences, the critics of the Communist press,
following the examples of Béla Balázs and Edwin Hoernle, accepted
the standards of production and reception, translating them into criteria
for analyzing Soviet films. Until the end of the 1920s, reviews of Soviet
films distinguished almost no aesthetic differences. Although Soviet filmmakers such as Eisenstein and Pudovkin had developed diverging models
of production and reception,[19] the critics for *Die Rote Fahne* and IAH
newspapers perceived one relatively undifferentiated body of Soviet filmmaking. For them the power of the Soviet film derived foremost from its

ability to evoke an emotional response, to encourage audience sympathy for the protagonist. Otto Steinicke's reviews of Eisenstein's *Battleship Potemkin* (1925) and Pudovkin's *Mutter* (*Mother,* 1927) exemplify the lack of differentiation (*Die Rote Fahne,* 1 May 1926 and 25 February 1927). Steinicke's references to suspense, nerves, and a thrilling quality indicate the significance of emotional experience.

According to these and other Communist critics, Soviet films succeeded, i.e., they evoked an emotional response and moved the audience to accept a proletarian perspective, because they were realistic. Reviewers characterized the films as "close to life," "natural," "objective," "real"— in large part because their characters were effective. As a review of *Sohn der Berge* (*Son of the Mountains*) in *Die Welt am Abend* (29 November 1926) explained: "The actors disappear, one is no longer able to perceive the action as the performance of an actor, only as 'art'; real powerful life is what transpires with real people before us." While Alexander, Steinicke, and others attacked the film industry for falsifying history, they affirmed the use of its techniques for influencing audience reception. It was acceptable, even praiseworthy for Soviet filmmakers to create the illusion of reality, encourage uncritical sympathy for fictional characters, and ultimately reinforce aesthetically the audience's dependence on authoritarian structures, as long as they promoted what the critics perceived as an accurate perspective.

As the KPD's dependence on Soviet leadership and its willingness to accept the Soviet Union as a social model increased, so, too, did the uncritical acclaim for Soviet films in the Communist press.[20] By praising Soviet film art and the portrayal of Soviet society's achievements in its films, the Communist critics encouraged German workers to follow the Bolshevik path. In the process, reviewers often contrasted Soviet and German films. They characterized the former as infinitely superior, advocating a socialist revolution as the precondition for higher film quality.[21] Even Eisenstein, who refused to follow existing narrative trends and consequently lost the support of most film critics and spectators, continued to receive positive reviews for his films from *Die Rote Fahne* and the IAH critics. They were confused by his persistent experiments with nonnarrative montage but defended his work anyway.

Just as the KPD can be criticized for its close allegiance to the Soviet Union, the film critics for *Die Rote Fahne* and the IAH newspapers must also be criticized for their uncritical evaluation of Soviet films. Their unbridled praise may have alienated more than attracted those readers who were still in the process of regaining a sense of security following the postwar crisis years. They seemed far more attracted to cultural endeavors geared toward helping them in that recovery process than to those that suggested the need for a radical break with everything familiar in favor of what appeared to be a relatively exotic social system.

Willi Münzenberg fueled the enthusiasm for Soviet film in his *Erobert den Film, Winke aus der Praxis für die Praxis proletarischer Filmpropaganda* (*Conquer Film, Hints from Praxis for the Praxis of Proletarian Film Propaganda*, 1925). Münzenberg documented the advantage enjoyed by nationalist and militarist interest groups in the realm of film propaganda and implored his readers to compete.[22] Under Münzenberg's leadership and following the guidelines he outlined in *Conquer Film*, the IAH, in cooperation with the Comintern and KPD, took significant steps during the years of relative stability to expand its film production and distribution programs.

THE FILM PROGRAM OF THE IAH, THE BIRTH OF PROMETHEUS, AND *BATTLESHIP POTEMKIN*

Following its initial experience with film screenings in Germany and other European countries, the IAH increased its production capabilities in 1924. It established the Meschrabpom-Rus film company in the Soviet Union and accelerated production of films for distribution all over the world. According to Münzenberg, the IAH's films should challenge mainstream cinema's portrayal of historical and current events, inform audiences about the Bolshevik revolution and the developing Soviet society, document and solicit support for the activities of the IAH, and provide campaign publicity for Communist politicians.

Like the film critics for the Communist press, Münzenberg criticized commercial film content but affirmed existing forms of production and reception. As he explained in *Conquer Film:*

What makes the film [*His Warning*] valuable is its exact execution of a closed narrative with gripping, tragic elements and an accomplished artistic interaction of the cast. The wonderful emotional engagement of the children in the film is especially noticeable. . . . In short, in the content as well as in the ideological orientation, strictist unity, lively images, a rapid succession of scenes which hold the viewers in constantly mounting suspense so that the final images can transform the tension into the desire to help—to cooperate in achieving the monumental goals which the proletarian movement has set for itself. (103)

The list of descriptive but also prescriptive characteristics provides a precise account of the most effective elements of cinematic narration in Germany during the second half of the 1920s. For Münzenberg, if films with those elements promoted nationalism, militarism, or blind faith in religion, they were to be condemned. If they told the story of workers in the November Revolution, outlined the history of revolutionary struggle in general, demonstrated the effects of bourgeois politics and economics on workers, or even increased the popularity of Comintern leaders, they deserved praise and support. Münzenberg's orientation demonstrated that the contradiction between manipulative forms of production and reception, on the one hand, and allegedly socialist film content, on the other, continued in Communist film politics.

In Germany, where at the time "proletarian" film production seemed implausible, Münzenberg encouraged the IAH, KPD, and other working-class organizations to integrate Meschrabpom-Rus and other Soviet-made films into their cultural programs. Following two years of success and failure with IAH distribution, Münzenberg advocated the development of a central office to coordinate distribution and establish guidelines for film events. Like the SPD and its FuL, the IAH, while striving to build an efficient national program for film distribution, increased the power of centralized bureaucratic positions and minimized productive initiative at the grass-roots level. By 1927 the IAH, in cooperation with the KPD, had founded the Film-Kartell "Welt-Film" GmbH with headquarters in Berlin and offices in 15 other German cities.

The IAH also established formats for film events that facilitated their use for influencing public opinion on specific issues. At the end of 1928, for example, the IAH predicted that the German economy would weaken and that a debate would develop over allocations for the construction of the Panzerkreuzer A. To influence public opinion on the issue and solicit support for their organization, leaders scheduled a film tour for the industrial *Ruhrgebiet* and distributed circulars outlining eighteen specific steps to be taken in preparing local film events. Among the suggested steps were two in particular that revealed just how far the IAH had moved toward central control from above:

16. . . . The use of the event for recruiting members is one of the most important points. . . . Consequently, it is advisable to initiate the recruiting process quickly and effectively after the speech. . . .
18. Criticisms about the mistakes and shortcomings of the event should not be presented in front of all the visitors, rather in the meetings of the organization's functionaries.[23]

The noncommercial IAH and KPD film events minimized democratic participation in the organizational and ideological activities just as energetically as did the SPD events. The major difference between the film activity of the SPD and IAH-KPD during the years of relative stability developed in the realm of commercial competition. The SPD virtually abandoned attempts to produce and distribute films commercially after its experience with *Liberated People,* but the IAH and KPD, after initiating their efforts in 1926, persisted until 1931–1932.

Until the end of 1925 the AIH coordinated the distribution of Soviet films for the IAH in Germany. At that time a revision in the Weimar government's contingency law threatened to disrupt IAH distribution. Only those companies that distributed German films in Germany, the new law stipulated, would be allowed to distribute foreign films. To comply with the regulation, the IAH merged with a small private film producer, the Deka-Compagnie Schatz und Co. The new firm, the Prometheus Film-Verleih und Vertriebs-GmbH (Prometheus), emerged in December 1925 with a stock fund of 10,000 reichsmarks.[24] Although it is likely that the IAH and KPD were the real contributors, according to the original contract the official partners, Emil Unfried, Richard Pfeiffer, and Willi Münzenberg, contributed 4,500, 3,000, and 2,500 reichsmarks, respectively.[25] Unfried and Pfeiffer were listed as the original directors, but a change in the contract, which was registered on 9 January 1926, designated Ernst Becker and Richard Pfeiffer as the directors.

Emil Unfried had served in a number of leading positions in the KPD and participated in many Comintern congresses. Of greatest significance for Prometheus, he was the head of the Deka-Compagnie Schatz und Co. Richard Pfeiffer also was a leading KPD member. His functions included managing business transactions for *Die Rote Fahne,* serving as a central committee member for the factory councils of greater Berlin in 1923, and representing the KPD in the Comintern. Ernst Becker was a pseudonym for Ernst Christian Rath. Becker specialized in illegal activities for the party. Each of the original Prometheus directors had experience in leadership and management, but none of them, except to a limited extent

Unfried, had any experience with film. Nevertheless, after distributing their first film, Eisenstein's *Battleship Potemkin*, Prometheus had enough capital to begin producing its own films for the commercial market.

According to Carl Junghans, Münzenberg had attended the premiere of Eisenstein's film in Moscow and, despite its cool reception there, agreed to distribute the film in Germany.[26] Following a closed screening to commemorate Lenin's death at the Großes Schauspielhaus in Berlin on 21 January 1926, Münzenberg asked the Albert Angermann Filmverleih in Hamburg to submit the film to the national censorship bureau. The censors decided to prohibit public screenings of *Battleship Potemkin* at the end of March, triggering a wave of protests from well-known intellectuals, artists, and political activists. As a result of mounting public sentiment in favor of *Battleship Potemkin*, the censors accepted a substantially edited version at the beginning of April, and Prometheus scheduled the commercial premiere at the Apollo Theater in Berlin on 29 April 1926. During the rest of 1926, the film was either censored or threatened with censorship repeatedly, and public curiosity steadily increased. Interest grew so quickly that, whereas Pfeiffer and Unfried had struggled to find a theater for the initial screening in Berlin, they were for a time unable to meet the demand for film copies in the summer and fall of 1926.[27] For months *Battleship Potemkin* attracted full houses in dozens of theaters all over Germany.

Film historians generally attribute the commercial success of Eisenstein's film to his innovative use of photography and montage, his orchestration of dramatic mass scenes, and more generally to the exotic quality and monumental treatment of the subject matter. These factors were certainly important. But the coverage the film received in the press, the endorsements of famous personalities, and even the repeated intervention of censors attracted far more attention to *Battleship Potemkin* than it could have created by itself and with the marketing efforts of the tiny, inexperienced Prometheus.[28]

ÜBERFLÜSSIGE MENSCHEN (SUPERFLUOUS PEOPLE), KLADD UND DATSCH, DIE PECHVÖGEL (KLADD AND DATSCH, THE UNFORTUNATE FELLOWS), AND MIRAKEL DER LIEBE (MIRACLE OF LOVE)

With the profits from *Battleship Potemkin*, Prometheus submitted three of its own films to the censors by the end of 1926: *Superfluous People,*

Kladd and Datsch, the Unfortunate Fellows, and *Miracle of Love.* The censors approved all three films; however, Prometheus was able to distribute only the first.

There are numerous plausible explanations for the company's failure to distribute the latter two. It is possible that Prometheus produced them quickly and inexpensively as contingency films which would enable the firm to distribute commercially attractive Soviet films and generate enough capital to expand production capabilities.[29] If this is true, theater owners and the press perhaps ignored the films because of their poor quality. The commercial failure of *Superfluous People* provides another possible explanation. Theater owners perhaps grew skeptical about Prometheus productions and preferred to wait for another guaranteed attraction like *Battleship Potemkin.* It is also possible that theater owners, despite their willingness to screen Eisenstein's film, were less anxious to support the production of what they likely perceived to be a leftist, if not Communist, film company. Although there is no clear evidence to corroborate such claims, the political conservatism of the German theater owner's organization and their caution during a period of crisis in the German film industry at least suggest the possibility that commercial and political factors played a role.

Kladd and Datsch, the Unfortunate Fellows and *Miracle of Love* have been lost, and there was little press information about them. What is known indicates that Prometheus considered them to be important. Each was a full-length feature film, and Heinrich George, a leading film personality, had a major part in *Miracle of Love.* In addition, their titles betray an attempt to associate them with popular film genres, a strategy suggesting that Prometheus intended to attract large audiences. *Kladd and Datsch, the Unfortunate Fellows* evoked an association with the very successful *Pat und Patochon* film series. *Miracle of Love* is a title that belongs to the long tradition of *Aufklärungsfilme* and street films—a title that appealed to the erotic fantasies. The choice of titles and the decision to engage Heinrich George also indicate the company's efforts to assimilate and practice commercial production and marketing techniques.

The same strategy characterized the production of *Superfluous People.* To match the popularity of *Battleship Potemkin,* Prometheus executives asked Eisenstein to recommend subject matter and personnel for their first film.[30] Like others who produced films that could be associated with *Battleship Potemkin* (Cecil B. De Mille with *The Volga Boatman* in 1926, for instance), Unfried engaged a Russian director, Alexander Rasumny, and chose an adaptation of material from the works of Anton

Chekov.[31] Prometheus also attracted some of Germany's leading film stars. Among others, Werner Krauss, Heinrich George, Fritz Kampers, and Fritz Rasp accepted leading roles in *Superfluous People*. In addition, the company initiated the popular practice of advertising coming attractions to stimulate the interest of theater owners and distributors.

In July of 1926 announcements about the production of *Superfluous People* appeared in the *Film-Kurier* (15 July 1926) and in the *L.B.B.* (31 July 1926). In August Prometheus claimed that Rasumny would direct two monumental films, *Superfluous People* and *Heimchen am Herd* (based on Charles Dickens's *Cricket on the Hearth*). In September *Miracle of Love* replaced *Heimchen am Herd* in Prometheus announcements, and in the end only *Superfluous People* premiered. Following its one-week run at the Capitol in Berlin, the film virtually disappeared until December, when a revised version resurfaced for short engagements with very little success ("Überflüssige Menschen"—"Superfluous People," *Film-Kurier,* 4 December 1926).

It is possible that the film failed because it did follow commercial guidelines so closely. As Kurt Grimm explained: "Germany was shaken by the crisis years. Widespread unemployment prevailed. After the 'Potemkin' film, theater owners and audiences expected from Prometheus under the title 'Superfluous People' a powerful social film that would deal with the problem of unemployment."[32] Instead, *Superfluous People* provided a slapstick account of very loosely connected events in a Russian village before World War I. It met the standard for cinematic entertainment but perhaps failed to meet the expectations of filmgoers who had seen *Battleship Potemkin.*

The film begins with a long expositional text, setting the time and place. The first sequence introduces various inhabitants of the village by juxtaposing shots of them and intertitles, proclaiming "Werner Krauss in the role of . . . ," "Fritz Kampers in the role of . . . ," etc. The narrative progresses with humorous scenes depicting the experiences of the local band's members. A magician seduces the wife of one band member, Sigajew. In a dream sequence, Sigajew imagines shooting both of them. In real life, he decides only to buy a butterfly net. Another band member, Bramsa, learns that his wife, whom he has mistreated for years, is fatally ill. He is full of remorse and decides to demonstrate it by building a beautiful casket for her. He even measures her body while she watches. In the meantime Sigajew has drowned his sorrows in alcohol, and upon returning to his home, he accidentally starts it on fire. Juxtaposed sequences portray his neighbors, who extinguish the fire only after the house has been ruined, and the inept village firemen, who sleep, initially don't hear the alarm, drive in slow motion, arrive much too late, and conclude: "Then we rushed here for nothing!" The film culminates with an appearance by the band at a wedding in the mayor's house. On the way to the ceremony Sigajew passes a pond and decides to swim. The bride's brother steals his clothes. Then the bride appears and she decides to swim. Her brother steals her clothes too, and Sigajew offers to hide the bride in his bass violin case. After many other coincidences, she emerges from the case at the mayor's house. Despite the embarrassment, the wedding proceeds, and the film ends.

Rasumny may have intended to use humor as a vehicle for calling into question the value of a bourgeois society inhabited by laughable characters. He chose material from a number of Chekov stories, including *Love Affair with a Double-Bass* (1886) and *Rothschild's Fiddle* (1894), but relied solely on the common setting and the band to associate the protagonists with one another. Rasumny showed little regard for narrative cohesion, but unlike Eisenstein, he offered no explanation. Consequently, it seems unlikely that he envisioned an aesthetic alternative. Instead of encouraging spectators to share in organizing the cinematic material into something meaningful, Rasumny alienated them with his random sequential organization.

The reviews were generally negative. They confirmed Grimm's perception of the public's desire for social criticism, asserting that *Superfluous People* did have a socially critical orientation, but one that belonged to Chekov's world of the late nineteenth century. They also criticized the alienating quality of the film's structure. According to the *L.B.B.* review (3 November 1926), which was very generous, the lack of cohesion was part of a Russian tradition Germans should learn to enjoy. The less generous *Film-Kurier* review (3 November 1926) claimed that Rasumny had learned nothing from the masters of Soviet filmmaking and had wasted the talent of his crew.

PROMETHEUS DISTRIBUTION OF SOVIET FILMS AND THE PRODUCTION OF *EINS + EINS = DREI (ONE + ONE = THREE), KINDERTRAGÖDIE (TRAGEDY OF THE CHILDREN),* AND *SCHINDERHANNES*

Following the commercial disappointments with its own films, Prometheus distributed a number of Soviet films during the first half of 1927.

Two of the films, *Iwan, der Schreckliche* (*Ivan the Terrible*) and *Zar und Dichter* (*Czar and Poet*), focused on prerevolutionary themes; a third, *Zwischen Himmel und Erde* (*Between Heaven and Earth*), depicted the feats of a Soviet pilot. None of them was politically controversial.

Following its censorship difficulties with *Battleship Potemkin*, Prometheus may have concluded that it could minimize the financial risk associated with possible censorship by selecting films with less blatantly political themes. The company's experience with a fourth Soviet film, *Die Todesbarke* (*The Death Barge*), demonstrated again the sensitivity of the censors. *The Death Barge,* which portrayed a dramatic episode from the Russian civil war and praised the efforts of the Red Army, spent over one month traveling between the censors and the Prometheus editors before the censors accepted a substantially edited version. None of the Soviet films attracted as much attention as *Battleship Potemkin* had in 1926, although *Ivan the Terrible* and *Czar and Poet* were modest commercial successes.

Prometheus produced only one film, *Das Mädchen aus der Fremde* (*The Maiden from Abroad*), at the beginning of 1927. It premiered on 4 April 1927. The press ignored it, and the film quickly disappeared. For several months Prometheus supplied little information about its production plans. The *Film-Kurier* (2 March 1927) mentioned that Prometheus planned to produce an adaptation of Upton Sinclair's *King Coal,* and the *L.B.B.* (23 May 1927) reported that Erwin Piscator would direct a film about the 1848 revolution, but that was all.

There are various possible explanations for the long pause before Prometheus began to produce again in 1927. In addition to its desire, and perhaps need, to accumulate sufficient capital from the distribution of Soviet films to finance production, the performance of company executives may have motivated Münzenberg to hesitate and to contemplate administrative changes. In letters to Eisenstein, the composer of the musical scores for *Potemkin* and *Superfluous People,* Edmund Meisel, explained that Münzenberg supervised the Prometheus executives closely and that he was disappointed with their performance.[33] Meisel, like Kurt Grimm, noted that they had made major errors. The Russian Trade Bureau in Berlin initiated negotiations with other German film companies late in 1927, and Münzenberg eventually transferred Jefrem Schalito from Meschrabpom to Prometheus in 1928.

Finally in September 1927 notices in the trade journals announced the new Prometheus program under the heading "Our Slogan: Not Quantity, but Quality!" (see *L.B.B.,* 10 September 1927). The program included

One + One = Three: "A Film Jest from Béla Balázs," *Illustrierter Film-Kurier* program. (Staatliches Filmarchiv der DDR)

three Prometheus productions: *Schinderhannes, One + One = Three* and *Tragedy of the Children*. Prometheus was able to finish only *One + One = Three* and *Tragedy of the Children* by the end of 1927.

Prometheus engaged Béla Balázs to write the script for *One + One = Three*; Felix Basch was the director. Balázs, who had written scripts for commercial films, paid close attention to production techniques that intensified film's suggestive power.[34] In his *The Adventures of a Ten-Mark Note*, in 1926, for example, a banknote provided the narrative cohesion by circulating from one group of people to another and causing sorrow in each case. In contrast to that script, in which striking workers finally destroyed the banknote, the script for *One + One = Three* lacked any blatant social criticism.

The film tells the story of Paul, who falls in love with Anni and proposes to her. Unfortunately he is poor, and Anni's patriarchal father prefers a wealthy son-in-law. Balázs integrates a deus ex machina: Paul inherits a fortune from a deceased uncle. But there is a condition: he may not marry a young maiden. To solve the dilemma, Paul asks his friend, Peter, to marry Anni yet allow him to be Anni's real husband, while Peter maintains the facade. Peter agrees. He and Anni marry, but then become amorous. After further conflicts and resolutions, Peter and Anni divorce so that Paul finally can marry Anni—who can no longer be considered a young maiden.

It is difficult to explain the intentions of Prometheus in producing *One + One = Three*. It is again unlikely that the company wanted to produce an inexpensive film quickly to acquire a contingency certificate. As was the case with *Superfluous People*, Prometheus engaged established personalities such as Veit Harlan and Claire Bloom to play the leading roles, and for the first time, even commissioned the *Illustrierter Film-Kurier* to produce an accompanying program. In addition, *One + One = Three* was one of the films that Prometheus had described with the slogan "Not Quantity, but Quality!"

It is possible that Prometheus and Balázs had agreed to make further concessions to the perceived tastes of the public. Balázs had struggled intensely with Fox Europe, the producers of *The Adventures of a Ten-Mark Note,* to maintain the critical quality of that film, but ultimately acquiesced to the company's desire for less social criticism, more romance, and a happy ending.[35] If concessions were intended here too, it also would corroborate the claim that Prometheus strove to strike a balance between the socially critical Soviet films, its own critical documentaries, and less provocative entertainment films.[36]

The most plausible explanation is that *One + One = Three* was produced as a parody of commercial romances.[37] Following his experience with Fox Europe, it seems likely that Balázs would perceive some value in undermining the compensatory potential of idealized love in mainstream cinema. According to his comments in "Der Film arbeitet für uns" ("The Film Works for Us," *Film und Volk,* February/March 1928: 6–8), film could and should have such a subversive effect on audiences: "Film is the art of seeing. Its fundamental tendency is to nurture revelation, exposure. . . . In the struggle for truth there is no better weapon than the presentation of reality. It demands taking sides. . . . It can never develop fully in the hands of those who have much to hide and disguise" (8).

At the same time, Balázs considered it essential to make concessions to audiences that demanded entertainment. For him the model compromise existed in the films of Charlie Chaplin. With this in mind, and considering the Prometheus desire for commercial success, it seems likely that *One + One = Three*—with its subtitle "A Film Jest from Béla Balázs"— was intended as a parody of commercial romance films that also would entertain.

The synopsis in the *Illustrierter Film-Kurier* program, which uses many of the film's intertitles, also suggests that *One + One = Three* was a parody. In its explanation of the conflict between Paul and Anni, for example, the program describes the father's role in the following way: "He makes a scene, because he had envisioned a rich son-in-law. His sensibilities demand that, just as they require the domestic discipline that corresponds to the precision of a petty officer. Seven regimented children and a charming housewife submit to his dictatorship." The references to the father as a "petty officer" who has established a domestic "dictatorship" indicate that Balázs also intended to criticize the patriarchal quality of traditional romances by portraying the father as laughable. This becomes especially clear in scenes depicting the family at the dinner table and on a walk in the country. In each case mise-en-scène strengthens the critique. The exaggerated facial expressions and gestures that accompany the father's commands, as well as the well-choreographed responses of the children, who eat and walk with military exactness, heighten the comic aspect of the patriarch's control.

The film raised questions about the romance film genre by comically subverting many of its other narrative elements as well. The subversion begins even before the actual plot gets under way with an innovative animated segment that accompanies the credits. The clever segment portrays with slapstick the efforts of the animated production crew to construct the set. In the process it draws attention to the fictional/farcical quality of the narrative. As the plot unfolds, these subversive techniques continue. For example, when Paul grows desperate after Anni's father has forbidden him to see his daughter, one of Paul's friends makes an unexpected appearance and exclaims, "Why this desperation? Where the need is greatest, a filmic wonder is close at hand!" Later, instead of resolving the conflict between Paul, Peter, and Anni plausibly, the narrative employs another farcical deus ex machina and moves toward a relatively grotesque but comical happy ending. Dr. Pinner, who had suggested the substitute marriage between Peter and Anni, intervenes with the solution to the complicated triangle. As the *Illustrierter Film-Kurier* program summarizes: "But how to find a way out of this dilemma. Pinner knows all and he also knows the way to a happy ending. The will is consulted and look there: Paul may not marry a maiden, but a divorced woman is no maiden! In that way morality is upheld. Paul has his lover and Anni has hers." The reference to a "happy ending" and the somewhat sarcastic " . . . and look there" further reinforce the film's subversion of the romance narrative in which heroic deeds ensure a happy ending and conventional morality remains unscathed. The necessity of a divorce only strengthens the comical twist of the resolution.

According to the press responses, *One + One = Three* was a commercial success. The *Film Journal* praised it as one of the best German films ever produced (see *Film-Kurier*, 14 December 1927). Hamburg distributors also described it as a hit.[38] Apparently Prometheus had found a formula for attracting audiences to films that criticized mainstream cinema, including its compensatory illusions of reality. As the animated opening segment, the plot development, the intertitles, and the use of slapstick indicate, the formula included devices that undermined the authority of cinematic narratives to organize their material for film audiences.

The second Prometheus film, *Tragedy of the Children*, never premiered. The only available information about the film comes from preproduction announcements and a two-page program that Prometheus produced and distributed independently. A brief *L.B.B.* announcement (28 September 1927) summarized the plot:

In rare cases émigrés leave their children behind and surrender them to an uncertain future. So it was, too, for the little Hermi who was left alone and forced to fend for himself. A variety of experiences led him to Marseilles, where he made himself useful as a coal carrier until one day he got mixed up with some criminals who misused the helpless child for their shameful plans. However, Hermi was lucky because chance led him into the arms of his parents, who happily took their son, whom they had given up for lost, into their home. This story is the subject of the major German Prometheus film *Tragedy of the Children,* in which Hermi Lutz, the German Jackie Coogan, plays the leading role.

The announcement suggests that Prometheus hoped to attract large audiences. It associated Hermi Lutz with Jackie Coogan, who had achieved instant stardom in 1921 with Charlie Chaplin in *The Kid,* and the entire film with other popular child tragedy films such as *The Illegitimate* and *Die Ausgestoßenen (The Rejected,* 1927).

Prometheus also produced four short documentaries and one major documentary, *Die rote Front marschiert (The Red Front Marches)* in 1927.[39] Just as the FuL solicited support for Social Democrats and the commercial newsreels promoted the more conservative political parties, the Prometheus documentaries focused on the leadership of the KPD and encouraged support for the party's program. Except for *The Red Front Marches,* which was censored drastically before being released for public screening (Filmoberprüfstelle No. 621, Berlin, 12 July 1927), Prometheus produced its documentaries for noncommercial distribution only. Weltfilm assumed responsibility for noncommercial production in 1927, freeing Prometheus to focus even more on commercial production and the distribution of its own and Soviet films.

Prometheus continued to function as the primary German distributor of Soviet films, but the Soviet film industry negotiated another cooperative relationship in 1927. The Soviet Trade Bureau in Berlin had established a Foto-Kino Abteilung, and its director, Edmund Zöhrer, agreed to found a Deutsch-Russische Film-Allianz (Derufa, later Derussa) with the Gruppe Sklarz-Phönix-Film in October 1927.[40] The initial stock fund for the new firm was 200,000 reichsmark (twenty times the Prometheus amount). As Zöhrer noted, although the Trade Bureau valued its cooperation with Prometheus, the Derussa program would be much larger ("Deutsch-russische Filmgemeinschaft"—"German-Russian Film Cooperative," *L.B.B.,* 13 October 1927). The partners planned to begin by distributing six Soviet and six German films and initiating joint film projects.

While Derussa's plans took shape, Prometheus opened its program in 1928 with *Schinderhannes, the Rebel of the Rhine.* Carl Zuckmayer and Kurt Bernhardt collaborated on the script, and the young Bernhardt directed the film. A mixture of established and less well known actors including Hans Stuwe, Lissi Arna, Fritz Rasp, and Albert Steinrück assumed the leading roles.

The plot for the film originated with the true story of Hannes Bückler (Schinderhannes). Bückler was a thief from the Hunsrück who was executed in Mainz at a time when the French occupied the entire left bank of the Rhine.[41] During the nineteenth century a Schinderhannes legend developed and flourished. A number of poets, novelists, and singers incorporated the legend into their works, portraying Schinderhannes as a Robin Hood figure, an opponent of the French, etc.

When the French occupied the Ruhr River Valley in 1923, the legend became very popular again. For many Germans, Schinderhannes, like Leo Schlageter, was a martyr of French aggression.[42] In 1922 Carl Zuckmayer composed his *Mainzer Moritat von Schinderhannes,* and in 1927 he completed a four-act play entitled *Schinderhannes.* In contrast to other versions of the Schinderhannes legend, which concentrated on national oppositions, Zuckmayer juxtaposed rich and poor, powerful and exploited.

In Zuckmayer's play, Schinderhannes appears at the outset as an established criminal with a tough personality. He cunningly and, when necessary, forcefully wields his power against the hated merchants, soldiers, and aristocrats, but exercises patriarchal generosity with his family, followers, and the peasants. After positing the opposition between rich and poor in the first act, Zuckmayer portrays in the second an alliance between the princes of the Rhine and the French army to defeat Schinderhannes and his band.

Zuckmayer's play challenged popular nationalistic interpretations of the French occupation in 1923 with a class-oriented explanation and a cynical conclusion. In the third act Schinderhannes attacks the French army, suffers a bitter defeat, flees from one village to the next, and finally attempts to integrate himself into society by joining the Prussian army. In the last act of the play, he is caught and executed, not by the French, but by the Prussian army in Mainz. For the Prussians, Schinderhannes's allegiance to the peasants against the rich overshadows his new national allegiance. When he complains about his arrest by referring to his enlistment papers, the adjutant remarks, "Do not forget that you are a political criminal." A loyal follower attempts to intervene, but Schinderhannes steps in: "Let the man go! He opened our eyes, that's all! Now we finally know what 'political' means!" (IV, 117).

Zuckmayer and Bernhardt reworked the play substantially, but the ideological message remained basically intact in the film. It begins with an omniscient narrative text, describing the sociohistorical context: "The left bank of the Rhine was occupied by the French army. . . . The German princes of the Rhine had allied themselves with the French army and paid little attention to the fates of the people. The land was impoverished and plundered by the endless state of war. The peasants, artisans, and workers lived under wretched conditions. Ruthless requisitions increased the bitterness in the land. . . . For unpaid high taxes, heavy penalties were inflicted." What Zuckmayer waited until the play's second act to reveal became a catalyst for the film's plot development. In the opening scenes Schinderhannes and his friends disrupt conscription proceedings in a small village. The magistrate catches Schinderhannes, jails him, and eventually has him flogged. When he is freed, Schinderhannes joins a band of robbers to seek revenge. Together they plunder and burn the magistrate's house, and one of the robbers kills the magistrate.

In what follows, the original head of the robber's band, Leyendecker, meets with Picard to discuss plans for arming the peasants against the French army and the princes of the Rhine. Picard, who controls the weapons supply, expresses skepticism about Schinderhannes's fervor. Schinderhannes then justifies the skepticism. He challenges Leyendecker's leadership, takes control, and foils the effort to arm three thousand peasants. As he does in the play, the rebel more or less spontaneously decides to attack the French headquarters when reinforcements arrive. He fails and eventually is executed.

The film also emphasizes class instead of national differences, but there is one major change. The addition of Leyendecker's role suggests an alternative to the play's cynical ending. If Leyendecker's followers had resisted the charismatic appeal of the anarchistic Schinderhannes and remained loyal to their patient leader, perhaps they would have succeeded. For revolutionary workers, who had experienced the October uprising of 1923, the transition in leadership from the Fischer/Maslow faction to Ernst Thälmann, and the KPD's growing allegiance to the Comintern under Stalin's leadership, the film's message was clear. It encouraged them and everyone else to accept central party leadership and follow a more disciplined course toward revolutionary action.

Although Bernhardt might have used various common narrative techniques to underscore the authenticity of his story, he relied almost exclusively on omniscient narrative texts. Whereas Lamprecht had used Berlin dialect for the intertitles in his Zille films, those in *Schinderhannes* appeared in High German, despite Zuckmayer's use of the Hunsrück dialect in the play. And, in contrast to the tendency toward shooting historical pageants in real-life settings, the Prometheus team shot most of the film in the studio, where set designers had constructed a noticeably artificial environment, and characters performed in what were only relatively believable costumes.

Bernhardt and his cameraman, Günter Krampf, did incorporate a wide variety of popular camera angles and montage techniques that encouraged the audience to sympathize with Schinderhannes and associate ideologically with those characters who sought to temper his headstrong personality. The opening scenes provide a good example of this practice. Following the expositional narrative text and a sequence in which Schinderhannes disrupts the conscription process, he is seen caught and arrested. The juxtaposition of the text with the first sequence suggests that Schinderhannes sides with the peasants in their struggle against an exploitive ruling class and therefore deserves the spectators' sympathy. The next sequence reinforces the suggestion considerably. The audience first observes Schinderhannes in his cell; he moves to the window, looks out, and sees (spectators see from his perspective) a series of storm images. A cut returns the spectators to a neutral position, from which they now watch as Schinderhannes rages. By forcing them to see the storm through his eyes and then depicting his anger, Bernhardt and Krampf encouraged them to understand his emotional condition and to share his experience.

A fade-out and fade-in provide a transition to shots of the magistrate, who taps rhythmically on his record book with a pen. A cut follows; in the next sequence, depicting the flogging of Schinderhannes, it becomes apparent that the magistrate had been tapping in time to the cracks of the whip. The subsequent close-ups shift from the satisfied face of the magistrate to the protagonist's agonizing expressions to his friends and their expressions of sympathy. When Schinderhannes cringes there is a cut. The onlookers cringe, but cuts to the magistrate reveal that he continues to tap in enjoyment. Finally the punishment ends, and the jailers release Schinderhannes. The camera perspective allows the spectator to see him fall to the ground but then switches to his perspective (foggy, soft-focus), suggesting that Schinderhannes can barely see. At the end of the scene, the camera resumes an observer's position, and spectators watch Schinderhannes as he flees into the forest.

In this scene, as in the entire film, changing camera perspectives and transitional elements, such as the tapping pen and the cracking whip, encourage the audience to share the protagonist's emotional experience and to sympathize with him while condemning his evil opponents. When

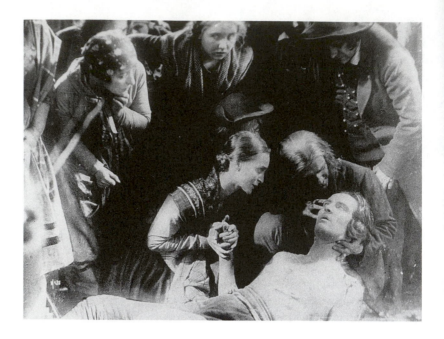

Schinderhannes, the Rebel of the Rhine: peasants comfort Schinderhannes after his flogging. (Staatliches Filmarchiv der DDR)

Schinderhannes and his band make their way to the guillotine, the film encourages a transformation of this sympathy into a desire to prevent the executions. Leyendecker represents the alternative. If spectators rejected radical leftist positions, affirmed the leadership of the KPD, and followed its guidelines for change, then perhaps similar casualties could be avoided.

The trade journals generally praised *Schinderhannes*.[43] According to Prometheus advertisements, it attracted large audiences in major urban centers (*Film-Kurier,* 15 March 1928). Nevertheless, the company once again hesitated with its feature production while its relationship with Meschrabpom changed significantly. The *L.B.B.* reported that seventeen Meschrabpom officials had been arrested and charged with embezzlement ("Moskauer Filmskandal"—"Moscow Film Scandal," 9 March 1928). A short time later Edmund Meisel reported in a letter to Eisenstein that Prometheus had completely exhausted its operating capital (6 June 1928). Following the reorganization of Meschrabpom,[44] the two companies negotiated an agreement whereby they would begin to coproduce films.

Although Meschrabpom had produced commercially successful films, including *Mother* (1927), it seems likely that, because of the embezzlement report and Meisel's description, financial problems more than anything else stimulated the negotiations. By producing films cooperatively, Prometheus and Meschrabpom could share production costs, and Prometheus could take advantage of Soviet talent. In the process, Prometheus might increase the attractiveness of its films, decrease the cost, and, by claiming that the co-productions were German films, continue to receive contingency certificates.

FALSCHMÜNZER (COUNTERFEITERS) AND OTHER CO-PRODUCTIONS

The People's Commissar for Education in the Soviet Union, Anatoli Lunatscharsky, wrote the script for the first Prometheus-Meschrabpom co-production, *Counterfeiters* (released as *Salamander* in the Soviet Union). He based his story on the case of an Austrian biologist, Paul Kammerer.[45] Kammerer had promoted Darwin's theory of evolution and, as a result, suffered persecution. In the Soviet version of the film, which premiered in Moscow before Prometheus submitted its version to German censors, the protagonist is Professor Zange, a biologist who experiments with salamanders to determine if there is a connection between inherited and acquired traits. Academics, priests, and aristocrats who fear that Zange's research will undermine their authority challenge his findings. One of Zange's students, Prince Karlstein, seduces the professor's wife, yet wins his confidence and becomes his assistant. Karlstein then sabotages Zange's experiments just before a commission arrives to evaluate the work. The commission denounces Zange, and having to leave his position at the university, he becomes destitute.

In the meantime, Zange's wife has decided to live with the prince, who also forges money with a banker. She is caught with some forged bills, but the prince denies any connection with her, and the police believe him. While her downfall unfolds, Zange recovers. A loyal assistant describes Zange's persecution to the People's Commissar for Education, played by Lunatscharsky, and requests him to invite the mistreated professor to continue his research in Moscow. Lunatscharsky agrees. While Zange contemplates suicide, his assistant attempts to reach him in a speeding train. The assistant arrives just in time. The film ends happily for Zange but unhappily for his wife.

Counterfeiters: cold, calculating aristocratic students and clergy. (Staatliches Filmarchiv der DDR)

Although the co-producers shot most of the film in Germany, and despite Lunatscharsky's role (with the flag of the Soviet commissars in his buttonhole), Prometheus attempted to appease the German censors by changing titles, names, and props to imply that the story was set elsewhere and that a German Minister of Culture had invited Zange to Germany. The effort outraged the censors who wrote in their explanation that the portrayed nation—in which representatives of all social institutions were either inept, corrupt, or both—was clearly recognizable as Germany (Filmoberprüfstelle No. 21, 17 January 1929:4). The censors' anger derived from their perception that Prometheus, under a very thin disguise, intended to criticize German social institutions. They prohibited public screenings, describing the film as an "anti-German agitational film" that offended the national unity and degraded Germany's reputation.

The censors' criticism was partially unjust; in reality the film criticized only specific social institutions, not the German nation. But they correctly assessed its portrayal of characters. *Counterfeiters*, despite the general accuracy of its critique, posited less convincing oppositions between totally negative representatives of the church, state, aristocracy, and the business world, on the one hand, and the very positive figure of Zange, his assistant, and the People's Commissar, on the other.

The film developed the oppositions with fairly sophisticated montage techniques. For example, one sequence uses stream-of-consciousness montage to identify the church as corrupt, in opposition to the virtuous Zange. The sequence portrays a priest verifying Zange's findings and contemplating his response. The spectator sees first the priest in his laboratory, then an image of Jesus on the cross, the priest again, the salamanders in their aquarium, and then the Bible. The priest finally smashes the aquarium and then prays, as the shot fades out. The sequence suggests that the church fosters lies to maintain its authority.

Other montage techniques strengthen the oppositions and encourage the audience to adopt correspondingly opposing evaluations of the characters. For example, by juxtaposing shots of the decadent Prince Karl-stein, who seduces Zange's wife, and others, focusing especially on the diligent Professor Zange in his laboratory, *Counterfeiters* nurtures a negative impression of the prince and sympathy for Zange. In the final scenes parallel montage further solidifies Zange's sympathetic image by juxtaposing his wife's demise and his recovery, as well as by shifting from Zange's assistant in the speeding train to Zange. The growing suspense stimulates an even closer emotional link to Zange and his benefactors by encouraging the audience to hope that the assistant will arrive before Zange commits suicide.

While Prometheus cooperated with Meschrabpom in producing *Counterfeiters*, their relationship developed further. According to the *L.B.B.* ("Die Neugestaltung des russisch-deutschen Filmgeschäfts"—"The Reformation of the Russian-German Film Business," 13 September 1928), the Soviets decided to shift much of their cooperative activity from Derussa to Prometheus. Only one year after its inception, the Derussa venture deteriorated. Although the company had announced grandiose plans for co-productions, it continued to emphasize distribution.[46] The shift from Derussa to Prometheus increased the Prometheus operating capital from the original 10,000 reichsmarks to 100,000 reichsmarks, and work on the next Meschrabpom-Prometheus co-production, *Der Lebende Leichnam* (*The Living Corpse*), began.[47]

Prometheus also distributed a number of Soviet films in 1928. They included Eisenstein's *Zehn Tage, die die Welt erschütterten* (*Ten Days That Shook the World*) and *Eisbrecher Krassin* (*Icebreaker Krassin*), an expedition film, portraying the heroic rescue of the Nobile expedition. Eisenstein's belated contribution to the tenth anniversary celebration of the Russian Revolution attracted a tremendous amount of attention initially, but it in no way matched the success of *Battleship Potemkin*. Eisenstein, who by this time had developed his theory of the intellectual film, experimented freely with narrative techniques to nurture critical reception. Because of the film's nonnarrative structure, most critics and filmgoers rejected it or at least expressed confusion. *Icebreaker Krassin* was significant because it initiated a new trend in Soviet filmmaking. Between 1928 and 1933 Soviet filmmakers paid less attention to historical subjects and more to the developing Soviet society. Many of their films, including *Icebreaker Krassin,* were documentaries that glorified Soviet achievements while claiming objectivity.[48]

Prometheus contributed to the trend with feature-length documentaries such as *Quer durch Sowjetrußland* (*Straight across Soviet Russia*). The film documented the journey of a German workers' delegation in 1927 and highlighted developments in Soviet agriculture and industry. Like the Soviet documentaries, this one was less than objective. The censors initially refused to permit children to see it, claiming that they would be unable to distinguish between the film's images of prosperity and the reality of a slowly developing society.

In their documentaries German and Soviet filmmakers marketed the Soviet Union to German audiences. They emphasized the best elements, withheld information about serious problems, and hoped to convince spectators to support the IAH, KPD, and Comintern. While attempting to demonstrate the model quality of Soviet society, filmmakers ran the risk of transforming it into a commodity and did little to nurture the critical skills the German people would need to build their own socialist society.

THE BIRTH OF THE VOLKSFILMVERBAND: PARTISAN NONPARTISANSHIP AND GRASS-ROOTS ORGANIZATION FROM ABOVE?

While Prometheus adapted to the conditions of commercial film production and the IAH together with Weltfilm concentrated on noncommercial programs similar to those of the SPD, a number of left-leaning intellectuals and artists joined Social Democrats and Communists to found the Volksfilmverband für Filmkunst (later Volksfilmverband, VFV) at the beginning of 1928.[1] After numerous discussions about the need for and possibility of organizing a nonpartisan, grass-roots film organization at the end of 1927, the VFV emerged on 13 January 1928. The founding proclamation emphasized that the organization would follow in the footsteps of the Volksbühne and challenge the aesthetic as well as the ideological quality of commercial film (*Film und Volk*, February/March 1928, preface).

As the proclamation indicated, the founders of the VFV intended to create a forum in which spectators could express dissatisfaction with commercial film, transform that dissatisfaction into constructive criticism, and influence production. Initially, the VFV planned to exert influence by acquiring a theater, like the Volksbühne, to screen only those films that it considered aesthetically and ideologically acceptable. It also planned to publish critiques and suggestions for production in its own journal, *Film und Volk*. The VFV hoped to increase grass-roots participation in setting standards for film quality and to pave the way for less centralized production. Ultimately, the VFV expected to produce its own films.

The VFV appeared to be a catalyst for the democratic participation in film production and reception that neither the SPD nor the KPD had provided. A closer look at its structure and program reveals that the VFV, too, abandoned much of its democratic impetus. From the beginning the leaders of the VFV relied on personalities to attract attention and set guidelines for the organization. Correspondence between the VFV business manager, Rudolf Schwarzkopf, and Heinrich Mann reveals that, as the official president, Mann functioned primarily to enhance the organization's image.[2] Schwarzkopf reported to Mann on the VFV's activities, requesting that he make appearances at special events and write short articles on particular occasions. By selecting Mann as its president and inviting prominent artists, intellectuals, and even film stars to join its honorary board of directors, the VFV demonstrated that it was willing to use the tactics of the existing culture industry. Like mainstream cinema with its star system, the VFV at least indirectly reinforced the belief in the authority of a few gifted artists and unusually intelligent intellectuals.[3]

Film und Volk, the first journal of the German left devoted exclusively to film, followed the same course. In its inaugural issue the names of those renowned individuals who belonged to the executive committee and the honorary board of directors were listed to legitimize the organization and stimulate interest. Initiatives from above to expand and guide the allegedly grass-roots organization characterized contributions to *Film und Volk* throughout 1928. Most contributors were well-known authors, film experts, or VFV leaders. Their articles criticized the film industry in more detail than most articles in the SPD, KPD, and IAH press. Some even discussed the need for radically democratic change. But the initiative regularly came from above.

In addition to reviews and reports on the organization's activity, feature articles criticized the film industry. They exposed the influence of conservative and reactionary interest groups (Alfons Goldschmidt, "Die Filmwirtschaft"—"The Film Economy," February/March 1928:21). They described the dictatorial rule of company executives over directors and other personnel (Rudolf Schwarzkopf, "Abenteuer um Abenteuer"—"Adventure after Adventure," April 1928:1). And they exposed connections between producers and critics (see Hermann Hubner, "Diese Filmkritik"—"This Film Criticism," August 1928:8). A few articles even focused on production techniques, but none challenged the narrative quality of commercial film and its effect on reception.

Instead, most of the contributors to *Film und Volk* challenged the authority of producers to dictate standards of film quality in general. Articles such as "The Film Works for Us" (Béla Balázs, March 1928:6),

"Künstler und Volk gehören zusammen" ("Artists and People Belong To-gether," Carl Zuckmayer, March 1928:16), "Eroberung des Films" ("The Conquest of Film," Franz Höllering, June 1928:4, and August 1928:4), "Revolution von unten" ("Revolution from Below," S. Alher, August 1928:6), and "Arbeiter dreht Filme!" ("Workers Make Films!" Felix Lange, November 1928:9–10) encouraged the German public from a variety of perspectives to build its own alternative cinema. Except for beginning a seminar on film production at the end of 1928, the VFV did little organizationally to encourage initiative from below.

As mentioned above, Social Democrats and Communists participated actively in the VFV. The SPD perceived it as an appendage to the Volksbühne, with which it could attract new members and support for its political programs. The KPD hoped to use it as a forum for broaden-ing its sphere of influence. Both factions were interested less in enhancing critical skills than in asserting the authority of their parties and programs. By April 1928, when the VFV held its first national conference in Erfurt, the SPD had decided to leave the organization and attack it as a front for Communist propaganda.[4] Despite the SPD's decision, a number of Social Democrats remained, and the VFV's leaders continued to assert the or-ganization's nonpartisanship. To prove their claim they worked diligently to sustain the visibility of prominent members who could not be associ-ated with a specific party. They also strove to increase membership, and initially succeeded.

VFV groups from eighteen German cities, including Berlin, sent dele-gates to the national conference, and during the second half of 1928 the number of groups steadily increased. Franz Höllering, editor of *Film und Volk,* reported to Heinrich Mann in July that the journal's circulation was approaching five thousand. The time had come to schedule monthly VFV film events.

At the same time, Höllering complained about the difficulties associ-ated with selecting appropriate films, finding suitable theaters, and ex-panding the organization so that it could become more than just a film club for people who were attracted by less expensive prices. Distributors refused to allow the VFV to screen first-run features. Even cooperative theater owners granted the VFV access to their facilities only on Sunday afternoon. Ufa boycotted the organization, and independent production seemed impossible.

Faced with these problems, Heinrich Mann, in a proclamation pub-lished in the November 1928 issue of *Film und Volk,* announced that the VFV had a dynamic program for its second half-year, including film events, courses, and production. To convince its members that production was possible, the VFV requested and received permission from Prometheus to screen another of the documentaries that it had produced in 1927–28: *Das Dokument von Shanghai* (*The Document of Shanghai*).[5] The film premiered on 9 November 1928 in the Tauentzienpalast in Berlin and ran for two weeks, but the VFV program continued to stagnate.

PART THREE

THE END OF THE WEIMAR REPUBLIC: 1929–1933

By the end of 1928 the German economy had begun to weaken. In the wake of the New York stock market crash in October 1929, a major economic crisis once again threatened the stability of the Weimar Republic. Weimar's parliamentary democracy began to disintegrate under the pressure of the crisis in the spring of 1930.[1] Less than three years later, Adolf Hitler and the Nationalsozialistische Deutsche Arbeiterpartei (NSDAP), who were able to attract only eight hundred thousand votes in the Reichstag election of 1928, assumed leadership in Germany.

While relations of political power shifted, German cinema also experienced a dramatic change. The economic and political crisis, as well as the introduction of sound, initiated a new round of national and international competition between producers, distributors, and theater owners. The largest companies increased their strength while smaller companies struggled, were subsumed, or simply ceased to exist. The film organizations of the German left also struggled to compete commercially and ideologically, but one by one they vanished.

12

THE GREAT COALITION AND THE DISINTEGRATION OF PARLIAMENTARY DEMOCRACY

Following a series of power struggles between the Zentrum Partei (Catholic Center party), the Deutsche Volkspartei (DVP), and the Deutschnationale Volkspartei (DNVP), the *Bürgerblock* collapsed at the beginning of 1928. In the ensuing Reichstag elections of May 1928, the Social Democrats achieved their greatest success since 1919, attracting nine million votes and justifying the organization of a coalition cabinet under their leadership. By June the SPD's Herman Müller had assembled a somewhat tenuous cabinet, consisting of representatives from the SPD, the Deutsche Demokratische Partei (DDP), Catholic Center party, DVP, and the Bayrische Volkspartei (BVP). General Groener represented the military as the minister of defense.

At approximately the same time, the economy showed signs of stress. By the beginning of 1929 unemployment rose above peak jobless rates for the past four years. When the New York stock market crashed in October 1929, the bottom fell out of the German economy, and the SPD again found itself in an uncompromising position. As the leading party of the governing coalition, it appeared responsible for the nation's crisis, just as it had been perceived to be responsible for the postwar crisis.

While the SPD's Great Coalition worked to maintain the social status quo and reinforced the perception that its members were devoted republicans who accepted responsibility for the spreading economic crisis, an ever-growing political right dissociated itself from the republican government and advocated various forms of authoritarian rule.[1] In June of 1929 Hugenberg succeeded in expanding the antirepublican front by forming a committee in opposition to the ratification of the Young Plan. Members included representatives from the Pan-German League, the Stahlhelm, the Reichsverband der deutschen Industrie (Reich Association of German Industry), and Adolf Hitler. They condemned the SPD and its republican allies for accepting the Treaty of Versailles and refused to agree to a plan that called for reparations payments until 1988. Although their plebiscite campaign failed in the fall of 1929, it strengthened the perception that the SPD and its coalition partners had mismanaged the original peace negotiations and Germany's economy. The campaign also defined the crisis more as a national rather than a class conflict.

Over the next three years powerful interest groups, under the leadership of Hugenberg and Fritz Thyssen (leader of the Reich Association of German Industry), strove to sustain their wealth and authority. As the economic crisis intensified, the German people, although they partially blamed the Social Democrats and the republican government, also blamed greedy speculators. They recognized that powerful industrialists and investors had maximized profits by speculating and either forming or joining national and international cartels with little concern for German workers. Now the same people were closing plants and exporting capital.[2] The best strategy for Germany's capitalist elite was to support campaigns that emphasized the national character of the economic crisis and blamed the republican government. For the most part they supported the Nationalsozialistische Deutsche Arbeiterpartei (NSDAP).[3]

As the antirepublican front around Hugenberg grew, the KPD returned to an ultraleftist course.[4] Among the contributing factors were (1) during the years of relative stability, the membership of the KPD slowly decreased from 180,000 to 130,000; (2) during the same period, the German electorate shifted slowly to the left; (3) in 1928 the Comintern and the KPD anticipated that the German economy would peak and start to decline; and (4) after defeating his opposition on the political left in 1926, Stalin was initiating an attack on those to his political right in an attempt to consolidate his power in the Soviet Union and in the Comintern (Flechtheim, 248). Beginning in the summer of 1928 the triumvirate of Ernst Thälmann, Hermann Remmele, and Heinz Neumann positioned itself solidly within Stalin's camp and moved to exclude both the so-called appeasers and the right-wing leaders in the KPD. By the end of the year they had assumed party leadership.

Toward the end of 1928 and in 1929 the developing economic crisis and the SPD's policies intensified KPD opposition to Social Democracy. The Great Coalition's decision to begin construction of Panzerkreuzer A motivated the Communists to organize a campaign to stop funding for the project in October 1928. In May 1929 the Communists staged their annual May Day March, despite the refusal of the Social Democratic coalition in Prussia to lift its ban on such demonstrations. The resulting confrontation between marchers and the police (who were under the direction of the SPD police chief, Karl Zörgiebel) concluded with twenty-five civilian casualties and thirty-six seriously injured. When the Prussian minister of the interior, Carl Severing, banned the Rot Frontkämpferbund throughout Prussia at the end of May, it only strengthened the perception that the SPD had united with antirepublicans in support of fascism.

In response to these developments, the KPD accused the SPD of complicity in the rise of National Socialism. Between 1929 and 1932 Communists refused to join the SPD in united actions and attempted to win support from the Social Democratic rank and file. The KPD's approach was understandable but counterproductive. At critical points, the KPD missed opportunities to slow or stop the progress of National Socialism and occasionally even seemed willing to cooperate with the nationalist opposition.[5]

Finally in 1932 the KPD seemed to realize its mistake. In the spring and summer of that year the party gradually abandoned the theory of social fascism and proposed united actions against the nationalist opposition. However, the solidified animosity toward the KPD among SPD leaders and the KPD's continued cynicism about the Social Democrats rendered virtually impossible any productive cooperation. Neither party was willing to make the compromises necessary to unite in what might have been a successful coalition against National Socialism.

In addition to the lack of cooperation between the SPD and KPD, various other factors contributed to the rise of National Socialism. As mentioned above, leading industrialists, agrarians, and aristocrats opportunistically supported the NSDAP. Of even greater significance was the appeal of National Socialism to large numbers of dissatisfied and disoriented civil servants, other white-collar workers, small merchants, and other petty bourgeoisie.[6] When the economy weakened in 1929 and 1930, Germany's middle classes once again faced the prospect of downward social mobility, unemployment, and other severe hardships. Many middle-class Germans grew skeptical of capitalism (as evidenced by the decrease in electoral support for those political parties most closely associated with German capitalism, the DVP and DNVP). For them, the Social Democratic program also was unacceptable because Social Democrats bore at least partial responsibility for economic dependence on

Western banks and consequent economic instability. In addition, as the party most closely associated with the republic, the SPD appeared responsible for a government in which the polarization of special interests hindered the formation of national consensus.

At the same time, the Communists, who implied that middle-class Germans should abandon their national and class identity in favor of a more egalitarian society, posed an even greater threat. According to the KPD, Germany should become a soviet republic, and middle-class Germans should accept the dictatorship of the proletariat.[7] For most nonproletarians, fears about losing their national and individual identities far overshadowed the potential advantages associated with the KPD plan.

Large numbers of lower-middle- and middle-class Germans searched for a third way—an anticapitalist and anti-Marxist alternative.[8] The National Socialists provided the most attractive ideological alternative. The NSDAP advocated a strong national identity associated with precapitalist Germany.[9] It fulfilled the middle-class need for security by positing a regressive utopia and suggesting that Germany could regain its former glory by embracing that utopia in the future.[10]

The National Socialist ideology galvanized the national identity by attributing blame for present social problems on dangerous "others."[11] The NSDAP attracted middle-class support by shifting blame from the German people to foreign influences. The instigators of Germany's economic crisis were not German capitalists—or even Germans: they were Bolsheviks and Jews. Such explanations confirmed middle-class fears about Marxism and capitalism without questioning the German identity. On the contrary, they united "Germans" against a common enemy. As the Weimar era drew to a close, the success of National Socialism depended to a large extent on its ability to use a nostalgic nationalism and xenophobic racism to attract and unite dissatisfied middle-class Germans. Mainstream cinema played an increasingly important role in the process.

13

SOUND, THE ECONOMIC CRISIS, AND COMMERCIAL FILM'S IMAGES OF THE PAST, PRESENT, AND FUTURE

Even before the economic crisis hit, the transition to sound dramatically affected the development of German cinema.[1] In 1927 Ufa's executives discussed the company's contracts with the Triergon A.G. in Zürich (the inventors of the most advanced sound film system in Europe) and decided against further investments in sound film experimentation.[2] Two years later, after unsuccessful attempts to find distributors for Ufa's silent films in the United States, Ufa's Ludwig Klitzsch returned to Germany and hurriedly began construction of a sound studio.[3] In 1929 a few producers used sound as a novelty element in their films, but Ufa's *Die Melodie des Herzens* (*Melody of the Heart*) was Germany's first 100 percent sound film. Following its commercial success in December 1929, German film producers gradually acknowledged that silent films were a thing of the past.

Once again commercial cinema in Germany underwent a process of concentration. During the second half of 1928, the Tonbild-Syndikat A.G. (Tobis) emerged and claimed to possess the European licenses for sound film production.[4] At approximately the same time, the two largest German electrical concerns, Siemens & Halske and A.E.G., founded the Klangfilm GmbH and made similar claims. Early in 1929, following an intense patent war, the two competitors agreed that Tobis would hold a monopoly in the realm of production; Klangfilm would control that of projection. Together Tobis and Klangfilm entered another round of competition with major U.S. patent holders over control of the world market. In July 1930 the participants decided to divide the world into spheres of influence, allowing Tobis and Klangfilm to control much of Europe.[5]

In the meantime, Tobis had established conditions for the production of sound films that virtually excluded all but the largest producers in Germany.[6] Between 1929 and 1931, there were 71 production companies in Germany with a combined operating capital of near sixty-one million marks. The eight largest producers had a combined capital of fifty-eight million marks, or 95 percent of the total. Of these only Ufa, Emelka (which came under the indirect control of Ufa in 1929), and Tobis possessed licenses for sound film production. Tobis required the others to request permission to use its equipment. The company demanded extremely high prices for production rights and granted rights only to those producers whose scripts it deemed acceptable.[7]

The monopolistic control exerted by Tobis and Klangfilm greatly improved the positions of Ufa and a few other large producers. The rapid rise in the cost of production and the correspondingly great financial risk forced smaller companies to depend on commissions for production from larger companies, to limit production to between one and three films per year, and to concentrate on less costly and far less profitable silent films.[8] As the return on silent film production dwindled, ever-increasing numbers of small producers went out of business.

The economic crisis only exacerbated the problem. Between 1929 and 1932 Germans allocated more of their income for basic needs and less for entertainment. Annual movie theater attendance sank steadily from, approximately, 328 million to 238 million. At the same time, the credit available for small film producers became much tighter.

Simultaneously, the conservative and (to an ever-larger extent) reactionary character of mainstream cinema intensified. Among other things, the transition to sound and the economic crisis enabled Alfred Hugenberg to expand his influence in the industry. By 1931 Ufa encompassed 71 companies, including 6 production, 5 distribution, 37 theater, 19 foreign, and 4 miscellaneous companies.[9] Ufa operated 115 major movie theaters and served almost 2,000 theaters with its massive distribution network. With the Ufa concern, Hugenberg and his nationalist opposition worked more and more overtly to promote an antidemocratic, nationalist alternative to the Weimar Republic. For example, as early as 1929, at the time of the Reichstag debate on the Young Plan, Ufa executives planned and produced an anti–Young Plan film (R109, 1027b, 13 November 1929).

Although that film clearly demonstrated Ufa's intention to influence public opinion, its executives remained hesitant about expressing their opinions publicly. Nevertheless, there were numerous opportunities for

Ludwig Klitzsch and his associates to advocate nationalism openly. In 1929 and 1930 the attempts of Hollywood companies to monopolize the European market affected public opinion as it had at the time of the Dawes Plan. As was the case then, producers, journalists, and others in the industry opposed the efforts of U.S. companies to control the German market. Many critiques identified the German film industry with the German nation and suggested that Hollywood's threat to the industry was a threat to the national identity.

At Ufa's annual convention in 1930, for example, Ludwig Klitzsch outlined the concern's development during the past two years and emphasized the national character of the struggle between Ufa and its Hollywood competitors: "The past two years were probably the most difficult that a company ever had to experience. For a time there was even grave doubt that a German film industry with a worldwide reputation could survive. . . . It is foremost thanks to Ufa that this goal was achieved."[10] Klitzsch continued by projecting a positive image of the German cinema in the future: "These considerations demonstrate . . . that Germany will be the future center of production in Europe. You can imagine yourselves what task will fall to Ufa in this process. These developments simultaneously demonstrate the crucial importance of maintaining protective trade regulations."

Klitzsch was correct in describing Hollywood's threat as a threat to the entire industry, but he also implied that Ufa was interested in its general well-being. His real interest lay in protecting and, if possible, strengthening Ufa's position in its competition with foreign as well as domestic companies. Klitzsch referred to the German film industry only to convince his audience to perceive Ufa's interests as national interests and, as he suggested, to assist Ufa in fulfilling its goals. His strategy was no different than that of Germany's most influential industrialists who, as proponents of a nationalist opposition, described their efforts to sustain their own economic and political power as a national mission.

Until 1932 Ufa continued to promote an antirepublican, antidemocratic, and nationalist alternative indirectly with references to competition against U.S. companies and with films that most Germans accepted as cinematic entertainment. According to a speech given at Ufa's 1931 convention by the production director E. H. Correll, Ufa strove to fulfill the needs of the German public ("Tag der großen Referate"—"Day of the Big Speeches," *L.B.B.*, 15 July 1931). He indicated that in 1931 Ufa was satisfied with producing films that "lifted the spirits" of increasing numbers of Germans who were suffering severe hardships. A production strategy that focused on entertainment was especially sound business at a time when deteriorating economic and political conditions intensified the public's desire for relief from everyday anxieties. Films such as the anti–Young Plan film remained the exception to the rule. Only in Ufa's newsreels did the concern's ideological orientation manifest itself openly.

At the annual convention in 1932, Correll finally advocated nationalism as a goal of Ufa's production: "We are beginning to make films, whether serious or lighthearted, in which not only pleasantly diverting events are portrayed. They are films in which questions are asked, questions that we must answer. In the future, we want to see people in films who pursue clear goals, who because of their character take up the struggle with external forces and who nationally or in purely human terms strive to achieve a worthy goal. They succeed neither through coincidence nor through deceit. . . . We must have filmmakers with German poetic sensibilities who, of course, must first master the technique of scriptwriting." [11] Although Ufa's executives waited until just six months before Hitler's takeover to promote an openly political production strategy, Correll's comments accurately describe much of Ufa's production between 1929 and 1932.

The transition to sound and the economic crisis also forced the entire industry to rely even more on production strategies that increased the ideologically conservative nature of mainstream cinema. Ufa's persistent caution about films that openly referred to social issues reflected the concerns of most producers. To remain competitive, producers had to attract large audiences. The best formula for filling theaters continued to be to offer compensation for perceived inadequacies in everyday life. As production costs rose and the number of patrons steadily decreased, companies also redoubled their efforts to standardize production. They cut production schedules, engaged the most popular stars, and focused more intensely on those subjects that had demonstrated public appeal. Film production became even more autocratic, the number of genres gradually decreased, and producers worked even harder to create films that encouraged audiences to sympathize with their protagonists. [12]

At the same time, the tolerance of producers for journalistic criticism diminished further. To guarantee that potential customers would receive positive information about their films, Ufa's executives founded yet another film journal, *Die Film-Welt.* Many of the journal's editorial pages contained information only about Ufa's production, and Ufa's press office supplied the photos and text directly. Other producers were unable to create their own critical acclaim. Nevertheless, they, too, attempted to maximize positive publicity by influencing the press with advertisement contracts and through SPIO.

In 1929 theater owners, distributors, and producers spent a total of thirty million marks on advertisements in the German press. The industry continued to use advertising contracts as a lever to force German newspapers and trade journals to print favorable reviews. In response, the Reichsarbeitsgemeinschaft der deutschen Presse (Reich Study Group of the German Press) created a set of policies in 1929 designed to ensure the independence of journalists from the film industry's influence.[13] A year later the SPIO published an official communiqué expressing the industry's disgruntlement over what it characterized as subjective and extremely political critiques. Here, as well, the arguments of the SPIO, in which Ufa's executives held leading positions, emphasized the necessity for journalists to disregard any ideological distinctions and defend German films in the interest of the entire nation.[14] Finally, in November 1930, a group of Berlin critics organized the Verband der Berliner Filmkritiker (Association of Berlin Film Critics) to protect their journalistic freedom.

Despite these and other attempts to maintain independence, the character of mainstream film criticism generally became more conservative. Of course, the Berlin critics association could expect little cooperation from the *Kinematograph, Ufa Wochenmagazin,* and *Die Film-Welt.* Although the *Kinematograph* maintained its relatively neutral coverage of Soviet and Prometheus films, it and other Scherl publications enthusiastically promoted Ufa's films and the SPIO's policies.

The editors of major newspapers and film journals who sustained the critical quality of their coverage bemoaned Ufa's expanding influence. In extremely blatant cases, they criticized the content of films that overplayed the myth of upward social mobility and advocated monarchism, nationalism, or militarism. However, as the economic and political crisis escalated, the threat of Hollywood domination increased, and pressure from clients intensified, most newspapers and trade journals softened their criticism.

Coverage by the *Lichtbild-Bühne* (*L.B.B.*) offers a good example of this development. When Geheimrat Kuhlo entered negotiations for the purchase of Emelka late in 1929, the *L.B.B.* printed an article exposing Kuhlo as a member of Ufa's board of directors and criticizing Ufa for its attempt to monopolize the film industry and use film as an ideological tool.[15] The *L.B.B.* implied that Ufa had begun to produce openly anti-republican and nationalistic films. Less than one year later the journal responded to an invitation from Ufa to participate in a tour of its new production facilities with an article, "Appell an die Presse. Die nationale Funktion des Films" ("Appeal to the Press: The National Function of Film," 5 June 1930). The article included the following statement: "The actual *point of departure* for all manifestations of crisis in German film is *the false relationship of the German public sphere to German film in general.* A comparison with certain other countries proves with painful clarity that the particularly national function of an independent cinema has not yet clearly impressed itself on the consciousness of our people and their leaders."

Like Ludwig Klitzsch, the editors of the *L.B.B.* were correct to perceive a threat to an internationally competitive German film industry. They also emphasized that the *L.B.B.* had had no reservations about criticizing Ufa in the past when it felt that Ufa had not served Germany's national interest. But, in the end, the *L.B.B.* reinforced the association between Ufa's interests and those of the entire industry, while suggesting even more generally that Ufa's interests could be equated with those of the nation. By implication the article legitimized Ufa's efforts to organize the extremely varied experiences of an economically and politically heterogeneous society into a single national perspective. It praised Ufa for completing new facilities, congratulated the concern for saving German cinema, and encouraged the press to convince the German people of German (i.e., Ufa) film's value. With their appeal the editors of the *L.B.B.* typified the general direction of mainstream film criticism for the remainder of the Weimar era. Whether they hoped to appease their clients or truly believed that the films of Germany's major producers were "precious cultural artifacts of the great German people" is unclear. But the critics for the *L.B.B., Film-Kurier,* and *Der Film,* in addition to critics for newspapers and journals associated directly with the Hugenberg Concern, generally praised the artistic quality of German film, concentrated primarily on plot summaries, avoided overtly ideological evaluations in all except the most blatant cases, and continued to offer allegedly conclusive opinions.[16]

The government also attempted to support the domestic film industry by extending contingency regulations. According to most industry representatives, however, the heavy taxes levied on ticket revenues offset any advantage gained over foreign competitors through import controls. During the final years of the Weimar Republic, producers, distributors, and theater owners persisted with requests for tax relief and stricter contingency laws, as well as for the establishment of a special fund to help producers compete with Hollywood.[17]

Although the government was unwilling and/or unable to support the entire industry with new legislation between 1929 and 1932, as the power of the nationalist front expanded, censors increasingly privileged nationalistic and militaristic films produced by Ufa, Emelka, Terra, and other major producers. At the same time, they closely scrutinized, partially censored, and sometimes prohibited discernibly pacifistic and socialistic films.[18] While rejecting *All Quiet on the Western Front* (1930), *Ins dritte Reich* (*Into the Third Reich*, 1931), *Kuhle Wampe* (1932), and *Enthusiasmus* (*Enthusiasm*, 1932), the German censors accepted *Die letzte Kompagnie* (*The Last Company*, 1930), *Berge in Flammen* (*Mountains in Flames*, 1931), and *Der Kongreß tanzt* (*The Congress Dances*, 1931).[19]

The latter films exemplify three of the most popular genres in the last phase of the Weimar era: the Prussian history film, the World War I film, and the film operetta.[20] It must be noted that the industry produced affirmative and critical films in each genre. However, in virtually every case the largest producers, including Ufa, Emelka, and Terra, were responsible for the overwhelming majority of pro-Prussian, militaristic, and affirmative films. Much smaller companies, such as Seymour Nebenzahl's Nero-Film,[21] produced many of the films that criticized the patriarchal Prussian order, advocated pacifism, or posited a more sober image of the economic and political crisis in Weimar Germany.[22]

Germany's largest companies produced films about Prussian history and World War I which, with few notable differences, followed narrative trends that had emerged earlier in the Weimar era. They used omniscient intertitles, costumes, sets, and documentary footage to suggest authenticity. They focused on stories about the Prussian aristocracy and military heroes. And, except for the first sound films, in which preoccupation with the new component generally decreased attention to camera perspectives and montage techniques, they offered cohesive narratives that nurtured the audience's emotional engagement.

In addition to using sound, one of the most significant changes in Prussian history films from the major producers after 1929 was their shift in focus from reconstruction following the Seven Years' War to the Napoleonic Wars.[23] Films such as *Waterloo* (Emelka, 1929), *The Last Company* (Ufa, 1930), *Luise, Königin von Preussen* (*Luise, Queen of Prussia*, Henny Porten, 1931), *Yorck* (Ufa, 1931), and *Die elf Schillschen Offiziere* (*The Eleven Schill Officers*, Märkische, 1932) depicted a Prussia threatened by or under the control of a foreign aggressor and governed by a weak and indecisive king.

In each film either France occupied Prussia or its spies, lecherous diplomats, and other despicable representatives threatened Prussian integrity. Often the symbol of that integrity was a Prussian woman, whose safety was endangered by a Frenchman. The threat to women and the threat to Prussia by what were portrayed as evil foreign forces encouraged German audiences to sympathize with Prussian patriots who united the Prussian people in defense of themselves, their families, and their homeland. Just as the period of reconstruction after the Seven Years' War provided the best context for promoting authoritarianism during the stable period, the Napoleonic era offered the best material for those who claimed that exploitation by the Western Allies and the compliance of a weak German government had caused the economic crisis.

The World War I films produced by Germany's largest companies between 1929 and 1933 had a similarly reactionary orientation. In World War I films, including *Mountains in Flames* (Luis Trenker, 1931) and *Morgenrot* (*Dawn,* Ufa, 1933), German soldiers and sailors united in defense of their homeland and, with their experience as soldiers on the front, provided a model for the National Socialist concept of the *Volksgemeinschaft.*

Ufa's *Dawn,* a film that had its premiere just one day after Hitler became *Reichskanzler,* exemplifies this type of film. In the film a group of submarine sailors exhibit solidarity while fighting the British navy. The suspense suggested by the portrayal of the vulnerable submarine and the ever-present threat of attack by an unseen enemy intensified the association between the audience's perspective and that of the sailors. The scriptwriter, Gerhard Menzel, and director, Gustav Ucicky, exploited the possibilities for such an association, encouraging spectators to perceive themselves as vulnerable to an unexpected attack and extremely dependent on each other. The film moved toward a climactic scene in which two of the ten sailors commit suicide so that the remaining sailors can save themselves as their submarine slowly sinks.[24]

While Germany's largest producers reinforced and encouraged nationalism with their Prussian history and World War I films, smaller companies produced films that criticized the Prussian heritage and advocated an antimilitaristic, humanist standpoint. Like their more affirmative and more expensive counterparts, such films employed standard narrative devices and new sound techniques to establish narrative cohesion and guide reception. Although their plots deviated from those of films from larger producers, many were at least as commercially successful as films like *Yorck* and *Mountain in Flames.*

Maidens in Uniform: a unique critical image of Prussian discipline in mainstream cinema. (Staatliches Filmarchiv der DDR)

Mädchen in Uniform (*Maidens in Uniform*), for example, which was produced by an independent cooperative, the Deutsche Filmgemeinschaft, attracted widespread attention in 1931.[25] The film portrayed the effects of authoritarianism in a Prussian boarding school whose headmistress terrorizes her female pupils with extreme measures of discipline and order. The film's protagonist, a sensitive newcomer named Manuela, breaks under the rule of the headmistress and tries to jump from a staircase.

The organization of shots in the attempted suicide scene typifies the film's narration. It invites sympathy for Manuela, criticism of the headmistress, and an association between her measures and Prussian discipline in general. A parallel montage sequence shifts attention from the suicide attempt to an argument about Manuela between the headmistress and a sympathetic teacher, as well as to shots of the other students who search for Manuela and call her name. The montage heightens suspense

The Captain of Köpenick: comic presentation of Prussian cult of authority, *Illustrierter Film-Kurier* program cover. (Staatliches Filmarchiv der DDR)

and encourages the audience to hope someone will stop the attempted suicide. After the students save Manuela, they confront the headmistress with accusing stares, and she retreats.[26]

The second film of the genre, *Der Hauptmann von Köpenick* (*The Captain of Köpenick*, Richard Oswald, 1931), used humor instead of potential tragedy to critique Prussian values. The film, an adaptation of Carl Zuckmayer's 1928 play, relates the story of Wilhelm Voigt, an un-employed cobbler who has served time in prison. Voigt is unable to find employment because the police refuse to give him a passport; however, the police reject his requests because he has no job. As the scenario un-folds, the friendly ex-convict tries to follow the rules of an impersonal bureaucracy. Finally he buys an old uniform, commandeers two squads of soldiers, and takes control of the Köpenick town hall. The ease with which he accomplishes the coup makes the depicted reverence for Prus-sian authority seem comical. Unable to locate a passport office, Voigt ultimately retreats unscathed. When the story circulates in the press, everyone, including the kaiser, laughs—inviting the audience to laugh along, to enjoy the realization that Prussian authoritarianism deserves criticism.

The films of smaller companies, such as *Westfront 1918* (Nero, 1930), *Kameradschaft* (*Comradeship*, Nero, 1931), and *Niemandsland* (*No Man's Land*, Resco, 1931), portrayed World War I far more seriously.[27] They depicted its violence and death as realistically as possible, suggest-ing to spectators that the French, English, and other supposed enemies were human beings with whom Germans could easily sympathize. *No Man's Land* demonstrates especially well the humanistic perspective of these films.

The film follows the lives of an English gentleman, French proletarian, German carpenter, Jewish tailor, and black cabaret artist from peaceful existence in each of their homelands to the battlefront. It frequently uses parallel montage to associate the five men and deemphasize national dif-ferences. For example, when the war begins, a sequence depicts their enlistment, training, and departure for the front. The narration rapidly cuts from the scene of a drill in Germany to one in England, to one in France, to one in Turkey as if each were a continuation of the previous one. It subsequently portrays the sadness of each major character as he takes leave of his family and departs by train or ship for the front lines.[28] Similar techniques portray the five soldiers when they confront one an-other in an abandoned house between the trenches. There they recognize shared interests, defend each other in a mortar attack on the house, and

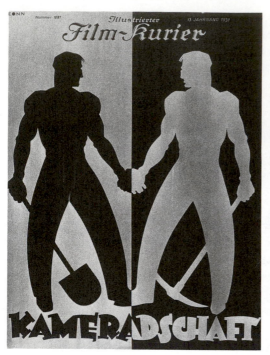 

Comradeship and *No Man's Land:* pacifistic films about World War I, *Illustrierter Film-Kurier* program covers. (Staatliches Filmarchiv der DDR)

in the end leave the house, united in their rejection of war. The camaraderie here crosses national, racial, and class barriers.

In addition to the historical and World War I films, operettas had proven commercially viable during the years of relative stability and continued to receive attention between 1929 and 1933. The realization that well-known male vocalists such as Richard Tauber and Jan Kiepura could attract large audiences made them especially popular for profit-hungry producers. Following the success of Wilhelm Thiele's *Liebeswalzer* (*Love Waltz*) in 1930, producers feverishly plotted ways to adapt popular stage operettas for the screen. One of the most popular films of the genre was Ufa's *Die Drei von der Tankstelle* (*The Three from the Gas Station*, 1930). In a parody of more serious operettas, three bankrupt friends sell their car to buy a gas station, compete for the attention of their most

The Three from the Gas Station: lighthearted, compensatory entertainment of the film operetta, *Illustrierter Film-Kurier* program cover. (Staatliches Filmarchiv der DDR)

dedicated patron, a consul's daughter, and conclude that friendship is more important than money. It is easy for them to reach the conclusion because, although only one of them can marry the wealthy daughter, all three regain their former wealth as their business, for no apparent reason, flourishes.

The Three from the Gas Station is significant because it typifies the film operetta, but also because it unites elements from other genres that appealed to insecure middle-class and lower-middle-class audiences. Wilhelm Thiele, the film's director, worked consciously to integrate music, dialogue, dance, and song in a cohesive narrative structure, governed by the concept of a dance rhythm and well suited to encourage uncritical reception, i.e., to maximize the film's entertainment value.[29] Thiele also engaged actors who had succeeded in the profession, including Lillian

Harvey, Willy Fritsch, and Heinz Rühmann, thereby indirectly reinforcing the film's myth of upward social mobility. Of even greater significance for worried middle-class Germans who desired a nonintellectual distraction from their everyday anxieties and a confirmation about the possibility of upward social mobility was the quality of the myth. In contrast to films of the stable period that upheld the myth only for those who were truly talented and perseverant,[30] more optimistic films that appeared during the final Weimar years stressed either that money was unimportant (*Ein blonder Traum, A Blond Dream,* Ufa, 1932) or that luck could bring prosperity overnight (*Man braucht kein Geld, One Doesn't Need Money,* Ufa, 1932). *The Three from the Gas Station* united both elements.

One of the few critical responses to the optimistic film operettas of the major producers was *Die Dreigroschenoper* (*The Threepenny Opera,* Nero, 1931).[31] Based on Bertolt Brecht's adaptation of John Gay's *Beggar's Opera* (1728), the film portrays the story of a gangster, Macheath; his marriage to Polly, the daughter of the beggar king, Peachum; and Peachum's attempts to disrupt their marriage by arranging Macheath's arrest and execution. The film posits the conflict of interest between the lumpen-proletarian beggars and the state, represented by the Queen and her police; exposes the corruption of the police, whose chief is Macheath's best friend; and suggests that the bankers are criminals. In contrast to operettas such as *The Three from the Gas Station,* which affirmed the existing social order and the possibility of relatively effortless upward social mobility, *The Threepenny Opera* encouraged spectators to perceive capitalistic societies as corrupt systems that allowed success only for those who could exploit others.

Nero bought the rights to produce a film based on *The Threepenny Opera* after Brecht's successful stage production in 1928. The company then sold the rights to Tobis–Warner Bros. However, it continued to function as producer and negotiated with Brecht about the script and the direction of the film (Gersch, 58). By 1930 Brecht had been studying Marxist political and cultural theory for over three years. His reception of Marxism focused his attention on the ideological character of artistic production and reception. Realizing that traditional dramatic aesthetics inhibited spectators from formulating their own critical responses, he developed and practiced his concept of the epic theater as an alternative.[32] While adjusting his dramatic theory to changing social conditions in Germany, Brecht welcomed the opportunity to experiment with film. Neben-

The Threepenny Opera: critical response to optimistic film operettas, *Illustrierter Film-Kurier* program cover. (Staatliches Filmarchiv der DDR)

zahl, who had attracted a number of renowned film artists to Nero with his reputation for being less autocratic than other producers, soon quarreled with Brecht. Their controversy illustrates well the limits for experimentation in the industry at the beginning of the 1930s.

Although Nero had obtained the rights to Brecht's material in May 1930, Brecht and Nebenzahl reached no agreement about the decision-making process for production until the beginning of August. Three weeks later Nero dissolved the contract and engaged Béla Balázs to finish the script. It is likely that Nero based its decision on a combination of economic and political factors. Faced with steadily rising production costs and with protests about the political orientation of the stage production from the president of the Verband deutscher Lichtspieltheaterbesitzer (Association of German Movie Theater Owners), Nero almost certainly felt insecure about the film's commercial viability.[33]

With Balázs in control of the script, most of Brecht's alienation effects either disappeared or were aestheticized. Except for adding the transformation of Macheath's gang into a group of bankers, he returned to the stage script. G. W. Pabst, the film's director, followed Balázs's script closely and, together with the set designer, created a mysterious atmosphere, devoid of the provocative and alienating elements Brecht had envisioned (Gersch, 69). Needless to say, the film attracted filmgoers interested foremost in entertainment, and Bertolt Brecht was deeply disappointed.

Despite following the existing trends toward cinematic entertainment, films such as *The Threepenny Opera, No Man's Land,* and *Maidens in Uniform* demonstrate that even within the realm of mainstream cinema it is difficult to locate reflections of a single national mentality. Commercial films of Weimar's final phase, as was the case throughout the Weimar era, reflected, modified, and generated a variety of ideological positions under the influence of political, economic, and psychological factors. Although the popularity of nationalistic Prussian history films, militaristic World War I films, and optimistic film operettas increased as the economic and political crisis intensified—and as middle-class and lower-middle-class insecurity deepened—companies such as Nero preferred to appeal to republican, pacifist, and humanist sentiments in Weimar society. While Ufa, Emelka, Terra, and other major producers maximized profit with films such as *Yorck, Dawn,* and *The Three from the Gas Station,* political considerations also influenced their decisions. Instead of merely calculating audience desires and making films to satisfy those desires, Hugenberg's Ufa and other leading companies concentrated increasingly on production with an ideological orientation corresponding to the political, economic, and psychological interests of the national front.

In the end, whether one factor or another played a dominant role in the ideological orientation of a plot, or whether a film advocated militarism or pacifism, was only of limited significance. Equally important for ideological development in Germany was mainstream cinema's continued emphasis on entertainment and its dependence on standard cinematic techniques—factors that perpetuated structures of uncritical reception and reinforced authoritarian structures in Weimar society. By encouraging uncritical affirmation of an ideological perspective, commercial films, to some extent independent of their specific orientation, only increased the susceptibility of their audiences to authoritarian figures with ideological agenda for Germany's social development. Before turning to the response of the German left, the contribution of sound to the process deserves some additional attention.

Sound developed in three phases between 1929 and 1933.[34] Initially it possessed only a novelty quality in films that continued to emphasize visual images. During most of 1929, producers experimented with sound techniques and attempted to overcome restrictions caused, for example, by the stationary microphone and its sensitivity to undesirable sounds. To avoid such problems and to test sound on audiences who were accustomed only to silent films, producers used the new element sparingly. The first German sound film, *Ich küsse Ihre Hand, Madame* (*I Kiss Your Hand, Madame,* January 1929), was almost completely silent, except for one scene in which Harry Liedtke, with the dubbed voice of Richard Tauber, sang the title song to Marlene Dietrich. The next sound film, Walter Ruttmann's *Die Melodie der Welt* (*The Melody of the World,* March 1929), used sound only to supplement visual images. Films like Ruttmann's, referred to by contemporaries as synchronized films, were silent films with music, sounds from nature, and other sound effects added in a postfilming production phase.

As mentioned above, Ufa's *The Melody of the Heart* (December 1929) was the first 100 percent sound film produced in Germany. Toward the end of 1929 and in 1930, technicians overcame the initial restrictions, and actors were permitted to speak more and more. The result was that filmmakers at least temporarily focused their attention on dialogue, once again depended on theatrical conventions, and neglected the visual

M: Lang's ambiguous portrayal of Weimar society. (Staatliches Film-archiv der DDR)

element. In some cases they reverted to filming what were little more than stage productions with almost no attention to mise-en-scène and montage.[35]

Within a very short time the industry also overcame its dependence on theater and began to experiment with methods for combining audio and visual elements to enhance film's narrative capacity.[36] Some filmmakers united sound and image to uphold an illusion of reality. The producers of film operettas, for example, often felt compelled to associate music in their films with a source such as an orchestra, musician, etc.[37]

G. W. Pabst was the most energetic advocate of empirical authenticity.[38] *Comradeship,* Pabst's film about solidarity between French and German miners, offers the best example of his model.[39] In it sound combined with visual images so that spectators could perceive the cinematic fiction as they would the everyday world. The voices of characters who appear to be far away are more difficult to discern than those of characters who seem to be closer to the spectator. When a mineshaft caves in, the coinciding noise is deafening; as a truck full of German miners embarks on the rescue mission, the sound of its engine diminishes as it moves away from the mining camp where the camera has assumed the perspective of waving family members.

Other directors paid far less attention to empirical authenticity but employed sound with equal care as a narrative device that guided audience reception. Fritz Lang described his efforts in the film *M* (Nero, 1931) as follows: "At that time I realized that not only could one use sound as a dramaturgical component, but one should. In *M*, for example, when the stillness on the street is destroyed by the shrill police whistles or the unmelodic, recurring whistling of the child murderer. . . . I also believe that for the first time in *M*, I allowed sound—a sentence—to overlap from the end of one scene to the beginning of the next. That not only accelerated the film's tempo; it also strengthened the necessary intellectual association between two consecutive scenes." [40]

Lang integrated sound, as did other German directors of the period, to intensify suspense, to communicate the thoughts and emotions of his fictional characters, and generally to guide reception with associations between characters, other visual images, and events. However, unlike most directors, who used sound to entertain in a way that nurtured uncritical reception, Lang challenged audiences with ambiguity. In *M* sound and camera techniques motivate sympathy for the child murderer's victims and their families. But Lang also portrayed the police as inept and allowed the organization of criminals to catch the child murderer for selfish reasons; he associated the police with the criminals and, in the end, even invited sympathy for the murderer, who cowers before the criminals' tribunal and argues convincingly that other forces control his behavior. In this way Lang was calling into question simplistic notions of morality at a time when many Germans found it increasingly tempting to affirm such notions.

14

THE SPD AND FILM: THE INTENSIFYING CRITIQUE OF POLITICAL REACTION IN COMMERCIAL FILM AND THE PARTY'S PROGRAM OF CINEMATIC PROPAGANDA

Between 1929 and 1933 film coverage in the SPD press and the SPD's program for production, distribution, and screening changed only minimally.[1] The central party newspaper, *Vorwärts*, paid limited attention to film, a policy it had initiated in 1928. In 1929 the *Monatliche Mitteilungen*, the journal of the Film und Lichtbilddienst, began appearing monthly, then every two months, and finally on a quarterly basis in May 1930. Its reports in no way matched those of *Vorwärts* prior to 1928. Instead of following the development of the film industry and reviewing films, the *Monatliche Mitteilungen* reported almost exclusively on the activity of the party's program. Some issues also included excerpts from reviews printed in *Sozialistische Bildung*, an educational journal which also began appearing in 1929. But the general trend here and in the entire Social Democratic press was to shift attention from commercial film and intensify efforts to build the FuL.

Vorwärts film coverage sustained many focal points that had been established earlier in the Weimar era. An example was its interest in technological innovation. Articles such as "Der erste 'Farben-Tonfilm'" ("The First 'Color-Sound Film,'" 9 March 1930) and "Die Lunge wird gefilmt" ("The Lung Is Filmed," 15 May 1930) demonstrated that the interest remained uncritical.[2] The newspaper uncritically affirmed innovation as a contribution to the general progress of humanity.

Vorwärts critics also continued their campaign to expose the influence of conservative and reactionary interest groups on commercial production. Articles, including "Milliardenverlust der Terra" ("Terra's Loss of

Billions," 8 January 1930), informed readers about the further concentration of power among the most wealthy antirepublican interest groups in the industry. Others, such as "Filmzensur und Ufa-Monopol" ("Film Censorship and Ufa Monopoly," 31 December 1930), reported on the national censorship board's activity, arguing that its decisions increasingly favored the militaristic and nationalistic films of Germany's largest producers while restricting the efforts of smaller companies, including the FuL. The newspaper paid particular attention to the censorship of *All Quiet on the Western Front* in December 1930 and *Into the Third Reich*, produced by the Film und Werbeabteilung of the SPD and submitted to the censors in January 1931. In both cases *Vorwärts* articles criticized the censors' decisions but withheld judgment about public demonstrations. The SPD remained loyal to parliamentary democracy.

As had been the case earlier, Social Democratic journalists based their support for films such as *All Quiet on the Western Front* primarily on plot analysis. Erich Gottgetreu's comments in "Neue Filme" ("New Films," 6 March 1932) typify SPD commentary: "Socialism and truth and art are a holy trinity, for which there is no exception. . . . The *Maidens in Uniform* . . . in the forced uniformity of boarding-school life . . . , the proof for the senselessness . . . of war in *No-Man's Land* . . . , the bitter satire of an inhumane bureaucracy in the *Captain of Köpenick*— all of that is propaganda for socialism, because it is propaganda for humanism." Each of the cited films employed techniques of narrative cohesion and incorporated sound in a way that encouraged spectators to affirm their ideological orientations, but Gottgetreu was satisfied. For him and other *Vorwärts* critics, mainstream films that criticized militaristic discipline, war, and inhumane bureaucracies were unconditionally praiseworthy.[3]

As the statement about socialism, truth, and art indicates, during the last years of the Weimar Republic *Vorwärts* film critics increasingly abandoned allegiance to concepts of autonomous art. The central party newspaper openly praised films with a clear connection to existing social issues as long as they posited what the editors perceived as a socialist perspective and characterized as the truth. By ascribing to socialist ideology the quality of truth and suggesting that the SPD was responsible for generating that ideology, *Vorwärts* critics claimed the authority to dictate to readers the criteria for evaluating films about everyday life in Weimar society. They now applauded films that in their estimation conveyed absolute truths about social development, while reserving the authority to evaluate what was true or false/good or bad for themselves and their party.[4]

The same logic also characterized the *Vorwärts* attitude toward the use of film for election campaigns. Articles such as "die Technik im Wahlkampf" ("Technology in Election Campaigns," 28 September 1932) expressed clearly the party's strategy: "The election campaigns of the future will be led foremost by engineers and technicians. Perhaps new occupations, which we do not yet anticipate, will emerge in this field."[5] In 1932 Social Democrats seemed more concerned about winning elections than they were about encouraging German voters to participate actively in organizing their experiences into an ideological strategy for social change. They relied on parliamentary democracy, deemphasizing the necessity for critical democratic interaction at the grass-roots level and reinforcing public susceptibility to authoritarian leadership. Similarly, *Vorwärts* critics asserted their authority and acclaimed or condemned socially critical films, assessing the ideological orientation of plotlines and their relation to the Social Democratic perspective. They rarely took the next step and criticized mainstream cinema's compensatory attraction. However, there were a few notable exceptions.

While the number of reports about developments in the film industry and reviews of individual films decreased, the number of short stories and serialized novels remained constant. Occasionally they assumed even more space than prior to 1929. The short stories and novels appeared to provide entertainment for readers who sought an alternative to the serious political and economic reports that filled the headlines. A closer look reveals that they also addressed pressing social issues and often suggested parablelike morals to their readers.

Occasionally the short stories depicted the interaction of the German public with commercial cinema and exposed the fictional world of films as a dream world. Stories such as "Arbeitslose gehen ins Kino . . ." ("The Unemployed Go to the Movies . . . ," 12 March 1930) and "Abschied nach einem Film" ("Farewell after a Film," 27 September 1932) portrayed the dissatisfaction of moviegoers who realized that most mainstream films offered only temporary and artificial relief from daily frustrations. They demonstrated the SPD's acceptance of commercial narrative techniques, but the SPD employed the techniques to maximize political success by criticizing their commercial and ideological orientation.

K. R. Neubert's "Farewell after a Film" illustrates well how such stories employed narrative techniques to persuade readers to accept their ideological viewpoints without critical participation. The story depicts an episode in the lives of Walter and Lola, an engaged couple. Walter is politically conscious and lower in the social hierarchy than Lola, the self-centered, politically naive daughter of a wealthy businessman. The story begins with a rendezvous at the Gloria-Palast in Berlin. Walter and Lola disagree about the film they should see; Lola prefers a *Manöverlustspiel* (military farce) in the Gloria-Palast, and Walter argues for a pacifistic French war film in a smaller theater across the street. Finally Lola suggests that they separate and meet again after the screenings. The narrator then assumes Walter's perspective as he realizes that Lola belongs to another world and that he must become politically active to stop the militarism at work in Weimar society. When Walter leaves the theater, he avoids Lola, returns to his home, and writes his fiancée, explaining why they must break their engagement.

"Farewell after a Film," like many commercial films, juxtaposed unambiguous images of its central characters. By portraying Walter as politically conscious, compassionate, and pacifistic while depicting Lola as a naive and egocentric bourgeois daughter, Neubert invited his readers to sympathize with Walter and condemn Lola. He motivated the evaluation further by associating the narrator's perspective with that of the protagonist, who supplies his arguments in favor of dissolving the engagement, while Lola remains silent.

Neubert asked his readers to accept Walter's evaluation as the unconditionally valid moral of the story: film has political significance even when it purports to entertain. Audiences, the story suggests, should recognize film's ideological significance, reject commercial entertainment, and embrace films that promote pacifism and other humanist values.

Only at the end of 1932 did *Vorwärts* editors initiate an alternative approach. After concentrating for over a decade on establishing and strengthening their own authority to evaluate the quality of Weimar culture, they invited readers to participate in an open discussion about Irmgard Keun's *Gilgi, eine von uns* (*Gilgi, One of Us*). The novel had appeared in the newspaper in serialized form in the summer and fall of 1932. On 9 October in "Ein Volksroman wird Film" ("A People's Novel Becomes Film") the editors announced the coming film adaptation and their intention to solicit readers' participation in evaluating the story. Approximately a week later the first group of responses appeared under the title "Eine von uns?" ("One of Us?" 18 October 1932). The article included the following comments: "In this way the novel of a young female author . . . becomes educational: it calls for criticism, it motivates us to think through a problem that concerns us all—and thus has a creative function. But this creative critique should not remain that of the individual. It should engage the public . . . it should be carried to the author and thus create a connection between artist and audience, as is— despite all the barons and the cultural reaction—appropriate for a democratic epoch."

The *Vorwärts* initiative was far less radical than Anna Siemsen had advocated, but it was a step toward the reintegration of art into everyday life. Female readers responded enthusiastically by evaluating Keun's novel and suggesting modifications. At least one contributor even expressed the wish that *Vorwärts* editors use their experiment as a model for future grass-roots discussions of literature ("Kunst/Kitsch/Leben?"—"Art/ Triviality/Life?" 28 October 1932). The editors neither accepted the suggestion nor repeated the experiment. The *Vorwärts* reaction to the film version of *Gilgi, One of Us* demonstrated just how limited the initiative was. The film had its premiere in Berlin's Capitol Theater on 20 October, and as usual, an authoritative review appeared the next day in *Vorwärts* (see "*Gilgi* auf der Leinewand"—"*Gilgi* on the Screen," 21 October 1932).

There are a number of plausible explanations for the onetime experiment with a more democratic approach to the evaluation of art in the Social Democratic press. It is possible that as the economic crisis intensified and the popularity of both the NSDAP and the KPD increased, party leaders became more sensitive to internal criticisms about their authoritarian rule and unwillingness to assume a more radical course.[6] Many of the SPD's left-wing critics, including Anna Siemsen, also had proposed changes in the party's approach to education and culture. It is equally possible that *Vorwärts* editors were emulating campaigns similar to those employed by the IAH newspapers. *Die Welt am Abend* and *Berlin am Morgen* had gained rapid and widespread attention during the years of relative stability (see Chapter 10). Both occasionally invited readers to submit evaluations of literature and other cultural products. Finally, the efforts of Heinz Lüdecke and Korea Senda to stimulate grassroots proletarian film criticism in the VFV *Arbeiterbühne und Film* (see Chapter 16) may have served as a model. Whatever the motivation, the enthusiastic response and the absence of any further invitations demonstrated both the desire of the *Vorwärts* readers to participate and the unwillingness of the editors to abandon positions of authority.

THE FuL AND ITS *MONATLICHE MITTEILUNGEN*

While the limited coverage of mainstream cinema persisted in *Vorwärts*, the SPD intensified efforts to build the FuL into a more effective organization for attracting the attention of German voters and persuading them to support Social Democratic candidates and policies. Just how significant the party's program for film production and distribution had grown by 1929 became evident in September of that year when the Sozialistischer Kulturbund devoted its national convention in Frankfurt to a discussion of film and radio.[7] The two-day event included an exhibition of FuL equipment, a film series highlighting the technical and artistic development of the medium, and a session in which SPD cultural leaders presented papers. Topics included the SPD's use of film, the significance of sound, music's role in film, and film censorship. Participants responded to the papers and suggested guidelines for the party's future film work.

The exhibition of equipment and the film series strengthened the impression that the SPD emphasized technical achievements and artistic quality. In his opening address "Film und Funk in ihrer Bedeutung für die Arbeiterschaft" ("The Significance of Film and Radio for the Workers," *Film und Funk,* 9–14), the president of the Kulturbund, Heinrich Schulz, reinforced the emphasis. He affirmed technological achievements in general and asserted that the organized working class was capable of employing technology for the public welfare, though technology maximized the profit of a select minority in the existing social context.

Schulz perceived film as a technological achievement but also as a form of artistic expression especially capable of generating the illusion of reality and more accessible than painting or theater. According to Schulz, it intensified dramatic effects and exerted them on a much larger segment of the German population. As such, he argued, film provided the most effective medium for SPD leaders to communicate to the masses, from above, their insights about social development: "The struggling and striving working class . . . does not wish to win with the armor of barbarians. . . . It wishes to win with the growing insight of the masses, with their insight into the causes of their problems and the means for their liberation. In this respect radio and film may help us, in this respect we wish to nurture them" (14). Here again, an SPD leader expressed the party's orientation toward reformism and legitimized parliamentary democracy as well as central party leadership. With the education of the masses in mind, Schulz advised the SPD to continue to expand its film program to promote candidates and policies, to attract members, to advertise its newspapers, and to increase the effectiveness of the party's educational program.

The second presentation, Siegfried Nestriepke's "Die technischen und kulturellen Möglichkeiten des Films" ("The Technical and Cultural Possibilities of Film," *Film und Funk,* 15–29), outlined in greater detail the use of film in Weimar society and the possibilities for a proletarian alternative. Nestriepke, the co-director of the Berlin Volksbühne, began his address, as had Heinrich Schulz, by affirming the use of film for scientific research, pedagogy, and political propaganda. He also characterized cinematic documentation and entertainment as worthwhile endeavors. Film's value for each of these activities, Nestriepke argued, resided in its capacity to expand the boundaries of human perception, to reproduce authentic images of reality, to illustrate concepts, and to evoke human emotions.

He supported Schulz's position by focusing on the medium's dramatic potential and evaluating it positively. However, in contrast to Schulz, who traced film's dramatic potential to its ability to suggest the illusion of reality, Nestriepke refused to acknowledge that filmic representation could equal the realistic quality of theater. For him film generated drama with its uniquely optical language: "A film text demands the engagement of only one sense—that of the eye—while the ear and the intellect, which transforms words into concepts, remain relaxed. . . . One should not underestimate the advantage that film consequently possesses" (17). Nestriepke's concept of cinematic reception is significant for two reasons. It indicated, as did the subsequent presentations on the role of sound and music,[8] that the SPD's film experts had only a very superficial understanding of sound's narrative potential. It also demonstrated that Nestriepke, like most other Social Democrats, had no reservations about the ideological impact of standard forms of cinematic reception.

Nestriepke outlined more specifically than other Social Democratic film critics and cultural activists the system of photographic and montage techniques used by commercial filmmakers to guide reception. He equated the mastery of the system with artistic achievement. He praised directors and cameramen who strove consciously to construct cohesive narrative structures, using shot composition and montage to induce audience responses. After citing a number of examples in which commercial filmmakers had integrated, in his estimation artistically, the various elements of the existing cinematic code to juxtapose fictional characters, create suspense, associate the spectators' perspective with that of the protagonist, and elicit their sympathy, Nestriepke criticized the aesthetic as well as political quality of most commercial films: "The great majority of ... films have little or nothing to do with art. ... Instead of offering logical plots with inner tension, they present a more or less senseless accumulation of events and adventures that intend nothing more than the satisfaction of superficial visual curiosity. ... These films are not only aesthetically but also ethically worthless, if not even dangerous. ... It is these films in which brute force is glorified, militarism is praised, stupid subservience to authority is valorized, and the command to be dependent is preached" (19).

According to Nestriepke, there normally was a connection between a film's aesthetic and ideological quality. Most ideologically unacceptable commercial films, he asserted, were also aesthetically inadequate. However, ideologically unacceptable films with a high aesthetic quality were praiseworthy: "The truly artistic enriches our knowledge of human beings and life so much that the specific ideological perspective of the artist by comparison no longer plays a significant role" (21). Here Nestriepke revealed his latent allegiance to a concept of autonomous art that considered aesthetic impact relatively independent of its ideological significance. While criticizing commercial film's militaristic and authoritarian tendencies, he suggested that its autonomous aesthetic qualities were more important.

Nestriepke also outlined possibilities for improving the aesthetic as well as the ideological quality of mainstream film. Each of his proposals envisioned increased democracy in cinema, but also perpetuated its fundamentally authoritarian structures. First, critics and other film experts should educate the masses about the medium's aesthetic and ideological qualities so that they could exercise a more informed influence on production. Secondly, although Nestriepke contemplated and even advocated nationalizing the industry in the future, he stressed that production would remain the responsibility of a talented elite. Filmgoers would influence production indirectly through consumer organizations. Communities could operate communal theaters and regulate the screening of films. In addition, organizations such as the FuL could influence production by selecting "worthwhile" films and promoting them through distribution programs. Finally, voters could appeal to their representatives to control film's aesthetic and ideological quality.[9]

The presentations by Heinrich Schulz and Siegfried Nestricpke included the most advanced statements of the SPD's film policy.[10] During the final years of the Weimar Republic, the SPD followed their suggestions and expanded its film programs. The FuL, as Heinrich Schulz had proposed, intensified efforts to attract the attention of German voters and win support for SPD candidates and policies. It also strove to educate party members and sympathizers about Social Democratic ideology. Following Nestriepke's argumentation, the FuL also increased its indirect influence on commercial production by selecting films for distribution. It worked to maximize effectiveness by producing films that guided reception with cinematic codes of narrative cohesion.

The journal of the FuL, the *Monatliche Mitteilungen,* which began appearing in 1929, provides the most detailed account of the SPD's film activity at the end of the Weimar era.[11] As mentioned above, it appeared monthly, then every two months, and finally quarterly in issues of ten to fifteen pages. Issues often began with articles such as "Vom Wert des Films für die Parteibewegung" ("On the Value of Film for the Party Movement," April 1930). They offered descriptions of and guidelines for the SPD film program. The contributors provided very specific instructions for organizing local film events. They advised local party leaders to publicize events with posters and advance ticket sales, decorate the theater or hall with SPD banners and other party symbols, open with a short, gripping speech, include a brief blatantly political film, follow with an intermission, and then screen a full-length entertainment film. By featuring entertainment, the authors explained, organizers could attract the less interested and then attempt to win their support.

Just as the FuL leadership minimized the initiative of local officials, so should the local officials minimize the critical participation of audiences. In "On the Value of Film for the Party Movement," J. Päckert directed his readers to maximize their influence on those who attended SPD film events; lure them with entertainment, stimulate their interest in the party with banners, then educate them with powerful oration and effective propaganda films. Neither Päckert nor any other contributor suggested that local officials invite discussion or encourage participant initiatives.

In addition to establishing guidelines for film events, the *Monatliche Mitteilungen* advertised FuL films. It also provided information, including short synopses about the other films it distributed. The FuL distributed a wide variety of films, ranging from what it considered to be socially critical commercial films, such as *The Illegitimate,* to Soviet films like *Mother.* It included Social Democratic films as well as Prometheus films.[12] The only excluded films were those that glorified the Prussian monarchy, mystified Germany's role in World War I, openly perpetuated the myth of upward social mobility, or seemed pornographic.

Finally, the *Monatliche Mitteilungen* reported on the SPD's use of film at the district level throughout Germany. After beginning very modestly in 1926 with just 15 films, the FuL increased its distribution to 2,645 in 1930 and consumed approximately one-third of the Reich Education Committee budget (Schumann, 84). Between 1930 and 1932 the most important function of the FuL was to provide films for election campaigns. The SPD incorporated film into three to four thousand campaign events yearly during the period and reached as many as 750,000 voters who otherwise received no substantial information from the SPD. At least some district officials asserted that film had helped them to increase the number of SPD voters (*Monatliche Mitteilungen,* October/December 1930).

The SPD was pleased with the success of its film program. Nevertheless, just two years later the National Socialists assumed power and the Weimar Republic dissolved. In retrospect, the SPD's strategy for building a united front in support of the republic and its reliance on film as a component of its strategy seem far less successful. A closer look at some of the campaign films suggests at least a partial explanation for the SPD's inability to generate the support necessary to counteract the National Socialist surge.

Social Democratic district officials reported in 1930 that they screened *Was wir schufen* (*What We Created,* 1928) and *Dem Deutschen Volke* (*For the German People,* 1928–1929) more often than other campaign films. The first film depicted the SPD's achievements with municipal programs, youth programs, and programs for the elderly between 1919 and 1927. In each case images and short texts introduced problems, then portrayed Social Democratic officials contemplating solutions, and ultimately presented average individuals and families taking advantage of Social Democratic programs: a worker traveling on the new subway system, young people receiving advice about employment, elderly citizens in nursing homes, etc. The film concluded with the imperative: "Vote for Social Democrats!"

The second film, *For the German People,* was one of many animated campaign films produced by the Film und Lichtbilddienst between 1929 and 1932.[13] This film criticized the programs of the other major parties. It begins with an image of the Reichstag building where the bourgeois coalition distributes money to landlords, high military officers, wealthy industrialists, and the agrarian elite. When a worker arrives and requests his share, he receives nothing. Then a short text explains that an emergency decree has led to the dissolution of parliament. Now an overweight, well-dressed man appears. He is a caricature of the bourgeois businessman. He eats abundantly, slumbers, and dreams about the evil worker. While dreaming, he repeatedly asks, "Who will save capitalism?" Images of party leaders appear after each repetition. Alfred Hugenberg promises to fight savagely for a dictatorship. Adolf Hitler proclaims, "Down with the Marxists!"—and explodes. A member of the bourgeois coalition is ready to invoke Article 48 to protect middle-class and upper-middle-class interests. Ernst Thälmann splits the workers movement. When the dreaming bourgeois asks the question a final time, the reply is "No one." The film concludes with a short outline of the SPD's plan to stop the present government's exploitive tax program and gives instructions to the audience: "So do this: Vote SPD 1 on 14 September."

The campaign films encouraged voters to consider the party's achievements and to contrast them with the achievements of the other major political parties. Between 1930 and 1932 such a strategy might have weakened rather than strengthened the SPD's position. By claiming that the SPD was directly responsible for municipal and social welfare programs prior to 1928, *What We Created* also invited audiences to hold the SPD directly accountable for the ensuing economic crisis. In addition, while films such as *For the German People* effectively identified the most powerful constituents of each political party, arguing that the SPD represented the working class, they offered no real incentive for voters from other social classes to unite with the SPD. On the contrary, they perhaps alienated potential voters by portraying them as enemies of the workers.

Perhaps even more important was the support of SPD campaign films for authoritarian leadership. The animated campaign films simplified the analysis of political relations.[14] They suggested that Social Democrats were competent and conscientious leaders, that the leaders of the other political parties were either dictators or the puppets of an industrial, agricultural, and military elite, and that German voters had only to vote for the correct leaders. With their simplified analysis and claim to documentary authenticity and narrative authority, the films encouraged audiences to accept uncritically simple explanations to complex social problems from authoritarian leaders. Of course, the success of the National Socialists depended on much more than the quality of Social Democratic campaign films. However, films such as *What We Created* and *For the German People* did nothing to counteract the voting public's susceptibility to simplistic analysis and authoritarian leadership. The campaign films also must be seen as symptomatic of the SPD's general response to the economic and political crisis. Its unbending allegiance to parliamentary democracy, at a time when the political right was exploiting the system to destroy it, and its unwillingness to cooperate with the KPD in a broad united front against the National Opposition only exacerbated the SPD's problems and accelerated the rise of National Socialism.

Social Democratic organizations also produced two feature films during the final years of the Weimar Republic: *Brüder* (*Brothers*, 1929) and *Lohnbuchhalter Kremke* (*Bookkeeper Kremke*, 1930). Both were silent films. Although the number of theaters that would screen silent films was steadily decreasing, the distributors of the films did attempt to market them commercially. *Brothers*, which was filmed in Hamburg, had its premiere in the Schauburg theaters in Hamburg on a Sunday morning just before May Day (28 April 1929),[15] and *Bookkeeper Kremke* had a normal evening premiere at the Phöbus Palast in Berlin on 15 September 1930. *Brothers* attracted sixty thousand people in three days in Hamburg, but was unable to draw as well in other German cities; *Bookkeeper Kremke* was even less successful. The *Film-Kurier* review (16 September 1930) offered a plausible explanation: "After months we again see a silent film. We are less puzzled by the absence of dialogue than by that of noises. When an accordion plays or a typewriter types, or when people sing, then we wait hopelessly for the sound."

The SPD did produce a campaign film with sound, *Die Sozialdemokratie im Reichstagswahlkampf* (*Social Democracy in the Parliamentary Election*, 1930), in which audiences could hear the speeches of Social Democratic party leaders. But it is very likely that the party was unwilling and perhaps even unable to invest the money necessary to produce a feature sound film. The SPD decided to concentrate on silent films, and while its features were unsuccessful commercially, the FuL distributed them widely for party events.

BROTHERS

The FuL distributed *Brothers*, but it was the Deutscher Verkehrsbund (German Transportation Federation) in Hamburg that commissioned the Werner Hochbaum Filmproduktion GmbH to produce it.[16] The film depicts the dockworkers' strike in Hamburg in 1896. Opening sequences introduce the dockworkers' milieu and juxtapose harbor images and symbols of the state: city hall, policemen, a bust of the kaiser. The story develops around one longshoreman's attempt to organize co-workers against unfair treatment by their employers. Eventually they form a strike committee and stop traffic in the harbor. While the strike proceeds, the male protagonist receives a visit from his brother—a policeman. The striking dockworker indicates that he is unwilling to tolerate his brother's presence. The brother leaves and the strike continues. Finally, at Christmas, the police arrest the rebel longshoreman at home and take him to jail.

In front of the jail his co-workers demonstrate, attracting the attention of the police and allowing his sympathetic brother to release him. Following his release, the protagonist returns to a meeting with friends in his home. There the police arrest him again. His friends threaten to intervene, but he dissuades them, arguing that they must organize to bring about change legally. Back in jail, the protagonist learns that the strike has failed. The film concludes with an intertitle, explaining that the strike provided a model and catalyst for working-class struggle over the next three decades: "In thousands and thousands of souls that until then had slumbered, in the souls of thousands and thousands of women and the maturing youth, the igniting spark of enthusiasm fell in these weeks."

The film's final statement demonstrates Hochbaum's effort to establish cinematic authenticity and narrative authority. From an omniscient point of view, the concluding text posits a direct connection between the fictional longshoremen's strike and the reality of Weimar society. It simultaneously implies that the fictional account is authentic, that the protagonist's strategy was correct, and that spectators, therefore, should accept his strategy. With the film the leaders of the German Transportation Federation hoped to convince their rank and file to support the union's program of legal struggle and to reject the more militant tactics of the KPD's Rote Gewerkschaftsopposition.[17]

Hochbaum initiates the film's narrative authority at the outset through an omniscient narrator who identifies the fictional portrayal with real historical events. Following the title, an intertitle proclaims: "The history of humanity is the history of its class struggles!" The intertitle suggests that the ensuing juxtaposition of harbor scenes and symbols of the state's power is the beginning of what will be an accurate account of life in Hamburg at the turn of the century. Hochbaum reinforced the illusion of reality by relying heavily on natural settings. He also employed nonprofessional actors.[18]

While suggesting authenticity, Hochbaum made little use of photographic and montage techniques to build suspense or associate the spectators' perspective with that of the protagonist. Instead, he concentrated on techniques designed to associate characters with one another and ascribe symbolic meaning to them. For example, in the opening sequence the camera focuses on a policeman and then slowly tilts to a bust of the kaiser. When the dockworkers enter their employer's office to request better wages, a portrait of the kaiser can be seen on one wall. When the police struggle with the rebellious protagonist in his home, a sequence juxtaposes shots of the Christmas tree with a close-up of the dockworker's hand as he falls back against a wall and a nail penetrates it.

Although Hochbaum limited the spectators' perspective to that of an observer, his narration encouraged them to associate the interests of the exploitive employer with those of the state, to criticize the police as the protector of the state's and consequently the employer's interests, and to sympathize with the longshoremen. Their leader appears as a Christ figure—someone who must suffer for the good of the masses. Unlike the SPD campaign films, with their heroic Social Democratic leaders and villainous opponents, Hochbaum's film invited the audience to sympathize with the policeman as well. *Brothers* implied that class differences could be reconciled peacefully. As the dockworkers proclaim while demonstrating before the police station: "The world is our fatherland and all humans are brothers."[19]

BOOKKEEPER KREMKE

The second Social Democratic film, *Bookkeeper Kremke,* was the only feature produced by the FuL between 1929 and 1933. It also was the only film associated with the German left during the Weimar era to be directed by a woman. The head of the FuL, Marie Harder, initiated the project in 1930 and, although she had no experience with production, persuaded Hubert Schonger, a producer of *Kultur* and *Heimat* films, to finance it (Schumann, 81).

The film focuses on a petty-bourgeois bookkeeper, Kremke, who loses his job when his employer decides to automate the bookkeeping process. The news devastates Kremke. He had placed all his trust in the existing social system and believed that the unemployed were parasites who should be held accountable for their fates. Kremke immediately looks for work, takes a job as a traveling salesman, has no success, must mortgage his belongings, eventually collects unemployment benefits, and in the end grows totally despondent and commits suicide.

Another story unfolds parallel to Kremke's—that of his daughter, Lene. At the beginning of the film Lene holds a job in a department store and is engaged to a university student. When the student learns of Kremke's predicament, he abandons his fiancée. Unlike Kremke, who becomes even more dejected as yet another connection with the middle class dissolves, Lene soon meets another man, a window washer named Erwin. Her new friend remains optimistic, although he also had lost his job as a chauffeur at the department store. Erwin ultimately finds a new chauffeur's position and asks Lene to marry him. She accepts, but Kremke refuses to abandon his allegiance to the middle class and join his daughter with Erwin in the proletarian milieu. Instead, he takes his life.

The parallel developments of Kremke and Erwin, with Lene moving from her father's petty-bourgeois world to that of the proletarian Erwin, establish the film's narrative structure. *Bookkeeper Kremke* addressed millions of insecure middle- and lower-middle-class Germans who had always dreamed of upward social mobility and feared the possibility of falling into the proletariat. It also challenged both the street film portrayal of the working-class milieu as a "quagmire" filled with criminals and prostitutes and the many commercial films' perpetuation of the myth of upward social mobility.

In contrast to Werner Hochbaum, Marie Harder engaged professional actors, including Hermann Valentin (Kremke), Anna Sten (Lene), and Kowal Samborski (Erwin). She also shot most of the film in the Hubert Schonger studios in Berlin. Nevertheless, she, too, attempted to generate the illusion of reality and portrayed Kremke's story as typical. Even before the title appears, numbers and dates roll by, indicating the ever-increasing rate of unemployment between 1927 and 1930. As the rate grows, the size of the numbers grow and the sequence accelerates until very large letters proclaim that the numbers refer to "UNEMPLOYED IN GERMANY!"

The next sequence begins and gradually accelerates as smaller, but progressively enlarging, words describe the condition of the unemployed, the international dimensions, and the narrator's emotions: "The hungry, helpless, despairing—in Germany, England, in America, ALL OVER THE WORLD!" Now the credits appear, and an intertitle establishes the connection between the everyday world of German workers and the fictional world of *Bookkeeper Kremke*: "This film reports a fateful story, just like the tragic, if not even more tragic stories that unfold daily—it is the story of—Bookkeeper Kremke." Again omniscient narration introduces the audience to the fiction and asserts the authority to indicate that Kremke's story is authentic and typical. At the same time, the sequential rhythm and the graphic progression of the texts convey the narrator's emotional intensity and encourage a similar audience response.

Photography and montage function similarly to guide reception. The first scene depicts Kremke and his colleagues hard at work. A new machine arrives, and a short, fast-paced sequence suggests its speed. One of the bookkeepers asserts that the machine will replace five of them, but Kremke disagrees. The presentation immediately stimulates skepticism about Kremke's perspective. Information about rising unemployment and the sequence depicting the machine's speed suggest that Kremke clings to the past and harbors false expectations about the future. By sharing information with the audience that Kremke either does not have or will not accept, the narrative invites spectators to transcend and criticize Kremke's perspective.

The process continues with a parallel montage sequence that juxtaposes shots of Kremke, waiting at home where he expects a visit from his daughter and her future husband, and shots of the couple at a dance. Kremke is seen playing with a neighbor's child, glancing at a clock, watching a military parade on the street, and marching to the music in his apartment with his petty officer's hat. After he impatiently opens a bottle of liquor, the sequence shifts to the dance. Lene prepares to leave, and her fiancé refuses to come home with her. With this information the audience realizes that Kremke's expectations are unrealistic. His perception of himself as a part of the student's middle-class world is just as illusory as his perception of himself as a part of the military parade.

Subsequent scenes reinforce the image of Kremke as a conceited petty bourgeois who considers himself upwardly mobile, disdains those below him, and refuses to accept reality. When Lene returns alone, Kremke conceals his disappointment and storms off to his *Stammtisch*. There he and his friends toast the figure of a knight and criticize unemployment insurance. Kremke asks, "Should we perhaps work so that the lazy ones can go for a stroll?" In the next scene Kremke and his colleagues lose their jobs, and Kremke's downfall begins.

Throughout the film, narrative signals encourage rejection of Kremke's attitude and acceptance of Erwin's position, as well as Lene's decision to abandon her father's world. Kremke maintains his belief in the existing social order and gradually deteriorates as he realizes that he has become a member of the social class he disdains. When he applies for unemployment benefits, he must sit among other workers who explain their situations. Parallel sequences illustrate their stories and indicate that they, too,

Bookkeeper Kremke: Kremke and his friends deride the unemployed. (Staatliches Filmarchiv der DDR)

are victims of automation. Kremke repeatedly denies it, but he is forced to realize that he belongs to the working class. In the meantime, Lene has met Erwin and has no reservations about being with him. In numerous parallel montage sequences Lene is shown enjoying her life with Erwin, while Kremke grows more and more despondent. After Kremke has refused to join Lene and Erwin to celebrate their engagement, a medium shot focuses on Kremke wandering aimlessly through the streets and finally jumping into a river. The running water fades out slowly and gives way to images of workers marching to the Reichstag and the final imperative exclamation emerging from the water and the workers: "GIVE WORK!"

Like Werner Hochbaum's film, *Bookkeeper Kremke* advocated unity between the working class and the petty bourgeoisie. However, only the final images of the marching workers and their imperative "GIVE WORK!" suggested united political action. For most of the film, it is more Erwin's ability to remain optimistic and find work that motivates Lene to join him than conviction that they must unite to demand employment for all. Perhaps the makers of *Bookkeeper Kremke* were cautious about communicating their message too clearly for fear that the censors would reject the film. By the fall of 1930 the Great Coalition had faltered and Brüning was governing by emergency decree; in December the censors did prohibit *All Quiet on the Western Front.* It is equally plausible that, while criticizing the impact of automation on employment, Harden intended to promote optimism about the economic system and suggest that workers should maintain their trust in the parliamentary democracy. Although *Bookkeeper Kremke* implied the necessity for more intense political activity, it perpetuated the image of parliamentary representatives as valid authorities to whom the demonstrators must make their appeal. During the final years of the Weimar Republic, Social Democratic leaders continued to assert their political authority to govern and strove to limit the initiative of the German masses.

THE KPD AND FILM: FROM STUBBORN PERSEVERANCE TO ELEVENTH-HOUR EXPERIMENTS WITH ALTERNATIVE FORMS OF PRODUCTION AND RECEPTION

While the KPD assumed a new leftist course based on the concept of social fascism, the party's cultural activists intensified efforts to gain leadership positions in existing working-class cultural organizations and to establish as well as expand their own organizations. In October 1928 a group of leftist and KPD authors founded the Bund Proletarisch-Revolutionärer Schriftsteller (Federation of Proletarian Revolutionary Authors, BPRS), and in August 1929 they began publishing their own journal, *Die Linkskurve*.[1] At the end of 1928 the more radical members of the VFV accused their leaders of reformism, and a member of the IAH, Erich Lange, replaced Franz Höllering as the chief editor of *Film und Volk*. In October 1929 the KPD founded the Interessengemeinschaft für Arbeiterkultur (Interest Group for Workers' Culture, IfA) to coordinate the party's cultural activities. In August 1930 party leaders expressed their intention to pay even greater attention to cultural activity as a component of what they referred to as the program for the national and social liberation of the German people.[2] During the same period, the IAH sustained and even expanded its already impressive network of cultural organizations and publications.[3]

THE CONTINUING DEBATE ABOUT MARXIST AESTHETICS

The process continued, as did the debate about a Marxist aesthetics. At this point, very few participants in the ongoing discussion about prole-

tarian culture insisted that such a culture depended entirely on the establishment of a socialist state.[4] Most agreed that the dominant culture in
Weimar society legitimized less democratic, more exploitive social structures by promoting a regressive ideology associated with the Prussian
monarchy. They also agreed that, while concentrating on political work,
the revolutionary working class, led by the KPD, must combat all manifestations of the dominant ideology if it hoped to change the ideological
orientation of noncommunist workers and transcend the existing social
system.

Although Communist cultural activists and those associated with the
KPD generally agreed about the goal of their efforts, discussion about
the quality of proletarian art continued, now focusing increasingly on the
relationship between production and reception.[5] Toward the end of the
Weimar Republic well-known KPD authors such as Johannes R. Becher,
who perceived Marxism above all as a system of analysis with which the
revolutionary working class could discern the laws of social development,
promoted art as a medium for communicating insights to noncommunist
workers.[6] Influenced in part by the emerging socialist-realist movement
in the Soviet Union, Becher believed that art should convey a Marxist
image of pressing social issues in a way that would allow proletarians to
understand the process of social development and enable them to influence the process to fulfill their individual and collective needs. Becher and
many other proponents of socialist realism commented almost exclusively on questions of content and only tangentially discussed aesthetic
form.[7] While affirming the new concept of realism, others, including
George Lukács, Friedrich Wolf, and Béla Balázs, paid more attention to
forms of aesthetic communication and promoted an Aristotelian model
of catharsis. Novels, dramas, films, and other art forms, they argued,
should portray typical figures from opposing social classes in contemporary society and employ techniques of expression capable of motivating
audiences to sympathize with proletarian victims of social injustice who
struggle for change.[8] A third group of participants in the discussion, theoreticians and artists who shared the desire to challenge the ideological
orientation of the dominant German culture, promoted those forms of
artistic expression that were deemed capable of reflecting reality most
authentically and providing a conceptual image of social totality. For example, Egon Erwin Kisch relied heavily on reportage techniques, John
Heartfield experimented with techniques of photomontage, and Erwin
Piscator integrated documentary film footage into his stage presentations.
They encouraged audiences to reject traditional concepts of social orga-

nization and development, internalize a Marxist viewpoint, and adopt the KPD's program for social change. Instead of appealing to the emotions of their audiences, they hoped to stimulate intellectual activity.

In contrast to each of the groups mentioned above, a final group, including Hanns Eisler and Bertolt Brecht advocated a radical departure from the traditional separation between production and reception. Influenced by radically democratic communists such as Karl Korsch and by members of the Soviet avant garde, including Sergei Tretjakov and remnants of the *Proletkult* movement, Eisler and Brecht challenged fundamental elements of the institution of art—professionalism, commercial entertainment, narrative cohesion, and emotional engagement. They argued that such elements established and reinforced the notion that only a small group of the most talented artists should produce art. Consequently, they asserted, an artists' elite assumed responsibility for organizing everyday experience into ideological perspectives for a much larger group of people who were restricted to consuming art and more or less uncritically assimilating the corresponding ideological evaluation. Brecht's experiments, first with epic theater and later with the *Lehrstück*, exemplified the development of the tendency among communist cultural theoreticians and artists to reject established techniques of reception and develop radically democratic models of artistic production as a means for the ideological organization of everyday experience.[9]

FILM CRITICISM IN THE COMMUNIST PRESS

In contrast to the SPD newspapers and journals, the KPD and IAH publications sustained their broad coverage of mainstream cinema as well as their own film activity. Only *Die Rote Fahne* struggled to maintain consistent coverage in 1931 and 1932 when the Brüning and Papen governments regularly censored it. Generally, the editors of *Die Rote Fahne* printed articles on cinema in the *feuilleton* and sporadically included a "Theater und Film" section. In 1931 the heading changed to "Film und Bühne" ("Film and Stage") and appeared even less regularly. In June/July 1932 the *feuilleton* slowly gave way to more articles about the escalating political struggle.

At the same time, the less blatantly partisan IAH newspapers avoided censorship and persevered with their coverage. *Die Welt am Abend* and *Berlin am Morgen* retained large *feuilleton* sections, frequently printed articles on cinema, and, like *Die Rote Fahne,* included special "Theater und Film" sections. Only the *AIZ* paid less attention to mainstream film than to KPD, IAH, and Soviet film activity. As had been the case previously, most *AIZ* articles on film publicized Soviet, Prometheus, Weltfilm, and VFV films. Exceptions included reviews of individual films, such as Lilli Kaufmann's critique of *Comradeship* (49, 1931), and reports on developments within the commercial film industry, such as Kaufmann's "Die Traumfabrik der Angestellen" ("The Dream Factory of the White-Collar Workers," 27, 1932).

Each of the tendencies outlined in the previous section found some expression in the coverage of cinema in the Communist press. The coverage in most Communist newspapers in many ways continued to emphasize the communication of insight from above. Recommending film to their readers is just one example. *Die Rote Fahne* continued printing its "Films of the Week"; *Die Welt am Abend* and *Berlin am Morgen* made suggestions under the heading "Filme, die man sehen soll" ("Films That One Should See"); and the *AIZ* experimented with its own rubric, "Die Welt der weissen Wand" ("The World of the White Screen," 23, 1931). As the *AIZ* explained: "In this space the AIZ regularly will provide an overview of the most important new films so that our readers do not have to risk falling prey to ostentatious advertising." Unlike the corresponding projects in other newspapers, the *AIZ* program ceased after one issue, and the newspaper devoted its energy to promoting Soviet, IAH, and VFV films.

In addition to recommending films openly, each newspaper followed the *AIZ* model, directing attention to specific films by reporting on their production and by featuring articles on topics related to their themes. During the fall of 1929, for example, a number of articles, including "Ein Zille-Film im Werden" ("A Zille Film in Production," *Die Welt am Abend,* 7 November 1929), "Wie der Zille-Film gedreht wird" ("How the Zille Film Is Being Produced," *Berlin am Morgen,* 9 November 1929), "Der richtige Zille-Film" ("The True Zille Film," *Die Rote Fahne,* 5 December 1929), and "Mutter Krausens Fahrt ins Glück" ("Mother Krause's Journey to Happiness," *AIZ,* 52, 1929), publicized the efforts of Prometheus to produce its film in commemoration of Heinrich Zille's death. With articles such as "Kinderhölle Sowjetrußland" ("Children's Hell in Soviet Russia," *Berlin am Morgen,* 25 January 1931) about the treatment of juvenile delinquents in the Soviet Union and *Der Weg ins Leben (The Way into Life,* the first Soviet sound film distributed in Germany), the Communist newspapers continued their campaign to generate interest in films they considered worthwhile. They did so by associating the fictional protrayals with existing social problems. Such articles advocated cinematic realism, ascribed authenticity to the featured film, and encouraged potential spectators to accept the corresponding ideological orientation.

The articles on commercial film in general and the authoritative reviews that appeared in the KPD and IAH newspapers provided much more powerful and explicit guidelines. Between 1929 and 1933 each newspaper relied on a small group of highly active journalists for film articles and reviews. Alfred Durus wrote many substantial articles and reviews for *Die Rote Fahne*. Kurt Kersten and Michael Mendelssohn contributed most frequently to *Die Welt am Abend*. F. C. Weiskopf, the *feuilleton* editor of *Berlin am Morgen*, Mersus (pseudonym?), and Hans Tasiemka shared responsibility for that newspaper's film coverage. Heinz Lüdecke contributed articles to all of the newspapers cited. Most *AIZ* articles appeared anonymously, but in 1932 Lilli Kaufmann emerged as that newspaper's film journalist. Each of the major contributors held a position of authority, communicating insights about the industry as unquestionable truths and positing general standards for film evaluation.

A major focal point remained the influence of right-leaning interest groups on commercial cinema. As the transition to sound progressed, articles such as "Hugenbergisierung des Tonfilms" ("Hugenbergization of Sound Film," *Die Rote Fahne*, 13 April 1929) discussed the ways in which the largest concerns used the innovation to increase their ideological control of the entire industry. Other articles, including "Die Ufa macht Politik" ("Ufa Politicizes," *Berlin am Morgen*, 9 July 1929) and "Kleiner Wahlfilm" ("Little Campaign Film," *Die Rote Fahne*, 13 March 1932), highlighted the explicit political activity of Ufa, Tobis, etc., to expose their ideological orientation. Contributors also criticized the ongoing manipulation of film criticism by producers and promoted journalistic independence ("Unabhängige Filmkritik"—"Independent Film Criticism," *Die Rote Fahne*, 5 November 1930; and "Um die Freiheit der Filmkritik"—"For the Freedom of Film Criticism," *Berlin am Morgen*, 4 January 1931).

Censorship decisions, especially after the prohibition of *All Quiet on the Western Front*, received even more attention. In articles such as "Die Filmzensur muß fallen!" ("Film Censorship Must Fall!" *Berlin am Morgen*, 9 December 1930) and "Filmzensur wütet" ("Film Censorship

Rages," *Die Rote Fahne,* 20 January 1931), contributors compared decisions on numerous films, noting that nationalistic and militaristic films passed while pacifistic and socialistic films were censored. The critics claimed that the government had begun to support cultural fascism openly.[10]

The articles on censorship reveal a second focal point of film coverage in the Communist press. When comparing the censors' decisions, contributors normally evaluated the films in question. As had been the case prior to 1929, they often accused mainstream filmmakers of falsifying history and perpetuating the myth of upward social mobility. Now they also more frequently distinguished general trends in production and referred at least vaguely to the relationship between production and reception. In "Rezept für Tonfilmpossen" ("Recipe for Sound Film Farces," *Die Rote Fahne,* 27 November 1931), for example, Heinz Lüdecke outlined the impact of standardization on production, suggesting that economic as well as political considerations influenced the quality of commercial film. Although individual film critics did recognize the influence of standardization on plotlines, it is important to note that its influence on production techniques and the effect on reception attracted almost no attention.

Between 1929 and 1933 those critics who consistently discussed audience reception more often criticized the cinematic appeal to the emotions. Michael Mendelssohn, in his review of *Cyankali* (*Die Welt am Abend,* 24 May 1930), exemplified the trend. According to Mendelssohn, Hans Tintner's adaptation of Friedrich Wolf's abortion tragedy only imitated the commercial techniques of catharsis. Although Mendelssohn and others criticized what they perceived as a manipulative emotional appeal, they rarely discussed in any detail how photographic techniques, montage, or sound generated and guided emotional responses. Instead of offering concrete evidence, in most cases they merely asserted their authority as experts. Mendelssohn's review also indicated that whereas the IAH newspapers originally moderated their criticism of commercial film to attract a broader, nonpartisan readership, the critical quality of their reviews now differed little from those of *Die Rote Fahne.*

In addition to guiding reception with its reviews, *Die Rote Fahne,* like the SPD *Vorwärts,* occasionally published stories about commercial films with a moral. E. Fritz, for example, narrated a story, "Kientopp" ("Nickelodeon," 12 May 1932), about a worker who temporarily escapes into the dreamworld of cinematic entertainment but then must return to the everyday world of exploitation, anxiety, and frustration. Like K. R. Neubert's "Farewell after a Film," Fritz's story instructed workers to reject cinematic entertainment and to strive for real social change. *Die Rote Fahne* also printed articles with titles from commercial films, such as "Drei von der Stempelstelle" ("Three from the Unemployment Line," 8 April 1932), and claimed to contrast cinematic fiction with reality. In this case the article referred to a film which invited the unemployed to trust resettlement schemes. While recalling the film, the article reported stories of three real unemployed workers who rejected the film's invitation, demanded work, and supported the KPD.

The attempt to draw a connection between leftist cinematic fiction and reality and the challenge to the authenticity of mainstream cinematic fiction demonstrated the general allegiance to the new concept of socialist realism among Communist film journalists. Alfred Durus reinforced the perception in his "Der Tonfilm, wie er ist und sein soll" ("Sound Film as It Is and as It Should Be," *Die Rote Fahne*, 25 June 1929). He asserted, "Sound film is most important as a medium for intensifying the power of realism in the revolutionary documentaries." Most of the regular contributors to the KPD and IAH newspapers perceived proletarian film as an element in the KPD's agitational work (*Kampfkultur*). They generally applauded emotional and intellectual approaches as long as filmmakers portrayed realistic struggles between typical figures from contemporary social classes, fostered a Marxist understanding of social totality, and encouraged audiences to participate in revolutionary social change.

While KPD and IAH journalists criticized commercial films as "sentimental" and "pathetic," they praised a similar aesthetic orientation in Soviet and Prometheus films as "gripping" and "compelling." The distinguishing feature was content. Films like *Cyankali* were unacceptable because their victimized working-class protagonists struggled unsuccessfully against social oppression. Such films evoked sympathy for proletarian heroes and perhaps even contributed to a Marxist understanding of social totality, but they provided no clear-cut guidelines for social change. Soviet films, on the other hand, won widespread acclaim among Communist critics by closely following the socialist-realist formula. As a review of Pudovkin's *Storm over Asia* in *Die Rote Fahne* (8 January 1929) explained: "The whole Mongolian world comes alive on the eve of its liberation. The barbarism of the White Guard officer's camarilla, the reactionary religious cult of the 'living Buddha,' and the misery of the plundered, deceived, and mistreated hunters and shepherds are shaped into the forces of play and counterplay from which inevitably and irresistibly the revolutionary conclusion, the tremendous compelling storm of freedom, the 'Storm over Asia,' arises."

Many critics preferred Pudovkin's emotional appeal to Eisenstein's experiments with intellectual stimulation. But they criticized Eisenstein's experiments only when they failed to meet the standards for socialist realism. The review of Eisenstein's *Der Kampf um die Erde* (*The Struggle for the Earth, Die Rote Fahne,* 12 February 1930) by Alfred Durus provides a good example; in it Durus notes: "Eisenstein wishes to assemble thoughts, but often only assembles images and 'emotions' where clear Marxist-Leninist thought patterns would be indispensable."

The reviews of Soviet and Prometheus films were often more extensive than those of mainstream films. They also included somewhat more detailed information about narrative techniques. Here, as well, the critics preferred narrative cohesion and cinematic catharsis but accepted experiments designed to stimulate intellectual activity as long as the ideological orientation associated with the plot was acceptable. Soviet films that portrayed the socialist construction were among the best films, according to Durus. His reviews in *Die Rote Fahne* of *Turksib* (29 December 1929), *The Struggle for the Earth* (12 February 1930), and *Enthusiasm* (26 August 1931) praised Soviet filmmakers for portraying examples of socialist construction with vivid authenticity and implied that such cinematic achievements were only possible under socialist conditions. Durus no longer intended to suggest that proletarian art was impossible in Germany, but he, F. C. Weiskopf, and others did present the Soviet Union and its cinema as models for German social and cinematic development. In each review Durus also praised the portrayed accomplishments of Soviet industry and agriculture, affirming the conquest of nature and asserting that under socialism humanity could accelerate its progress toward that goal ("Turksib," *Die Rote Fahne,* 29 December 1929).

Communist journalists during the final crisis years generally communicated insights about mainstream cinema and about their own film organizations in an authoritarian manner. They promoted film as a medium to educate the working masses about social development from the KPD perspective and to reinforce the model quality of the Soviet Union. They did not encourage readers to practice their own analytical skills and to engage in critical interaction with filmmakers, critics, and the films themselves. As the reviews of Soviet films by Alfred Durus demonstrate, Communists concentrated foremost on marketing the Soviet model.

There were apparent exceptions: *Die Rote Fahne* and *Berlin am Morgen* initiated limited campaigns to involve readers more in film criticism and production. For example, the KPD's *Arbeiterkorrespondenten* (worker correspondents) regularly submitted short reviews to *Die Rote Fahne*. As the newspaper explained: "In Germany all cultural correspondents of the *Arbeiterkorrespondenten* in *Die Rote Fahne* are part of our campaign to stimulate the creative initiative of the masses in the struggle against bourgeois ideology even before we assume power" ("Rotarmisten über Ermlers Films"—"Red Guards on Ermler's Film," 16 April 1930). The reviews of the *Arbeiterkorrespondenten* created the perception that grass-roots initiatives contributed significantly to the KPD's film program. The perception was at least partially false. *Die Rote Fahne* editors did encourage the *Arbeiterkorrespondenten* to participate, but their suggestions often took the form of directives from above. In "Filmkritik" ("Film Criticism," 10 September 1929), an Hungarian emigrant described his initiative in the following manner: "I received a ticket from *Die Rote Fahne,* with instructions to see an Hungarian film in the Primus Palast and to write a critique of it." A short time later a more experienced correspondent indicated even more clearly the relationship between the editors and the correspondents. In "Statt einer Filmbesprechung" ("Instead of a Film Review," 8 October 1929) the correspondent expressed appreciation to *Die Rote Fahne* for sending him tickets to a premiere but explained that he had joined a boycott of the performance with striking workers at the theater. The correspondent closed by apologizing for not submitting a review.

Berlin am Morgen relied exclusively on a core of experienced journalists for its articles on cinema and reviews. But in 1932 the newspaper began to encourage readers to participate more creatively in film production. In "Wer schreibt den besten sozialistischen Film?" ("Who Will Write the Best Socialist Film Script?" 2 June 1932) the editors announced their cooperation with Meschrabpom in a campaign to solicit exposés and scripts from readers. And in "Hallo, alle kommen mit" ("Hey, Everyone's Coming Along," 14 July 1932) they invited readers to attend a steamship cruise. During the cruise, passengers would generate ideas for a film script cooperatively. At approximately the same time, other articles, including "Warum Schmalfilm?" ("Why 8-mm Film?" 23 June 1932) and "Mit der Kamera in die Zeltstadt" ("Into the Tent Colony with the Camera," 9 August 1932), discussed the introduction of 8-mm film and its use by independent working-class collectives. The Meschrabpom contest, the steamship cruise, and the reports about grass-roots work with 8-mm film at least appeared to be more genuine attempts to challenge existing concepts of production and reception and to encourage readers to initiate their own projects.

It is important to note that the reviews of the *Arbeiterkorrespondenten* and the new approach in *Berlin am Morgen* were relatively isolated phenomena that coincided with the experience of crisis. When the KPD reevaluated its political strategy and abandoned the concept of social fascism in 1932, it is likely that cultural leaders also grew more susceptible to proposals for radically democratic cultural alternatives. As the popularity of National Socialism increased and the economic crisis intensified, the KPD leadership perhaps became more sensitive to criticisms and proposals from its political and cultural left wing. Ernst Thälmann had expressed the need to strengthen the democratic process within the party in response to criticism from Berlin delegates at the district party convention as early as May 1930 ("Genosse Thälmann über Selbstkritik und Massenarbeit"—"Comrade Thälmann on Self-Criticism and Work with the Masses," *Die Rote Fahne*, 27 May 1930). By 1932 the KPD's cultural leaders seemed willing to accept such criticisms and initiate campaigns to increase the participation of readers and moviegoers in the party's film program. In January 1933 before they could test the viability of their new approach, Hitler assumed power.

THE FILM-KARTELL "WELT-FILM" GMBH

Between 1929 and 1933 the KPD/IAH film production and distribution programs, like the coverage of film in the Communist press, followed developing trends in Marxist aesthetics. The Film-Kartell "Welt-Film" GmbH (Weltfilm) concentrated exclusively on noncommercial production and distribution, supplying films and guidelines for campaigns and other KPD and IAH events.[11] Weltfilm, like the SPD's FuL, distributed a small number of what it considered to be socially critical mainstream films, but relied heavily on Soviet films and Prometheus films to fill its distribution program. It also produced about thirty short documentary films with screening times of fifteen to twenty-five minutes. As was the case with the SPD's short documentaries, the films accompanied the feature and depicted KPD and IAH leaders, demonstrations, conventions, and sporting events. Weltfilm documentaries such as *Zwölfter Parteitag der KPD in Berlin* (*Twelfth Party Congress of the KPD in Berlin*, 1929), *Der erste Mai 1930 in Berlin* (*May Day in Berlin*, 1930), and *Rot Sport im Bild* (*Red Sport in Pictures*, 1930) functioned above all to promote the leaders and policies of both organizations to potential voters and sympathizers.

A smaller number of more extensive documentaries opposed dominant ideological perspectives with Marxist analysis. For example, *Zeitproblem. Wie der Arbeiter wohnt* (*Contemporary Problem: How the Worker Lives*, 1930), conceived by Weltfilm as the first in a series, challenged the orientation of mainstream newsreels such as Ufa's *Wochenschau*. Slatan Dudow, a young Bulgarian who had come to Berlin in 1922 to study drama and film, directed what became the only contribution to the series.[12] The film's abundant omniscient intertitles and simple juxtaposition of contrasting images betrayed Dudow's inexperience as well as the reductive approach of many German leftists toward documentary filmmaking. The intertitles suggested that corresponding visual images typified miserable living and working conditions for working-class Germans. With paratactic juxtapositions Dudow reinforced the suggested typicality of the misery being portrayed. For example, a selection of close-ups depicting the exhausted, sad faces of individual workers follows a sequence in which masses of workers leave a factory. In another sequence a crowd of people enter a streetcar followed by a single man who checks the ground around him for an unused ticket. After establishing an association between poor, exhausted individuals and the working masses, Dudow contrasted the living conditions of the rich and poor. An intertitle proclaiming "the unwelcome guest" introduces a scene in which a crippled salesman is turned away repeatedly by the occupants of villas and luxury apartments. Then the barracks of the poor appear, and an intertitle asserts "the irreconcilable differences." The narrative then depicts the living environment of the poor and portrays the police eviction of one family. Juxtaposed with shots of the eviction are close-ups of a fat, smiling bourgeois and the policeman's helmet. A final intertitle exclaims: "That is no solution!"

How the Worker Lives also exemplified a new trend in the KPD/IAH documentaries. While claiming all the objectivity of documentaries, it incorporated staged scenes such as the eviction to establish class distinctions, evoke sympathy for the poor, generate disdain for the rich, and encourage spectators to reject existing authority. *How the Worker Lives* employed the documentary medium and the omniscient narrative voice to maximize its authenticity and the authority of the KPD. Like the SPD's

FuL, Weltfilm used films such as Dudow's documentary and its distribution program to attract support for KPD/IAH leaders and perspectives. It did so in a way that encouraged spectators to rely on authoritarian direction.

PROMETHEUS: THE TRANSITION TO SOUND FILM AND MESCHRABPOM

While Weltfilm administered the noncommercial film programs of the KPD and IAH, Prometheus attempted to adapt to changes in the film industry and remain competitive. Just two weeks after the first major sound film, *Melody of the World,* had its premiere in Berlin, the leading trade journals announced that Prometheus and Meschrabpom were negotiating with British Phototone, a producer of sound film equipment, to co-produce films. According to the *L.B.B.* and the *Film-Kurier* (see reports on 16 April 1929), British Phototone had agreed to co-produce a number of sound films with Prometheus and Meschrabpom, including the next Pudovkin film, *Das Leben ist schön (Life Is Beautiful)*, *Das Wolgalied (The Song of the Volga)*, and *Die Premiere* with Anna Sten. None of the projects materialized. British Phototone had established an association with the Siemens-Halske Klangfilm company in January (*Kinematograph*, 22 January 1929). When Klangfilm merged with Tobis in the spring of 1929, it is likely that the Tobis-Klangfilm partnership superseded other agreements. Although Prometheus, Meschrabpom, and British Phototone had an agreement, they were unable to produce sound films independent of the large conglomerate.

Just one week after negotiating the British Phototone agreement, Prometheus and Meschrabpom further solidified their partnership. A report in the *L.B.B.* (23 April 1929) explained that Meschrabpom had granted Prometheus first access to its films for distribution. The change perhaps anticipated the co-production of sound films, but the increasingly tenuous status of Derussa also might have motivated the closer association between Prometheus and Meschrabpom. In September 1929 Derussa collapsed. It soon became clear that the German partners, the Sklarz brothers, had exploited the Russian Trade Bureau.[13] Without Derussa, the Soviet film industry depended even more on Prometheus in 1930 and finally declared the company to be its primary international distributor (*L.B.B.*, 15 October 1930).

In addition to negotiating with British Phototone and working more closely with the Soviet film industry, Prometheus modified its marketing program. Jan Fethke began administering Prometheus publicity in September 1929, and in November he was replaced by Wilhelm Giltmann, an experienced publicity executive for Gaumont who also could speak Russian.[14] During the final year in which silent films attracted large audiences, Prometheus used a wide variety of publicity techniques to maximize commercial success. It distributed production information to, and advertised often in, all leading trade journals; it commissioned the *Illustrierter Film-Kurier* to produce and distribute programs for its features and for many major Soviet films; and according to a report in *Die deutsche Filmzeitung* (26, 1929), it even experimented with recorded advertisements.

THE LIVING CORPSE

The desire for commercial success continued to influence the choice of subject material for Prometheus films. For their second co-production Meschrabpom and Prometheus selected an adaptation of Tolstoy's *The Living Corpse*. In 1928 Max Reinhardt had produced the play about a pathetic Russian bourgeois whose sense of propriety and honor hinder him from divorcing his wife when their marriage deteriorates. The success of Reinhardt's production almost certainly influenced the Prometheus and Meschrabpom decision to produce an adaptation. Fjodor Ozep, a young Russian who had directed *Der gelbe Paß* (*The Yellow Pass,* 1928), wrote the script and directed the film. Pudovkin played the leading role. In contrast to the drama's emphasis on the protagonist's psychological struggle, Ozep's adaptation concentrated on the injustice of the czarist social system.[15]

The story begins with the melancholic protagonist, Fedja Protassow, expressing his desire for a divorce to a priest in an Orthodox church. The priest refers to the inviolability of the church's law, explains that Fedja's case does not warrant divorce, and advises him to bear his cross as must everyone else. Fedja then appears in a bar where Artemjew, a lawyer, claims that, with his assistance, Fedja can pretend adultery and be divorced in no time. The scheme repulses Fedja. He contemplates running away but returns home where he finds his wife at the piano with her lover, Kerenin. Fedja flees to his gypsy friend, the beautiful Mascha, and following a confrontation with Kerenin, who also advises him to simulate adultery, he decides to attempt the deceit. Again the act of adultery re-

The Living Corpse: Illustrierter Film-Kurier program cover. (Staatliches Filmarchiv der DDR)

pulses Fedja. He finally accepts Mascha's suggestion to pretend a suicide attempt and begin a new life. The plot succeeds, but Fedja remains despondent. After years of wandering the streets as a living corpse, he reappears in the bar where Artemjew recognizes the lost husband and attempts to involve him in a scheme to blackmail his wife and her new husband. Fedja rejects the offer, and Artemjew betrays him to the police. In a final trial scene Fedja, confronted again by the inflexibility of the law, kills himself.

Unlike earlier Prometheus films, *The Living Corpse* made little use of omniscient intertitles to establish narrative authority or create the illusion of reality. For the most part intertitles communicated dialogues and occasionally revealed the content of letters from Fedja to his wife. However, Ozep did employ photographic and montage techniques to create a cohesive narrative structure and to guide reception. The reviews emphasized his use of montage, noting its similarity to that of the other Soviet directors. For example, the *Vorwärts* review (15 February 1929) explained: "Again and again we see the symbolic segments, so favored by the Russians. They represent the state, the church, the law, and remind the audience repeatedly that these are the things that cause all the suffering." The review accurately describes the narrative orientation but notes only one of many techniques that Ozep used to suggest social totality. The exposition provides an excellent example of Ozep's narration. The spectator first sees a cityscape dominated by church steeples; an intertitle explains: "Moscow, the city of a thousand towers." The next shot focuses on a single bell tower, and a second intertitle states: "The holy synod of the Orthodox church." Photography and montage now replace the intertitles in organizing and ascribing meaning to the visual image. The juxtaposition of a cityscape filled with church steeples and a single church's bell tower alone suggests that the Orthodox church is omnipresent and that the individual church represents them all. A split screen of many ringing bells reinforces the representative quality of the single bell tower, while their motion becomes a transitional element. Next a single incenser is seen inside the church, moving like the many bells and continuing the association between the general and the specific.

At this point the perspective moves outside the church and centers on its giant doors from a low angle. They seem to open automatically, and a short sequence presents still more shots of church steeples and icons of the Orthodox church. Finally, a man emerges as if from within the camera and climbs the stairs toward the entrance. As he climbs, images of religious statues and icons fade in and out. He enters the church, and the camera perspective moves to a high angle behind a priest, allowing the audience to observe the seemingly dwarfed man from above. Similar photographic techniques and montage symbolism organize the remainder of the scene as the man, whom the audience now recognizes as Fedja, communicates with the priest. Ozep's narration suggests throughout that the church's authority encompasses and dominates Fedja. Fedja's emergence from the spectator's perspective also initiates the association between spectator and protagonist.

In addition to depicting the priest as a cold and powerful representative of church law, Ozep employed an impressive variety of cinematic techniques to characterize most authoritarian figures as unemotional and selfishly calculating, while emphasizing Fedja's helplessness and encouraging audience sympathy. For example, the narrative juxtaposes the corrupt Artemjew and Fedja, the bigoted Kerenin and Fedja. It reveals the contents of a letter in which Fedja expresses his desire to ensure his wife's happiness. From an overhead angle the spectator looks down on a miserable Fedja after his pretended suicide. A sequence portraying a man who whips his exhausted horse follows shots of Fedja stumbling through the streets. Recurring shots of caged birds symbolize Fedja's condition. And parallel montage moves the spectator back and forth between images of Fedja, who begins the simulated adultery or contemplates suicide, and images of the bar, thus building suspense and heightening the spectator's emotional involvement.

After providing more than ample information for the audience to assimilate emotionally the narrative perspective, Ozep surprisingly disrupts the cohesion of his narrative somewhat and challenges the audience to participate both emotionally and intellectually in the concluding trial section. A symbolic montage sequence initiates the section, recalling the symbols of czarist authority. Following each image an intertitle proclaims: "The Law." The ensuing sequence depicts a crowd of people climbing a large stairway into a court building. For the first time Ozep composes the shots so that, from an observer's position, Fedja is perceived to be above those around him. He stands near the top of the stairs, separated by the crowd from his wife below. The statue of justice assumes Fedja's position, but his wife remains below with the crowd between them. The juxtaposition of Fedja and the statue at the top of each shot indicates that Fedja will no longer submit to the domination of the law, a suggestion that subsequent signals reinforce.

Once inside the courtroom, the camera's perspective changes periodically but establishes a base with the onlookers' point of view and draws special attention to the act of observation. Numerous shots present the onlookers, who are dressed formally and suddenly raise opera glasses in unison. This unexpected incongruity suspends the illusion of reality. By associating the audience's perspective with that of the onlookers, whose appearance and behavior are more like that of spectators at a cultural event than the gallery at a trial, it disturbs the audience's emotional engagement and invites them to participate intellectually in the decision-making process. The onlookers, lawyers, and Fedja take their places, but the judges' and jurors' seats remain empty. An intertitle announces: "The Law." Suddenly the judges and jurors appear. The intertitle solidifies the association between the general symbols of czarist authority and the specific authority of the court. The sequence further disrupts the illusion of reality, reminding spectators of the fiction.

As the trial begins, a high-angle establishing shot from behind the judges directs the audience's view down on Fedja, with onlookers behind him. The perspective returns for most of the proceedings to the judges', jurors', and onlookers' positions. A dialogue develops between the judges and Fedja, who challenges their authority by looking directly at them (and at the audience) and asserting: "Only a divorce could resolve these tensions—freedom! But you block the way to this freedom with countless obstacles." Fedja continues, but one of the judges rings a bell and ends Fedja's challenge. The judge's image slowly dissolves into the image of Fedja and supersedes it.

Now the public prosecutor presents his arguments, claiming the law's authority over the will of individuals: "And the law remains firm: in the interest of the state it demands punishment for every crime." Images of czarist authority accompany his arguments, and when the defense attorney questions the definition of crime and criminals, images of nature and the statue of Venus appear. The courtroom then empties as a theater would at intermission. While the jurors deliberate, Fedja (and the audience) learn that he will be exiled to Siberia or forced to resume his marriage. As the deliberation continues, Artemjew appears and gives Fedja a gun. The sequence then shifts between a scene of the judges and onlookers enjoying a feast and high-angle views of Fedja alone in the courtroom. The juxtaposition builds suspense until spectators see a judge suddenly jump, indicating a shot has been fired. Everyone rushes to Fedja who lies motionless on the floor. Images of Fedja and the familiar symbols of authority conclude the scene.

As the suicide sequence illustrates, although Ozep at least partially suspended the illusion of reality and encouraged the audience to contemplate the arguments raised during the trial, the narration also reinforced his image of social totality and reestablished the spectators' emotional association with Fedja. Ozep revealed the fictional quality of his portrayal and invited spectators to consider its significance for their everyday lives, but provided sufficient information to influence if not control their contemplation. *The Living Corpse* challenged spectators to condemn social systems in which authority and its representatives are cold, inflexible, bigoted. It asked them to sympathize with honest, compassionate individuals who are victimized by the system.

For German audiences in 1929 *The Living Corpse* was particularly relevant. In 1928 the German parliament had renewed a debate about divorce regulations that had begun in 1921.[16] The existing regulations were almost as strict as those described by the priest at the beginning of the film. In most cases, they allowed divorce only if a partner could be found guilty of malicious abandonment, extreme persecution, or adultery. A proposed reform would have permitted a partner to file for divorce based on irreconcilable differences, but the Catholic Center party campaigned successfully against it. Considering the easily discernible parallel to the contemporary social context and the rejection of *Counterfeiters* in January 1929, it is likely that Prometheus masked its social critique and moderated it, allowing Fedja to commit suicide instead of attempting to initiate social change. Even so, the censors reviewed the film twice and removed almost six hundred meters before releasing it for public screening. Critics and audiences responded positively, and *The Living Corpse* became Germany's tenth most popular film for the first quarter of 1929 ("Die besten Filme seit Januar 1929"—"The Best Films since January 1929," *Film-Kurier*, 5 April 1929).

The most popular film at the beginning of 1929 was another film distributed by Prometheus, Pudovkin's *Storm over Asia*. On 26 January 1929 the Marmorhaus in Berlin celebrated its fiftieth sold-out screening of the film, and according to an advertisement in *Film-Kurier* (26 January 1929), two hundred Berlin theaters were screening *Storm over Asia*. It was within the context of increasing commercial success that Prometheus negotiated with British Phototone, contemplated the construction of a film studio in Berlin, and announced plans to produce impressive sound films, featuring directors such as Ozep and Pudovkin plus stars like Anna Sten. A short time later, following the Tobis-Klangfilm merger, Prometheus realized that it would be unable to join major German producers in their transition to sound film. The company modified its plans and concentrated on the production and marketing of what it hoped would be commercially successful silent films.

BEYOND THE STREET

The success of *Storm over Asia* and *The Living Corpse* enabled Prometheus to produce its next film without assistance from Meschrabpom. The Prometheus executives commissioned Alfred Tuscherer, the brother-in-law of Kurt Bernhardt and his assistant in *Schinderhannes*, to manage production. Jan Fethke, who also supervised publicity, and Willi Döll wrote the script. Leo Mittler, a stage director with limited film experience, directed the film. As the title suggests, Fethke and Döll based their script on the commercially successful street films. Economic and political interests influenced the thematic orientation.[17]

Beyond the Street presents the story of a young unemployed man, an older beggar, and an attractive prostitute who are drawn together by a pearl necklace. The story begins with the young man. He meets the beggar and describes his unsuccessful search for work. The beggar sympathizes and invites him to stay in his dilapidated houseboat. The young man accepts and spends his days looking for work while his older friend sits on street corners, pretends to be blind, and solicits donations with his music box. One day the beggar watches an elegantly dressed woman drop a pearl necklace on the street. He recovers the necklace and tries to conceal it before anyone notices. But a prostitute observes the event and, although she leaves, is unable to forget what she has seen. Later, after an especially prosperous day, the beggar invites the young man to a neighborhood bar. There they see the prostitute. She recognizes the beggar and dances with the young man. He eventually rescues her from a drunken sailor, and she takes him home with her. The next morning the prostitute prepares breakfast for her new lover and offers to share her apartment with him. Just then the landlady interrupts them and demands payment. The prostitute gives her some money, promises to deliver the rest that night, and then dresses for work. Only now does the young man realize that he has fallen in love with a prostitute. He promises to free her from prostitution, and when she asks how, he mentions the beggar's necklace. The prostitute offers to sell it to a friend, suggesting that they all will profit from the sale. When the young man explains the proposition to the beggar, he rejects it vehemently, and the young man must return to his

Beyond the Street: Illustrierter Film-Kurier program cover. (Staatliches Filmarchiv der DDR)

Beyond the Street: the prostitute and the young man meet in a neighborhood bar. (Stiftung Deutsche Kinemathek)

lover with the bad news. She becomes cynical and exclaims: "Leave me alone! It doesn't matter anyway. You can't really get out of this filth." The young man flees, wanders through the streets, and eventually returns to the houseboat. There he fights with the beggar, then chases him along the waterfront. The beggar falls into the water and drowns while clinging to his pearl necklace.

The story differed significantly from those of earlier street films. Unlike films such as *The Street* and *Tragedy of a Prostitute* with their emphasis on middle-class protagonists, *Beyond the Street* presented working-class and lumpen-proletarian protagonists.[18] Instead of portraying them as inherently and unalterably criminal inhabitants of a self-perpetuating evil world, it suggested that the existing social system forced compassionate and honest people to adopt criminal methods of survival. *Beyond the Street* challenged the portrayal of the street in mainstream films by positing an image of social totality. According to its image, affluence and poverty coexisted in an interdependent relationship. And some of the impoverished rejected the consequences of the relationship for themselves but were unable to initiate change.

The narrative employed numerous techniques to convince spectators that its image of the street was more authentic and more representative than that of previous street films. Except for Lissi Arna, who played the prostitute, the actors were relatively unknown, and the characters were nameless. *Beyond the Street* encouraged spectators to accept its characters as types, not as unique individuals. In addition, documentary film footage of bustling harbor scenes, busy urban streets, and tenement housing areas suggested its characters were authentic inhabitants of contemporary society. However, the most effective element of the narrative's realism was its frame story.

Before the unemployed young man and the beggar meet, a well-constructed framing segment introduces the characters and plot. It does so in a way that suggests authenticity and typicality while stimulating curiosity. The frame begins with an establishing shot of a sidewalk café. The camera slowly tracks in to the café, makes its way between the tables, and stops behind a cigar-smoking man with a newspaper. The perspective allows the spectator to read the following headlines with him: "Last speech by Poincaré in Geneva," "Express Train Catastrophe," and "Boxing Match for the Heavyweight Title." An accompanying intertitle draws a connection between the individual headlines and the general course of events: "Newspaper copies in the millions . . . daily. Ten thousand stories . . . daily. Ten thousand fates, and who thinks about it between a mocha and a cigar?" The intertitle suggests that newspaper readers like this one have little concern for the individual stories.

The newspaper slowly rises, and beneath it the man (and the audience) can see the slender legs of a woman. During the following sequence, the camera first assumes an observer's perspective, allowing spectators to watch as the man moves his newspaper to one side and begins to flirt. At this point he can be identified as the well-dressed, overweight caricature of a Prussian bourgeois. In the next shot, the camera returns to his perspective and scans the woman's body from her waist down. Then the perspective resumes a position behind him, from which spectators watch the newspaper rise again. A close-up depicts the woman as she seductively crosses her legs. Now the man straightens his newspaper and reads an article: "Murder or accident? This morning the corpse of a man was pulled from the water at the Paris Bridge. His meager clothing was so badly torn in places that officials suspect he was in a fight. Remarkable in this regard is that the old man . . ." Finally, the camera tracks in on the last phrase of the interrupted report: "the old man . . ."

As the framing segment reveals, Fethke, Döll, and Mittler constructed a tightly knit narrative with conventional photographic and montage techniques to introduce the main plot. Infrequent omniscient intertitles and the newspaper suggest its authenticity and typicality, but the primary signifiers are the images and their presentation. Costumes, gestures, camera angles and perspectives, as well as montage indicate the attitude of the bourgeois man and identify the woman as a prostitute. By interrupting the story about the old man and formulating the headline as a question, the narrative stimulates curiosity. The track-in to the last phrase provides a transitional element from the frame to the main plot.

The next scene begins with a low-level street shot, depicting the swiftly moving legs of passing pedestrians. The perspective slowly moves along the curb, through the legs, and stops before the old beggar with his music box. The reference to the old man at the end of the frame and his appearance now suggest that the newspaper article was about this beggar. The juxtaposition of the anonymous legs of the passing pedestrians and the motionless old beggar suggests that the quick pace of modern society inhibits interpersonal contact and compassion. Like the disinterested newspaper reader, the pedestrians show no concern for the beggar. Suddenly, a small child emerges from the stream of pedestrians and watches with amazement as the beggar plays his music box. Although frightened by his expressionless face, the child shyly places a coin in the beggar's hat. Following a close-up of the hat, the beggar prepares to acknowledge the gift mechanically, but then returns the coin to the child with a smile. The child buys some ice cream with the coin and disappears into the traffic. As the scene concludes the beggar collects his gear, stands, and slowly crosses the street, intersecting the flow of traffic. A short symbolic sequence, including images of rhythmically moving plant life and water reflections, punctuates his movement and strengthens the contrast between the bustling pedestrians and the lethargic beggar. It also offers a transition to the location of the next segment: the rural environment of the beggar's home.

With absolutely no intertitles, the narration (which bears a striking resemblance to Eisenstein's in the street scenes of *Battleship Potemkin*) establishes a clear contrast between a fast-moving, anonymous, and unfeeling society and the compassionate, slow-moving beggar. It also initiates the audience's emotional connection with the film's protagonists while reinforcing a negative image of the existing social system. In the following scene, the beggar demonstrates his compassion again by offering to share his houseboat. Later, the prostitute expresses her dissatisfaction with her profession and her wish to develop a sincere, loving relationship. And the young man searches incessantly for employment. But in the end, the necklace destroys the relationships between all of them.

When the beggar sinks into the water, still clinging to the necklace, images of asphalt fade in, replacing those of water. The narrative now returns to the café and resumes the frame story. The bourgeois man continues reading the article, as the audience reads along: "Remarkable in this regard is that the old man held a pearl necklace in his fist which, upon closer inspection, turned out to be a worthless imitation. The suspect is a young unemployed man who lived with the old man. He has not been seen since yesterday." Beneath the article is an advertisement for a widower's ball. The man circles it with a pencil, shows it to the woman at the next table, and says: "There's where we'll go." For the first time the spectator sees the woman's face and realizes that she is the prostitute of the main plot. In the concluding sequence, the bourgeois and his escort emerge from the stream of pedestrians. The man's stomach completely overshadows his companion's figure. While he flirts, her glance comes to rest on the spot where the beggar sat. Her facial expression reveals the sad memory of what has transpired. As she and her admirer pass the spot, they merge again into the flow of traffic.[19]

The closing frame segment solidifies the narrative's image of social totality. By revealing that the pearl necklace was a worthless imitation, the newspaper article strengthens skepticism about existing social values and the protagonists' decision to accept those values, join the quest for material wealth, and ultimately destroy their relationships. At the same time, images of the self-satisfied and dominating man, who directs the remorseful but submissive prostitute into the stream of anonymous pedestrians, reinforce the initial image of the street. According to the film's narrative perspective, the street is a place where the rich and the poor coexist interdependently. It is a place where fast-paced, acquisitive modern society threatens what little compassion remains between human beings. It also is a place where those who would prefer to make an honest living and develop healthy interpersonal relationships often are forced to adopt cold and calculating methods of survival.

Beyond the Street had its premiere on 10 October 1929, in Berlin's Atrium Theater. The mainstream reviews were very positive (see, for example, "Prometheus Erfolg," *Film-Kurier*, 11 October 1929). The Communist newspapers also responded enthusiastically. Instead of drawing attention to the film's subtle social criticism and rejecting the conclusion for being too pessimistic, reviews in *Die Welt am Abend* and *Berlin am Morgen* contrasted the film with previous street films and emphasized its higher artistic quality and realistic portrayal of the working-class environment. Despite the positive press response, *Beyond the Street* was unable to generate as much profit as did *Storm over Asia* and *The Living Corpse*.

There were two major reasons for its lack of success. First, during the final months of 1929, as the economic crisis deepened, the German public spent less on entertainment, and as the transition to sound film progressed, the popularity of silent films gradually decreased. Second, the cost of production made it difficult for Prometheus to realize a substantial profit with *Beyond the Street*. According to Willi Döll, Tuscherer mismanaged the film's production.[20] Although the team finished much of *Beyond the Street* in the Jofa studios in Johannisthal near Berlin, Tuscherer also organized a filming expedition in Holland. There the Prometheus crew, including the cameraman Friedl Behn-Grund, collected documentary footage of harbor scenes and expended 30,000 marks. Tuscherer sacrificed another 30,000 marks to attract Lissi Arna and, Döll claims, retained 3,000 marks for himself. The remaining production required an additional 30,000 marks. For a small company like Prometheus with only a limited reputation (and budget), Tuscherer's expenditures were very high. As a result of his mismanagement, Prometheus replaced Tuscherer in September 1929. Juri Spielmann, whom Döll described as an indecisive party functionary, assumed the production manager's position, and following the premiere of *Beyond the Street,* Prometheus concentrated on its next film, *Mother Krause's Journey to Happiness.*

MOTHER KRAUSE'S JOURNEY TO HAPPINESS

During the production of *Beyond the Street,* one of Berlin's most popular artists, Heinrich Zille, died. Zille had attracted broad public interest with his sketches of working-class people and their environment beginning at the turn of the century. By 1925 his work was so popular that commercial filmmakers had begun to produce "Zille" films, including *The Notorious* and *The Illegitimate.* The portrayal of the working class and its environment in these films for the most part resembled that of the street in films such as *The Street* and *Tragedy of a Prostitute* (see Chapter 8). The Zille films characterized most inhabitants of the proletarian sphere as inherently bad, while suggesting that upper-class individuals were compassionate and philanthropic.

The Zille films stimulated at least as much criticism as the street films among the German left. Leftist cultural activists rejected them; they claimed that producers used the artist's name to maximize profit by suggesting that Heinrich Zille, whom the working class accepted as a trustworthy and sympathetic artist, endorsed or was in some way associated with them. When Zille died, some of his friends, including Otto Nagel, Hans Baluschek, and Käthe Kollwitz, encouraged Prometheus to challenge the ideological orientation of the commercial films with a true Zille film in commemoration of the artist.

Prometheus agreed and assembled a production team that consisted to a large extent of those who had produced *Beyond the Street.* The Fethke-Döll team provided a script, Robert Scharfenberg and Karl Haacker designed the sets, and Friedrich Gnass, the drunken sailor in *Beyond the Street,* played Max, a class-conscious worker. Only Mittler left the team. Phil Jutzi, who had worked extensively as a documentarist for Weltfilm and assisted cameraman A. Golovnja in *The Living Corpse,* took his place and functioned both as director and cameraman.

Mother Krause's Journey to Happiness portrays the plight of a proletarian mother and her two children.[21] Mother Krause's newspaper route and the rent collected from a man and his prostitute-girlfriend, who occupy one room of their apartment, provide the family's only source of income. A crisis develops when the son, Paul, squanders the money he

Mother Krause's Journey to Happiness: Illustrierter Film-Kurier program cover. (Staatliches Filmarchiv der DDR)

has collected for newspapers on beer. He leaves the family virtually penniless and forces each member to consider alternate methods for raising the employer's 20 marks. Numerous possible solutions emerge. Mother Krause tries to borrow the money, but none of the well-dressed men she contacts is willing to help her. Paul resorts to burglary, shoots at a pawnbroker in panic, and eventually surrenders to the police. Erna, Paul's sister, attempts prostitution. The middle-class man she solicits disgusts her, and she runs to her Marxist boyfriend, Max, who is participating in a demonstration. Erna joins him and later learns that he will provide the necessary money. Before the good news reaches Mother Krause, she becomes distraught and commits suicide. Max and Erna return too late to rescue her, and the film concludes with a flashback of the couple marching together in the demonstration.

In many ways the production of *Beyond the Street* served as a model

Mother Krause's Journey to Happiness: advertisement materials include posters by Käthe Kollwitz and Otto Nagel. (Staatliches Filmarchiv der DDR)

for the makers of *Mother Krause's Journey to Happiness.* Once again their intention was to convince audiences that the cinematic fiction was both authentic and typical. In contrast to the production of *Beyond the Street,* the Prometheus team also strove to minimize expenditures. For both reasons they engaged less well known stage players and relatively inexperienced film actors. In addition, Otto Nagel searched for and hired authentic Zille types to play minor roles. While Nagel looked for typical characters, Scharfenberg and Haacker walked through the working-class community Berlin-Wedding to find representative settings. At the same time, Jutzi, guided by the Fethke-Döll script, constructed a cohesive narrative, integrating documentary footage with staged scenes in natural settings and scenes filmed in the Berlin Jofa studios.

The exposition of *Mother Krause's Journey to Happiness* clearly illustrates the resulting effect. The film begins with a handwritten text, describing Berlin-Wedding as the home of enslaved workers, the poor, playful children, invalids, drunks, beggars, and prostitutes. The text is signed "Heinrich Zille" and followed by documentary shots that visually introduce the working-class environment. Individual segments of Zille's text interrupt the sequence, suggesting that the documentary footage portrays what Zille has described. Throughout the sequence a tracking and panning camera maintains the eye-level perspective of an observer, allowing spectators to imagine themselves moving within the milieu. The association between what the text describes and its visual representation invites the audience to ascribe the same degree of authenticity and typicality to the filmic portrayal as they do to Heinrich Zille's artworks.

Omniscient intertitles replace Zille's text and accompany a series of sequences; together they introduce Mother Krause and her family. Following the final text segment, the camera tracks from the street level over a narrow, enclosed tenement yard up to the window of an apartment. An intertitle explains that it is Mother Krause's apartment. The camera tracks into the apartment and stops with a medium shot of a dancing couple. After another intertitle, introducing the dancers as Mother Krause's daughter, Erna, and a boarder, a second sequence juxtaposes the dancing couple and people in the tenement yard. An association between the scene in the yard and the scene in the apartment begins with the connection between an organ-grinder, who entertains the people in the yard, and the dancers. The montage suggests that Erna and the boarder are dancing to the music in the yard, and the juxtaposition of women dancing below and the couple dancing in the apartment reinforces the association. When the boarder draws Erna closer and grabs her breast, she pushes him away and becomes visibly upset. Before her emotional response ends, the perspective shifts to the yard. There the organ-grinder's monkey, who wears a hat similar to Erna's, just behaves as Erna did in the previous shot. When Mother Krause scolds Erna's frivolity, she does so in Berlin dialect, and a cut to the yard shifts attention to a close-up of a crying child.

With a variety of signifiers—the Zille description, dialogue intertitles in Berlin dialect, montage juxtaposition—the narrative establishes a strong connection between the individual working-class family and what it portrays as an authentic working-class milieu. Throughout the exposition the narrative style resembles that of the frame segment in *Beyond the Street*; however, as the plot unfolds, a major difference emerges.

Although the working-class environments of *Beyond the Street* and *Mother Krause's Journey to Happiness* include similar lumpen-proletarian as well as proletarian types, their narratives organize them differently. Whereas the story of the beggar, unemployed young man, and prostitute progresses in a relatively straightforward sequential manner, the story of Mother Krause, her children, the proletarian Max, and the lumpen-proletarian boarder unfolds much more hypotactically, with frequent parallel montage sequences. Some sequences contrast the methods used by Mother Krause, Paul, and Erna to collect the money they need; others contrast Max and the boarder as they interact with Erna. In the process, the narrative encourages the audience to sympathize with Erna in her developing relationship to Max and ultimately to affirm their political solution to the family's problems. The scenes in which Erna turns to Max for help, Paul burglarizes a pawnshop with the lumpen-proletarian boarder, and Mother Krause commits suicide exemplify the narrative thrust.

Initially Erna and Paul accept the boarder's schemes to collect money. He proposes burglary to Paul and prostitution to Erna. After her well-dressed, overweight bourgeois client attacks her in his apartment, she flees. The spectator next sees Erna running to Max's apartment, where she learns that he is at a demonstration. Erna leaves the apartment slowly and stops twice. A close-up of her facial expression indicates that she has made a decision. She no longer hesitates. The narrative perspective moves with Erna, allowing spectators to imagine her perspective while following behind her. In the next scene the perspective shifts from long shots of Erna and the demonstrators walking in opposite directions to medium shots of the demonstrators marching toward what the spectator imagines to be Erna's position. In the background a sign demands: "Working women join the ranks!" Before Erna joins the demonstrators, the narrative perspective does. The spectator now observes Erna from within the ranks of the demonstrators as she continues to look for Max. Occasionally the perspective merges with hers, shifting from shoes of individual demonstrators to shots of their marching feet. Eventually, Erna recognizes something and begins to walk with the marchers. The narrative perspective again moves with her as she joins Max in the demonstration. The view now moves from their feet, which begin to march together, back to their smiling faces.

The scene encourages working-class audiences to identify with Erna as she joins the demonstration. The exposition earlier suggested that she and her family are typical representatives of the working class. Here Erna represents all working-class women whom the sign orders to "join the ranks." By staging the demonstration in the streets of Berlin and including hundreds of real workers, the filmmakers strengthen the association between working-class filmgoers, Erna, and the demonstrators. But the most effective technique is the use of photography and montage. With it the Prometheus team simultaneously conveys the dynamic quality of the demonstration and draws the audience and Erna into it.

The juxtaposition of segments following the demonstration further motivates identification with Erna. In the first scene Max and Erna decide to attend a workers' festival. Some workers remind Mother Krause of her woes by singing, "We will drink granny's little house away." She leaves, and when Max asks for an explanation, Erna describes the family's problems. Max immediately offers assistance. As the festival progresses, parallel montage sequences depict Paul and the unfolding burglary. When Max offers to help Erna, the sequence shifts again to the pawnshop, then repeatedly from the burglary to the apartment where Mother Krause worries. The audience, which knows that Max will help, must watch with increasing dismay, while the police arrest Paul, and Mother Krause commits suicide. The narrative's order of events urges perception of Paul's and Mother Krause's behavior as both futile and unnecessary, thus strengthening identification with Erna.

The narrative style employed by the producers of *Mother Krause's Journey to Happiness* enabled them to present a more differentiated image of the working-class milieu than appeared in the commercial street films, Zille films, or even in *Beyond the Street*. It distinguished between an older generation (Mother Krause), whose members accepted existing social values and blamed themselves for unemployment and poverty, and a younger, less fatalistic generation. It also distinguished between lumpen-proletarians (the boarder and Paul), whose rejection of social values manifested itself in criminal action, and the proletarians (Max and Erna) who demanded social change.[22] While positing their more differentiated image, the producers asserted an even greater claim to authenticity and associated the audience's perspective with that of fictional protagonists more intensely than Gerhard Lamprecht or Leo Mittler had done.

Mother Krause's Journey to Happiness had its premiere on 30 December 1929 in Berlin's Alhambra Theater. Although some critics characterized the film as agitational (*8-Uhr Abendblatt*, 31 December 1929), most trade journals and newspapers recommended it enthusiastically. The IAH newspapers were especially positive in their reviews, focusing specifically on the film's realistic portrayal and its emotional appeal. Even Alfred Durus found little to criticize (*Die Rote Fahne*, 1 January 1930). Durus outlined the differences between *Mother Krause's Journey to Happiness* and earlier Prometheus films, emphasizing its authenticity and revolutionary quality. For him, the choice of Berlin-Wedding as the center of production and the narrative differentiation between the criminal lumpen proletarians and the class-conscious proletarians made it a much better film than *Beyond the Street.* Its only weakness, in Durus's estimation, was the somewhat indirect and symbolic, instead of concrete, reference to the social causes for the family's plight.

During its first week in the Berlin theaters, the producers of another film, *Zwischen Spree und Panke* (*Between the Spree and Panke*), claimed that their film was the true Zille film and filed a protest against Prometheus for plagiarism (see "Polizei und Gerichte um den Zille-Film"—"Police and Courts on the Zille Film," *L.B.B.*, 8 January 1929). The first regional court in Berlin rejected the complaint, and the film began an extremely successful run in theaters all over Germany. According to a poll of 1,138 theaters taken by *Film-Kurier* (31 May 1930), it was the 24th most popular film in Germany of 1930.

THE DISSOLUTION OF PROMETHEUS AND *KUHLE WAMPE*

As the transition to sound progressed and the economic crisis intensified, Prometheus found it increasingly difficult to sustain itself. In 1930 the company produced only six short travelogues from documentary footage collected in Rotterdam, but it continued to distribute Soviet feature films, including *Das Lied vom alten Markt* (*The Song of the Old Market*), *Der Mann, der sein Gedächtnis verlor* (*The Man Who Lost His Memory*), *Der blaue Expreß* (*The Blue Express*), and *Igdenbu, der große Jäger* (*Igdenbu, the Great Hunter*).[23] Prometheus also tried to remain competitive by producing a sound version of *Battleship Potemkin* and by distributing an inexpensive sound film about bicycle racing, *Rivalen im Weltrekord* (*Rivals for the World Record*).

Each of the Soviet films received generally positive reviews, but none was successful enough to enable Prometheus to initiate its own sound film production. It is also likely that Münzenburg, the IAH, and the Soviet film industry were unwilling to invest in Prometheus significantly at a time when the Comintern and the KPD hoped that revolutionary political activity would render cultural activity temporarily superfluous. In 1931 distribution continued to be the company's primary activity. Three

The Way into Life: Prometheus distributes first Soviet sound film in Germany, *Illustrierter Film-Kurier* program cover. (Staatliches Filmarchiv der DDR)

Soviet films, Dovschenko's *Erde* (*Earth*), *Feuertransport* (*Fire Transport*), and the first Soviet sound film, *The Way into Life,* attracted large audiences.[24] Despite the relative popularity of the films, theater owners offered very little for the right to screen them.[25] Most owners booked Prometheus films, if at all, for two- or three-day periods and paid from one hundred to three hundred marks. At the same time National Socialist organizations began a boycott of all films they considered to be Bolshevist. The previously tolerant creditors withheld further support for Prometheus, and the company suspended payments at the end of 1931. In February of 1932, following a court settlement, Prometheus formally dissolved.[26]

As late as 1931 Prometheus announced plans for production, including a sound film comedy to be directed by Phil Jutzi and an adaptation of Émile Zola's *Germinal.* The company produced neither film but did assist in the first phase of another project. Following his work on *How the Worker Lives,* Slatan Dudow developed a plan to produce a sound feature with little or no money.[27] Bertolt Brecht decided to accept Dudow's proposal for enlisting the help of the Communist-led Fichte Sport Club. The club members responded enthusiastically, gathering over four thousand members from other sports clubs to participate in what was the German left's first sound feature and its last major film before Hitler assumed power in 1933. The film was *Kuhle Wampe.*

The interaction between Dudow, Brecht, and the Fichte Sport Club characterized the film's production. In addition to budgetary constraints, the radically democratic aesthetic models developed by Brecht and his colleagues significantly influenced work on *Kuhle Wampe.* By 1931 Brecht had formulated his *Lehrstücktheorie* and had completed a number of *Lehrstück* experiments.[28] With his new plays Brecht strove to increase the participation of players as well as audiences in production, to disrupt the dramatic illusion of reality, to encourage emotionally engaged and intellectually critical reception, and to orient reception toward reflection about the relationship between dramatic fiction and everyday life. Following an enthusiastic collaboration with Berlin's Karl-Marx-Schule in rehearsing, performing, and reworking the *Jasager* material in 1930, Brecht was ready to undertake a similar experiment with film.

As the project developed, Hanns Eisler, who was the leading KPD proponent of a radically democratic alternative to traditional forms of artistic production and reception, joined the collective and began composing music for the film. Once Brecht and Dudow had produced an exposé, Ernst Ottwalt, a member of the BPRS who had developed a narrative style similar to that of Brecht's epic theater, stepped in and assisted in completing the final script.[29] Prometheus provided its set designers, Scharfenberg and Haacker. In August 1931 Günter Krampf replaced Weizenberg, a cameraman whom the collective had perceived to be unwilling to adopt its aesthetic orientation. Members from leftist theater groups, including the Gruppe junger Schauspieler, and agitprop groups such as Das rote Sprachrohr played leading roles in the film, in addition to the volunteers from the various sports organizations. According to Brecht, as the collective grew, the interaction of its members became at least as important as the product of their efforts.[30]

Interruptions slowed the production of *Kuhle Wampe,* which lasted over a year. The producers periodically exhausted their operating capital, and their creditors occasionally threatened to withdraw support.[31] Filming began in August 1931, and after Prometheus dissolved in February

1932, the Prasens film company, with the financial backing of Lazar Wechsler, purchased the rights to *Kuhle Wampe* and finished production in March 1932. Prasens also submitted the film to the censors, who rejected it twice before accepting a substantially edited version at the end of April. Finally, on 30 May 1932, *Kuhle Wampe* had its premiere in Berlin's Atrium Theater.

The opening sequences of *Kuhle Wampe* depict unemployed workers racing on bicycles through the streets of Berlin in a futile search for work. One of them, the young Franz Bönicke, has been unemployed for six months. When he returns to his home for dinner, Franz learns that his unemployment compensation has expired, and his parents scold him. His sister Anni suggests that there are social causes for the family's predicament, but Father Bönicke continues to blame his son. In desperation the son commits suicide. In the aftermath of the suicide Anni asks the landlord and various welfare agencies for assistance with the family's rent payments. No one is willing to help, and a judge finally evicts them. Anni's boyfriend, Fritz, suggests that the family move to Kuhle Wampe, a large tent colony outside Berlin. There Anni becomes pregnant. Her father demands that she marry Fritz and arranges an engagement party. At the celebration Fritz reveals that he feels trapped by the marriage. Anni responds by breaking the engagement and moving in with her friend, Gerda. Anni also returns to her sports club where fellow members collect the money she needs for an abortion. Fritz, who in the meantime has lost his job, searches for and finds Anni with her friends at the sports club. He joins them in preparing for a festival, during which the participants interact and discuss politics. Anni races with her rowing team; she and Fritz join others in singing Eisler's song of solidarity; and everyone listens as an agitprop group depicts a family whose members deny a landlord the right to evict them. While returning home from the festival on the S-Bahn, some of the participants argue with a businessman who is indifferent toward farmers who burn coffee bean crops to inflate prices. The workers condemn the practice and ask the man, who will change the system? The film ends when they assert that the dissatisfied will change it.

The narrative style of *Kuhle Wampe* in some ways resembles that of earlier Prometheus films. As was the case in *Beyond the Street,* the incorporation of newspaper material establishes a solid connection with everyday life. Before the unemployed workers begin their search for work, a fairly rapid sequence of documentary shots depicts the Brandenburg Gate, factory yards with smokestacks, and blocks of tenement houses.

Kuhle Wampe: unemployed in search of work. (Staatliches Filmarchiv der DDR)

(Over 60 percent of *Kuhle Wampe* was filmed in everyday settings.) A second sequence presents headlines from recent Berlin newspapers. Toward the end of the sequence the tempo accelerates as headlines indicating the increasing unemployment replace general headlines about national and international political developments. Following a number of national unemployment figures, the final headline asserts: "315,000 Unemployed in Berlin—100,000 Unemployed without Support."

The sequences encourage the audience to accept what follows as an authentic portrayal of working-class conditions in Germany during the escalating crisis of 1931—and the Bönicke family as typical working-class Germans. The exposition resembles that of *Mother Krause's Journey to Happiness.* The sequence of headlines suggests that unemployment is a widespread problem in Germany, and the final headline asserts that the rate of unemployment in Berlin exemplifies the national problem. The focusing process continues: in the next sequence, a number of unemployed men are searching for work on their bicycles, implying that the cyclists represent Berlin's unemployed. Finally, Franz emerges from the group as he returns home for dinner, making the final connection between the group of unemployed workers and his family. The Bönickes, according to the developing narrative, typify unemployed, working-class Germans during the crisis of 1931.

Throughout the film the narrative reinforces the image of typicality. During the suicide sequence, for example, shots of the bicyclists from the previous segment interrupt the action. The shots renew the association between Franz and the unemployed masses while illustrating his thoughts. Later, after he has plunged to his death, some children gather and attempt to locate the window from which he jumped. Their indecisiveness implies that it could have been almost any window or almost any family.

In addition to ascribing authenticity and typicality to the fictional portrayal, the narrative invites spectators to draw connections between various elements and to complete the production of a partially programmed ideological viewpoint. The transition from the suicide to the eviction sequence provides a good example. At the end of the suicide sequence two women discuss what has happened. They uncritically recite typical comments and conclude: "Such a young person. He really had the best part of his life ahead of him." The final comment becomes the heading for what follows. Before the audience sees Anni and watches as she requests assistance with the family's rent payments, a title introduces the segment: "The Best Part of a Young Person's Life." The title prompts spectators to decide whether young Franz really did have his best years before him. Anni's failure, the family's eviction, and their marginal existence in the tent colony indicate that the cliché can be false.

Here, as at various points throughout the film, spectators are encouraged to challenge traditional perceptions of social organization and interaction, including that of mass media entertainment. One of the most impressive juxtapositions, the oft-cited Mata Hari sequence, motivates audiences to question the popular image of the culture industry as an apolitical institution of entertainment. The sequence also contributes to the narrative's effort to undermine its own authority.

At the beginning of the scene Father and Mother Bönicke appear at a small table in their tent. A tapestry with a traditional motto embroidered into it suggests that even here the Bönickes cling to the facade of a middle-class existence. Father Bönicke reinforces the impression by smoking a cigar, reading a newspaper, and paying no attention to his wife. He reads a *feuilleton* story about Mata Hari aloud: "I am a courtesan but not a spy, a courtesan who exacted a high price for her love. I was a courtesan who demanded and received fifteen thousand, yes, thirty thousand marks as the going price. That was the refrain of Mata Hari's defense." A close-up depicts the worried face of Mother Bönicke. During this and the following shots, Father Bönicke continues to read aloud a description of Mata Hari's sexual adventures. The sequence progresses with shifts from shots of the father, who raises the newspaper so that it blocks his view of Mother Bönicke, to shots of the mother, who calculates a grocery list, and to close-ups of individual items and prices. Finally, there is a pan to the right, Anni enters, and the sequence concludes with a shot of a worried look from Mother Bönicke.

During the sequence, the Mata Hari story gradually engrosses Father Bönicke and renders him oblivious to what transpires around him. While he escapes into the fictional world of the newspaper, the juxtaposition of his descriptions and his wife's calculations serves to remind spectators that mass media entertainment, by inviting audiences to associate themselves with fictional characters, provides only a temporary and artificial escape from everyday concerns. The sequence encourages spectators to reject the vicarious pleasure Father Bönicke derives from reading about Mata Hari and to sympathize with his wife by overlapping his audio description with the visual portrayal of her maternal concern for the entire family. By implication, the narrative draws attention to its own potential entertainment value and encourages the audience to challenge it.

Although some of the narrative elements in *Kuhle Wampe* ascribe authenticity and typicality to the fictional portrayal and occasionally allow spectators to sympathize with one of its characters, as the Mata Hari sequence demonstrates, others disrupt the dramatic illusion of reality and dissuade the spectator from associating uncritically with a specific character or ideological viewpoint. The titles that introduce each segment (for example, "The Best Part of a Young Person's Life"), like those of Brecht's epic dramas, interrupt the narrative flow and encourage the audience's intellectual engagement. They do so by commenting ironically on the unfolding plot, by foreshadowing what will transpire, and, in every case, by minimizing the potential for building suspense.

Sound, too, functions as a disorienting element. For example, when Franz returns from his unsuccessful search for work, the family members speak in a cold and detached manner, avoiding an emotional appeal to the spectator. Occasionally a commentator interrupts the action and offers an unemotional, factual report—for example, the introduction of the tent colony. The music also consistently prevents the audience from being drawn emotionally into the developing plot. Eisler explained the music's function well when describing his intention for the music that accompanied the exposition's visual images: "From *Kuhle Wampe*, 1931 by Dudow-Brecht. Deteriorated houses on the edge of the city, slum district in all its misery and filth. The mood of the image is passive, depressing: it invites melancholy. Counterposed to that is fast-paced, sharp music, a polyphonic prelude, marcato style. The contrast of the music . . . to the straightforward montage of images creates a shock that, according to the intention, stimulates opposition more than sympathetic sentimentality."[32]

Even at the end of the film, the narrative supplies no individual hero and posits no clear solution to the portrayed crisis. Instead, it suggests that working-class people, like those who attend the sports festival, must join together and develop their own strategy for social organization. When the festival participants finally ask who will change the world, the response is: "Those who are not pleased about it!" Exactly how they will change it remains unanswered. The concluding shots of the participants walking together into an S-Bahn tunnel and a final repetition of the song of solidarity suggest only that the dissatisfied must join forces and cooperate.

According to an advertisement for *Kuhle Wampe* in the *L.B.B.* (7 June 1932), fourteen thousand people attended performances at the Atrium Theater during the first week. The theater's owner prolonged the engagement for an additional week, and seventeen other Berlin theaters screened it in June. Nevertheless, *Kuhle Wampe* failed to sustain public interest in Berlin, much less in the rest of Germany. There are a number of potential reasons for its commercial weakness. The most obvious reason is that Brecht, Dudow, Ottwalt, Eisler, and the other members of the production team rejected commercial formulas. They defined success in part in terms of the degree of cooperative participation in production. From their perspective, by involving over four thousand people in making the film, the project at least partially succeeded.

The producers also hoped to involve audiences in producing the film's ideological orientation. Instead of inviting audiences to enter a fictional world where authoritarian heroes protect the masses from external as well as internal threats and where success is guaranteed for those who persevere, *Kuhle Wampe* confronted them with a plausible portrayal of the existing crisis. Instead of stimulating uncritical reception by constructing a cohesive narrative and encouraging spectators to sympathize with its protagonists, the film disrupted the dramatic illusion of reality in order to engage them intellectually. In short, *Kuhle Wampe* prevented spectators from interacting with it as they had grown accustomed to interacting with mainstream films.

The censors' decision to remove substantial segments further disturbed its cohesion, and consequently the film deviated from established codes of cinematic entertainment more than the producers had intended. *Kuhle Wampe* confused filmgoers who expected seamless entertainment. It shocked those who either were satisfied with the existing social system or promoted authoritarian alternatives.

The production of *Kuhle Wampe* posited a more radically democratic alternative to commercial German cinema than any other film of the Social Democratic or Communist left during the Weimar era. Films such as *Bookkeeper Kremke* and *Mother Krause's Journey to Happiness* reached larger audiences, but they did so by adopting established narrative techniques from the solidifying cinematic institution. The content of such films promoted a higher degree of social equity and a reliance on democratic forms of social organization. But, by reinforcing the authoritarian relationship between narrative and spectator, their codes of communication perpetuated the public's susceptibility to authoritarian leadership. Of the films produced by Prometheus, *One + One = Three,* the final segment of Ozep's *The Living Corpse,* and *Kuhle Wampe* were the only ones to experiment seriously with alternative narrative codes that encouraged audiences to exercise emotional and intellectual skills by participating in the production of their ideological orientation. And *Kuhle Wampe* was the only project designed specifically to maximize the cooperative interaction of everyone involved in production. As such, *Kuhle Wampe* provided the most advanced model for radically democratic film production and reception before 1933.

16

THE INEVITABLE DECLINE OF THE VFV

While Prometheus struggled commercially and finally dissolved in 1932, the VFV continued its campaign to develop a grass-roots alternative to mainstream cinema. Shortly after Heinrich Mann reasserted the VFV's intention to produce films ("Aufruf"—"Challenge," *Film und Volk*, November 1928: 2), the organization cooperated with Weltfilm and the Theater am Schiffbauerdamm in producing a film about the miserable working and living conditions in the coal-mining district of Waldenburg. Leo Lania wrote the script, emphasizing that *Hunger in Waldenburg* would present a realistic image of working-class Germany.[1] Phil Jutzi directed the film, and a number of amateur actors, such as Holmes Zimmerman (who appeared as Paul in *Mother Krause's Journey to Happiness*), and people from the Waldenburg area played the leading roles. *Hunger in Waldenburg* had its premiere in Berlin's Tauentzienpalast on 16 March 1929.

HUNGER IN WALDENBURG

The film tells the story of a young man who decides to seek new employment in a coal-mining town when he learns that the owners of the textile mill where he presently works have again cut his wages. After bidding farewell to his despondent parents, the son travels by foot past a snow-covered palace and enters the coal-mining town where black smoke billows from the stacks of huge industrial plants. There the young man searches for work; he grows hungry and eventually steals a fish from a display in front of a corner grocery store. A worker who has observed the theft convinces him to return the fish, listens to his story, and offers help. Together they go to the apartment of a young widow who allows the newcomer to stay with her.

The young man gradually learns that life in the coal-mining town is no better than in his previous home. The widow explains that three hundred families live in her tenement building. Seven people occupy a room, and the landlord evicts those who fail to pay their rent. The widow's husband died in the mines, and she believes that she would have committed suicide long ago if she had no children. In addition to hearing about the misfortunes of others, the young man receives a letter notifying him that his application for unemployment benefits has been rejected. When he enters the widow's room one night, apparently intending to sleep with her, he notices the slumbering children and retreats.

The film's concluding segment depicts events in the tenement house prior to the day when the tenants must pay their rent. The wife of a family in a neighboring apartment goes shopping and learns that her grocer refuses to offer more credit. When she tells her husband, he hangs himself. Later that day the landlord's daughter confronts the widow in the hallway and asks about the young man in her apartment. When he returns, the widow cries, because they have nothing to eat. At the same time, the landlord goes from door to door demanding the rent. When he comes to the widow's apartment, she admits that she is unable to pay. The landlord orders her to leave. The young man intervenes and picks a fight. The film ends when the landlord throws him down a flight of stairs, killing him.

The narrative style of *Hunger in Waldenburg* suggests Jutzi's relative inexperience with feature film production and the low production budget. Although many of its techniques are similar to those of *Mother Krause's Journey to Happiness,* the narrative is far less cohesive and convincing. As Leo Lania had explained, their primary intention was to construct a realistic narrative. Natural settings and amateur players contribute to the effect, but a substantial omniscient intertitle asserts authenticity even before the visual narrative begins: "The film was made in Silesia, in the Waldenburg coal region. It is a drama that reports on the life of the working class. No professional actors are in the film, and there is no studio footage of any kind."

As the narrative develops, monologues, such as the widow's description of living conditions in her tenement building, and other omniscient intertitles suggest that the fictional portrayal is also typical. When the young man leaves his parents, for example, an intertitle notes: "And so yet another leaves for the coal mines." Still other texts indicate contrasts between visual images. When the young man begins his journey, an intertitle orients the spectator's perception of what follows: "In the distance the specter of industry spreads over the winter landscape." A sequence of images begins, progressing from shots of the snow-covered palace to others of the dirty gray coal fields. Both the intertitle and the contrast between light and dark encourage the spectator to perceive the contrast between the wealthy aristocracy and the poor coal miners.

Whereas other directors had begun to guide reception with more differentiated photographic and hypotactic montage techniques, Jutzi relied to a large extent on omniscient intertitles, used relatively simple photography, and organized the filmic sequences for the most part paratactically. Only occasionally did he insert more complex montage sequences, to suggest the quality of various milieus. For example, the juxtaposition of the coal-mining area and the palace includes a rapid sequence depicting symbols of the industrial complex: steaming machines, buildings, and smoke billowing from imposing smokestacks. The most innovative sequence begins when the landlord throws the young man down the stairs. Following a shot of the motionless young man, a series of shots recalls the images of life in the coal-mining town and eventually returns to the image of the young man at the bottom of the stairs.

The narration of *Hunger in Waldenburg*, although less complex and innovative, functions similarly to that of other Prometheus films in 1929. Like that of *Beyond the Street* and *Mother Krause's Journey to Happiness*, the narration of *Hunger in Waldenburg* emphasizes that its portrayal is authentic and typical. It asserts that class struggle characterizes German society. The ruling class, represented by the landlord, selfishly exploits the working class and will resort to brutal violence to hold rebels, like the young man, at the bottom of the social hierarchy. The film's portrayal encourages the audience to sympathize with the figures of the working class while condemning their exploiters. *Hunger in Waldenburg* offered an ideological alternative to that of most mainstream films but adopted, albeit somewhat simplistically, the dominant codes of reception. It did little to stimulate grass-roots participation in developing a viable alternative to mainstream cinema.

Hunger in Waldenburg received generally favorable reviews.[2] Most critics emphasized its experimental nature and praised the film's realistic portrayal. Only the most ardent proponents of socialist realism (see Willi Bredel's review in the *Hamburger Volkzeitung*, 4 December 1929) complained that it was too pessimistic. Despite the generally favorable reviews, *Hunger in Waldenburg* attracted little attention from theater owners and quickly disappeared from public circulation. Except for the members of the VFV and those who attended the film events of the KPD and IAH, very few people saw the film.

SELF-CRITICISM AND CHANGE IN THE VFV

While *Hunger in Waldenburg* was being produced, the VFV slowly changed its orientation.[3] At the end of 1928 Erich Engel, an author who was active in the IAH, replaced Franz Höllering as the chief editor of *Film und Volk,* and the KPD's influence gradually increased. Lange's programmatic article ("Worauf es ankommt"—"What Is Important," *Film und Volk,* December/January 1928–29, 12) and an article signed "Jan" ("Das zweite Jahr"—"The Second Year," *Film und Volk,* April 1929, 14–15) outlined the dominant critiques of the VFV's activity during its first year as well as the organization's future orientation. Both articles emphasized that the VFV had concentrated too heavily on film events, and they complained that too many members and sympathizers perceived it as an organization in which they could participate passively. Without questioning the original plans of the VFV (acquisition of first-run theater, film production, educational programs), Lange proclaimed that it must become a force for active struggle against commercial cinema.

The second article challenged the VFV's original plans and outlined three major errors. According to its perspective, the leadership had overestimated its capacity to acquire a first-run theater and to confront the film industry effectively with its own production. Like Lange, the article's author also criticized the popular image of the VFV as a club for budget-minded film enthusiasts. Instead of following its original course, the author argued, the VFV should concentrate more on film criticism and on public lectures. Instead of organizing film events and producing films to counteract the influence of mainstream cinema, the VFV should produce and screen films to increase public interest in its own programs. In contrast to Lange, who continued to promote the critical participation of members, the author of "The Second Year" encouraged VFV leaders to work closely with the most class-conscious members of leftist political organizations to achieve mass education. Together they should communicate to the uninitiated a correct perception of commercial film's ideological orientation and exploit the medium's potential as an element in their ideological struggle with the dominant forces in Weimar society. The VFV generally accepted the recommendations in "The Second Year," but as its connection to the KPD strengthened and as the economic crisis escalated, polarization between the KPD and the other political parties intensified, and the VFV's base of support gradually disintegrated.

In 1929 the VFV organized numerous lectures by critics, directors, and other renowned film experts, such as Alfons Goldschmidt and Dziga Vertov. It also frequently scheduled film events, but the organization's primary activity became the publication of its journal *Film und Volk*. A group of regular contributors, including Egon Larsen, W. Nettlebeck, and Edgar Beyfuss, provided substantial articles about the effects of economic concentration, scandals, censorship, and technical/aesthetic innovations on production. They also exposed the influence of conservative interest groups, including the Catholic church. Well-known film personalities from the Soviet Union, including Pudovkin and Eisenstein, reported on their work and on general trends in Soviet cinema. The editors of *Film und Volk* also continued rubrics such as "Kritischer Filmbericht" ("Critical Report on Film"), where authoritative reviews of recent films appeared. They occasionally also recommended films under the heading "Mitteilungen des Volksverbandes für Filmkunst" ("Communiqués of the Volksverband für Filmkunst"). Like the *AIZ*, *Film und Volk* also publicized Prometheus and Weltfilm products. The editorial policy of *Film und Volk* restricted reader initiatives. While asserting its own authority over readers, the VFV increasingly accepted the leadership of the KPD. In October 1929, the VFV joined the Communist IfA,[4] and in January 1930 the KPD's *Arbeiterkorrespondenten* began contributing to *Film und Volk*. Simultaneously, reports in the journal revealed that the VFV had begun to flounder.

By April 1930 the VFV no longer could support *Film und Volk*. It merged with the journal of the Arbeiter-Theater-Bund Deutschlands, and the new *Arbeiterbühne und Film* appeared for another year. By the fall of 1930 only two local chapters remained active. In Hamburg Willi Bredel led a group that published the *Sozialistische Film-Kritik* until the end of 1931. In Stuttgart Friedrich Wolf helped that city's chapter survive well into 1932. In response to the VFV's steady disintegration, IfA founded a film department in November 1930. In the same month, a group of intellectuals and artists led by Hans Richter founded the Deutsche Liga für den unabhängigen Film (German League for Independent Film) with principles very similar to those of the VFV. Neither organization was able to stimulate as much interest as had their predecessor in 1928.

While the VFV slowly dissolved, the contributors to *Arbeitbühne und Film* sustained their efforts to mobilize the German masses in opposition to mainstream cinema. A number of contributors persisted with claims about the influence of interest groups on production (see, for example, "Die 'Ufa' dreht einen Nazi-Film!"—"Ufa Makes a Nazi Film!" November 1930, 28). In accordance with the KPD's concept of social fascism, the list of interest groups now included the Social Democrats. Substantial articles and reviews (K. A. Wittfogel, "Wirtschaftskrise—Krise der bürgerlichen Demokratie—Kulturkrise"—"Economic Crisis—Crisis of Bourgeois Democracy—Cultural Crisis," September 1930, 1–4; and L. A. K. Kaufmann, "Lohnbuchhalter Kremke"—"Bookkeeper Kremke," November 1930, 28) condemned SPD support for stricter censorship and the ideological orientation of SPD films. The journal also perpetuated the campaign to combat manipulation of film criticism by producers (see Heinz Lüdecke, "Unabhängige Filmkritik"—"Independent Film Criticism," December 1930, 20–22).

The critics for *Arbeiterbühne und Film,* while recognizing the development of standardized film subjects, continued to base arguments about the ideological impact of commercial film for the most part on the analysis of film content (see, for example, Alice Lex, "Die Frau und der Film"—"Woman and Film," May 1931, 12–13). However, there was an exception. In the final issue of the journal Trude Sand initiated a discussion of film's emotional appeal: "The . . . film presents cowboys and terrible wild horses. And the children are engaged to the point of forgetting themselves. They not only yell and rage, as if they were being chased. They also jump from their seats. . . . The question is, are children ever so taken by a book or the spoken word? No! The *visualized plot* works much more directly" ("Kind und Film"—"Child and Film," June 1931, 25–26).

Many other leftist film critics had recognized the emotional appeal of filmic portrayals, and Sand offered no new insights about the narrative stimulation of emotions. Nevertheless, her critique is significant. Sand's article was one of only a few in any newspaper or film journal of the German left to question such an appeal and suggest an alternative: "We must go to the movies with our children! Just as the husband does with his wife, just . . . as political groups should, so that afterward they can discuss what they have seen."[5] An editorial note accompanied "Child and Film," requesting that readers respond to it with their own opinions. That invitation and Sand's vision of collective film discussions reflected a desire to encourage the critical participation of the journal's readers. As had been the case elsewhere in the left, the editors of *Arbeiterbühne und Film* began experimenting with more democratic forms of production and reception at the end of the Weimar era.

It was Heinz Lüdecke who most diligently promoted grass-roots involvement in *Arbeiterbühne und Film*. Beginning with "Dringende Aufgaben der proletarischen Filmkritik" ("Urgent Tasks of Proletarian Film Criticism," June 1930, 23–25) and culminating with "Agitpropasierung des proletarischen Films" ("Agitpropization of the Proletarian Film," with Korea Senda, May 1931, 8–11), Lüdecke consistently challenged the journal's readers to submit reviews, organize boycotts, and, finally, build production collectives. After asserting in the initial article the necessity for working-class Germans to develop critical skills through practical experience, Lüdecke invited readers to submit their reviews in "Proletarische Filmkritik—Der Leser hat das Wort" ("Proletarian Film Criticism—The Reader Has the Word," September 1930, 22–23). A month later he reported that very few readers had accepted the invitation and once again challenged them to participate ("Noch einmal. Proletarische Filmkritik"—"Once Again: Proletarian Film Criticism," October 1930, 17). During the rest of 1930 space for readers' critiques in *Arbeiterbühne und Film* slowly increased. By January 1931 the editors allocated five pages for "Proletarian Film Criticism." Eight reviews, including one collective contribution, appeared.

Finally, in May 1931, after three issues had appeared with either very few readers' critiques or none at all, Lüdecke collaborated with Korea Senda, a representative of the proletarian film movement in Japan, to formulate a new approach to production in "Agitpropization of Film." Their article began by summarizing the efforts to combat the ideological impact of mainstream film and organize a proletarian alternative. While acknowledging the difficulties associated with alternative film production, Lüdecke and Senda asserted that such production was the only effective method to stimulate the initiative of unorganized workers. Referring to the VFV, they noted: "A magazine—proclamations, programs, major articles—could enlighten and have an organizational impact. That alone is not enough, because the masses came to see films." According to them, the best model was the agitprop movement in theater.[6] Lüdecke and Senda encouraged small collectives to produce 8-mm documents of working-class life and to screen them at the grass-roots level in industrial and agricultural centers. Members of such collectives would receive training in film production and Marxist ideology from KPD leaders and use their films to attract unorganized workers to the party. Although the potential for self-education through practical experience thus would be minimized, Lüdecke and Senda claimed, collectives would develop at the local level and work in close cooperation with industrial and agricultural workers. Prior to January 1933 a small number of collectives emerged and produced a few films in Berlin and other large cities, but the envisioned national organization of proletarian film collectives remained nothing more than a concept. As had been the case with every other experiment in grass-roots film activity during the last years of the Weimar Republic, the "Agitpropization of Film" was unable to attract enough interest to combat the influence of commercial cinema as the popularity of National Socialism rapidly increased.

CONCLUSION

A variety of interwoven and interdependent economic and technological factors, aesthetic models and perceptions, sociopsychological tendencies, and ideological competition between interest groups shaped the contours of the emerging cinematic institution in the Weimar era. At the beginning of the period, the culminating transitions from mercantile and agrarian capitalism to modern industrial capitalism, from monarchism to parliamentary democracy, and from idealist to materialist concepts of religion, science, and art provided the framework for the film industry's rapid growth and the initial challenges to it from a variety of aesthetic, philosophical, and political perspectives. Within the context of a swiftly changing German society, first expressionism, then New Objectivity, and ultimately even socialist realism and the *Proletkult* movement influenced the development of mainstream as well as alternative models for film production and reception. In addition, the experience of World War I, the postwar crisis, Germany's position between the Western Allies and the Soviet Union, and the challenge to and reassertion of patriarchal principles of social, familial, and interpersonal relationships contributed to the quality of each aesthetic trend and its effect on Weimar cinema.

At the same time, competition between Weimar's most powerful interest groups played an especially significant role in the development of mainstream and alternative models of film production and reception. Representatives of fixed-asset capital, who aligned themselves with conservative and reactionary political parties and were led by individuals such as Alfred Hugenberg, invested heavily in film and other media. By 1933 they exerted what was approaching a monopolistic influence on mass communication in German society. The representatives of liquid-asset capital, who split their allegiance for the most part between the DNVP, DVP, and the Catholic Center and were led by wealthy speculators in the electronics, chemical, and (to some extent) publishing industries, either founded film companies or invested, albeit less energetically than the fixed-asset capitalists, in the film industry.

While the members of Germany's most powerful interest groups recognized the ideological and commercial potential of film, groups within the German left struggled with the political right and with themselves for political control of Weimar society. Only in the wake of the crisis that ended in 1924 did the SPD, KPD, and other leftist organizations and individuals begin to develop serious programs for an alternative to the emerging cinematic institution.

The development of mainstream cinema in the Weimar Republic and the ineffectiveness of the German left's attempts to compete commercially and ideologically with the major producers, distributors, and theater owners to a large extent confirms the concept of modern culture outlined by Max Horkheimer and Theodor Adorno in *Dialectic of Enlightenment*.[1] Various trends indicate that capitalism maximized the influence of a small economic and political elite on the quality of cinema. The high degree of speculation within the industry between 1919 and 1924, the formation of horizontal and vertical cartels throughout the Weimar era, administrative influence on production, and the efforts of producers to market their products by influencing criticism, orchestrating publicity campaigns, and developing standardized production techniques—all provide good examples.[2] The standardization of specific subjects, including sexual promiscuity, upward social mobility, and adventures or exotic/luxurious life-styles, and the emerging paradigms of narrative cohesion reinforce Horkheimer's and Adorno's assertions about the entertainment quality of commercial cinema and its ideological significance.[3]

Films such as *Das Spielzeug von Paris* (*The Plaything from Paris*, 1919), *The Three from the Gas Station* (1930), and *Die Gräfin von Monte Christo* (*The Duchess of Monte Cristo*, 1932) offered many working-class, lower-middle-class, and middle-class Germans an escape from everyday anxiety and frustration. At the same time, developing film genres, including the Fridericus films and many World War I films, presented a positive image of Prussian history and appealed to Germans who struggled with guilt and shame about their national heritage and insecurity about the existing economic and political system. As Horkheimer and Adorno suggest,[4] in the process the mainstream cinema often nurtured unambiguous oppositions between the familiar and the foreign, the socially acceptable and unacceptable, and even between the various social classes in Weimar society. By entertaining and encouraging audiences to affirm uncritically their inadequately differentiated portrayals and uniform models of behavior, major film producers simultaneously diffused public dissatisfaction with the existing social system and inhibited the development of the critical skills necessary to initiate subversive cultural activity.

Despite the relative correspondence between the concept of a culture industry and the development of mainstream cinema in Weimar Germany, that concept requires further refinement. Adorno and Horkheimer overemphasize the influence of economic factors on the quality of mass media production. In addition to the desire to maximize profit, the desire to influence public opinion stimulated the interest of decision makers in the film industry during the Weimar era. When, for example, Alfred Hugenberg's Economic Association for the Promotion of the Intellectual Forces of Reconstruction invested, first in the print media and then in film, political motivations significantly influenced the decision. In 1914 the group strove to counteract the growing influence of Social Democracy, and in 1927 it hoped to inhibit the spread of what it perceived as a Bolshevist force in Weimar cinema. During the Weimar era, the political and economic interests of those who were significantly influencing the development of mainstream cinema frequently coincided. By appealing to the regressive psychological needs of filmgoers with standardized cinematic entertainment that advocated a nationalistic, militaristic, racist, and antirepublican ideological orientation, through content and form, Germany's wealthiest and most conservative interest groups were able to follow their economic and political agenda simultaneously.

Although the influence of the culture industry did increase significantly between 1919 and 1933, reaching more and more Germans with its expanding network of print media, film, and radio, Adorno and Horkheimer overemphasize its capacity to inhibit the development of subversive alternatives. The activity of the German left indicates that the culture industry did not completely stifle efforts to subvert mainstream cinema. Leftist film activity also suggests that, in addition to the impact of mass media, a variety of other factors contributed to its relative failure. The SPD, KPD, and other organizations of the German left recognized film's ideological potential only after the foundation for a German cinematic institution had been established. At the beginning of the 1920s, the SPD concentrated above all on stabilizing the new political system and asserting its leadership within that system. At the same time, the party continued to emphasize prewar principles of cultural equity without evaluating the ideological significance of its orientation. Within the KPD the advocates of militant revolutionary activity and radically democratic cultural activity refused to cooperate in formulating a strategy for social change based on the interdependence of "material" and "ideological" activity. Instead, the KPD accepted the leadership of the Comintern and followed an unsuccessful course of violent revolutionary action.

When the major political parties of the German left finally did initiate programs to combat its emerging influence, the cinematic institution was strong enough to withstand the challenge. However, there are other reasons for the ineffectiveness of leftist alternatives. As a consequence of their relatively late reaction to developments in cinema and their respective ideological orientations, the SPD and the KPD to a large extent challenged only the content of mainstream films. The SPD's dedication to parliamentary democracy, its affirmation of traditional aesthetic models, and a lack of experience with film production led the Social Democrats to assimilate uncritically the dominant trends in production and reception. Their major concern was to increase the base of support for the party's leaders and policies. According to them, the techniques employed by the film industry to influence public opinion were the most effective. With this in mind, the program of the Film und Lichtbilddienst and independent Social Democratic film production encouraged party members and sympathizers to support Social Democracy with cinematic codes of narrative cohesion that did little to stimulate collective critical thought and grass-roots initiatives. Consequently, the SPD's film program reinforced the German public's susceptibility to authoritarian structures more than it fostered a democratic alternative.

For different reasons the KPD, in cooperation with the IAH, the Soviet film industry, and independent leftist intellectuals and artists, followed a similar course. When the Communist left initiated its challenge to mainstream cinema, beginning seriously in 1926, the KPD's allegiance to the Stalinist Comintern and reliance on concepts of scientific Marxism, democratic centralism, and later socialist realism played a significant role. Like the Social Democrats, those who contributed to the Communist press, cooperated in the film production of Prometheus and Weltfilm, and participated in the Volksfilmverband generally challenged mainstream film content while adopting the existing codes of narrative cohesion. Alfred Durus, Hermann Duncker, Kurt Bernhardt, Phil Jutzi, and others relied in part on what they perceived as effective techniques of cinematic narration. The belief in the principles of dialectical materialism and in the necessity for party leaders to use culture as a medium for communicating their insight to unorganized working masses also influenced their models of production and reception. The Communist left also strove to educate its audiences from above, instead of stimulating the critical interest of working-class individuals by encouraging them to participate cooperatively in formulating an ideological orientation and strategy for social change.

In addition to the culture industry's influence on public opinion, it seems likely that the disregard for more radically democratic alternatives contributed significantly to the ineffectiveness of the German left's challenge to it.[5] Only at the end of the Weimar era, when it became apparent to the leaders of the SPD and the KPD that their political and cultural programs were failing and that the National Socialists had become a formidable opponent, did they begin to listen to the advocates of grass-roots alternatives. Although leftist intellectuals and artists, including Anna Siemsen, Heinz Lüdecke, Erwin Piscator, Franz Jung, Hanns Eisler, and Bertolt Brecht, had promoted and experimented with such alternatives at various times throughout the period, they received little support and were often criticized by the political parties of the left. For the most part they developed and practiced their models of artistic production and reception independent of the SPD's and KPD's cultural programs. The major political parties of the German left, therefore, shared responsibility for the ineffectiveness of their alternatives to the culture industry and specifically to mainstream cinema. With this in mind, the evaluation of the radically democratic experiments with production and reception that were initiated at the end of the Weimar era should be differentiated further. While it is necessary to acknowledge their relative lack of success, it is also important for all who wish to nurture democratic forms of social interaction to perceive the potentially model character of such experiments as the discussion about the impact of mass media on the development of public opinion continues today.

NOTES

INTRODUCTION

1. Among others, see Herman G. Weinberg, *The Lubitsch Touch: A Critical Study;* Lotte Eisner, *The Haunted Screen: Expressionism in German Cinema and the Influence of Max Reinhardt,* trans. Roger Greaves; Roger Manvell and Hermann Fraenkel, *The German Cinema;* and Lee Atwell, *G. W. Pabst.* The trend continues in the 1980s with a variety of publications, including the illustrated *Klassiker des deutschen Stummfilms. 1910–1930,* ed. Ilona Brennicke and Joe Hembus.

2. Among others, see Siegfried Kracauer, *From Caligari to Hitler: A Psychological History of German Film;* George Huaco, *The Sociology of Film Art;* and Paul Monaco, *Cinema and Society.*

3. For a recent account of filmmaking in the FRG during the immediate postwar period, see, among others, Claudius Seidl, *Der deutsche Film der fünfziger Jahre.*

4. Among others, see Peter Jansen and Wolfram Schütte, eds., *Film in der DDR,* 7–56. The volume includes a good bibliography.

5. In addition to the original English version, a revised German translation was published in 1958. See *Von Caligari bis Hitler. Ein Beitrag zur Geschichte des deutschen Films* (Hamburg: Rowohlt, 1958). For an unabridged translation, see Siegfried Kracauer, in *Von Caligari zu Hitler Schriften,* ed. Karsten Witte, vol. 2. Here, see the introduction: 3–11.

6. V. I. Lenin, *Collected Works,* trans. Bernard Isaacs and Joe Feinberg, ed. Julius Katzer, 20:24.

7. See, for example, Heinz J. Furian, "Zwischen 'Caligarismus' und Realismus," *Deutsche Filmkunst* 1–4 (1957) and 1–4 (1958). Here, 1 (1957): 10.

8. Among others, see Karl Tümmler, "Deutsche Arbeiterbewegung und nationaler Film," *Deutsche Filmkunst* 10 (1962): 384–385; Gerd Meier, "Materialien zur Geschichte der Prometheus Film-Verleih und Vertriebs-GmbH. 1926–1932," *Deutsche Filmkunst* 1–8 (1962): 12–16, 57–60, 97–99, 137–140, 177–180, 221–224, 275–277, 310–312; *Film und revolutionäre Arbeiterbewegung in Deutschland. 1918–1932 (FurAbiD)*, ed. Gertraude Kühn, Karl Tümmler, Walter Wimmer, 2 vols.; and *Mutter Krausens Fahrt ins Glück. Filmprotokoll und Materialien*, ed. Rudolf Freund and Michael Hanisch.

9. See, for example, Willi Lüdecke, *Film in Agitation und Propaganda der revolutionären deutschen Arbeiterbewegung (1919–1933)*; Toni Stooss, "Erobert den Film! oder 'Prometheus' gegen 'Ufa' & Co.," 4–47; Yvonne Leonard, "Die verdoppelte Illusion," 48–64; Peter Schumann, " 'Aus der Waffenschmiede der SPD.' Zur sozialdemokratischen Filmarbeit in der Weimarer Republik," 77–85, in *Erobert den Film!* ed. Die Neue Gesellschaft für Bildende Künste (NGBK) and the Freunde der deutschen Kinemathek e.V.; and Helmut Korte, ed., *Film und Realität in der Weimarer Republik*. In addition to these, see Stefan Swoboda, "Zur theoretischen und praktischen Aneignung des Mediums Film durch die revolutionäre deutsche Arbeiterbewegung bis 1933 unter besonderer Berücksichtigung von *Mutter Krausens Fahrt ins Glück* (1929) und *Kuhle Wampe oder Wem gehört die Welt* (1932)," *Diplomarbeit;* and Rudolf Schweigert, "Proletarischer Film und bürgerliche Reaktion. klassenkämpferische Auseinandersetzungen um die Zensur der Filme *Panzerkreuzer Potemkin* (1926) und *Kuhle Wampe* (1932)," *Magisterarbeit*. The interest in the relationship between film and politics in the Weimer Republic continues in the 1980s, although the interest is no longer linked as strongly to programmatic political struggle. See, for example, Sybille Engels, "Der Film im Propagandaverständnis deutscher Parteien in der Weimarer Republik," *Magisterarbeit;* and Monique Lavallée, "Ideologievermittlung im Film—untersucht am Beispiel des deutschen expressionistischen Films der Weimarer Republik," *Magisterarbeit*. See also the special issue of *New German Critique* 40 (1987), which was devoted to Weimar film theory.

10. The theoretical and sociological categories posited by Peter Bächlin in *Der Film als Ware* and Dieter Prokop in "Versuch über Massenkultur und Spontaneität," in *Materialien zur Theorie des Films,* 1–44, provide guidelines without restricting the analytical orientation.

PART ONE. THE BIRTH OF GERMAN CINEMA AND ITS DEVELOPMENT DURING THE POSTWAR CRISIS: 1919–1923

1. A number of film historians have outlined the birth of cinema in Germany. For a concise account, see Oskar Kalbus, *Vom Werden deutscher Filmkunst* 2:

5–17; Curt Moreck, *Sittengeschichte des Kinos*, 8–20; and Emilie Altenloh, *Zur Soziologie des Kinos. Die Kino-Unternehmung und die sozialen Schichten ihrer Besucher.*

I. 1896–1918: FROM COUNTRY ROADS TO MAIN STREET AND THE DISCOVERY OF FILM BY POLITICAL INTEREST GROUPS

1. Siegfried Kracauer, *Caligari*, 15. For more specific information about the development of the commercial film industry—production, distribution, and screening—see Bächlin, 19–33; Anton Kaes, *Kino-Debatte*, 1–36; and Jerzy Toeplitz, *Geschichte des Films 1896–1928*, trans. Lilli Kaufmann, 1: 36–42.

2. Producers also began to consider ways to minimize production costs while maximizing profit. Borrowing already existing stories from theater, literature, and folklore enabled producers to decrease the cost of script production and increase the potential for commercial success. For more information about the quality of such changes and their effect on the German public sphere, see Altenloh, *Zur Soziologie des Kinos*. See also Miriam Hansen, "Early Silent Cinema: Whose Public Sphere?" *New German Critique* 29 (Spring/Summer 1983): 147–184.

3. One of Germany's first film stars was Henny Porten. She began her film career in 1906 by appearing in her father's films. In 1910 Oskar Messter "discovered" Henny Porten and offered her an exclusive contract. She ultimately became one of the most popular film personalities of the Weimar era.

4. For more information, see Kracauer, 18, and Gerhard Zaddach, "Der literarische Film. Ein Beitrag zur Geschichte der Lichtspielkunst," 17, 22–29, 30–38. See also Anton Kaes's "The Debate about Cinema: Charting a Controversy (1909–1929)," trans. David J. Levin, *New German Critique* 40 (Winter 1987): 7–33.

5. Unless otherwise noted, translations are my own.

6. Franz Förster commented on the change in "Das Kinoproblem und die Arbeiter" ("The Cinema and the Workers," *Die Neue Zeit*, 26 December 1913, 484–487). "One speaks of falsified portrayals of our leaders' and government's actions. Of course, an enlightened working-class audience should have no time for that. However, those scenes from films about geography, folklore, and technology, which serve *instructional purposes*, are recommended" (484).

7. For more general information, see Arthur Rosenberg, *Imperial Germany: The Birth of the German Republic 1871–1918*, trans. Ian F. D. Morrow, 1–32; Gordon Craig, *Germany 1865–1945*, 39–60; and Wilhelm L. Guttsman, *The German Social Democratic Party, 1875–1933*.

8. See Craig, 181–186. The Wilhelminian educational system discouraged

working-class children from following the course of study that led to a university education. Those students from families with low incomes, who did attend the Gymnasium, found it difficult to raise the money necessary for a university education. And the conservative makeup of university faculties hindered those who criticized the existing order from surviving in the academic community. For more detailed information about the cultural program of the SPD during the Wilhelminian era, see Vernon Lidtke, *The Alternative Culture: Socialist Labor in Imperial Germany.*

9. See Georg Fülberth, *Proletarische Partei und bürgerliche Literatur.* As Fülberth noted: "Even in *Die Neue Zeit* the majority of contributions on literature is characterized by an attempt to interpret bourgeois ideology from an artistic point of view. The contributors attempted to distinguish clearly between politics and aesthetics without compromising themselves politically" (38). For a concise account of the development of the concept of autonomous art in the nineteenth and early twentieth centuries, see Peter Bürger, "Institution Literatur und Modernisierungsprozeß," in *Zum Funktionswandel der Literatur,* ed. Peter Bürger, 9−32.

10. During the 1890s a small but vociferous minority did challenge the belief in a separation between aesthetics and politics. Some, including Edgar Steiger, Heinz Sperber, and Lu Märten, even contemplated a Marxist aesthetics.

11. See, especially, 16−17. Wagner notes: "Observing the measures of our enemies teaches us clearly that, during these difficult times, it is absolutely necessary to pay attention to the mood of the people. As a result, we must pay attention to cinema, for it is cinema that is able to influence so decisively. The goal of our efforts consists in the use of cinema in the national interest. We must see to it that cinema serves to enlighten and at the same time is capable of influencing the emotions of the populace in an appropriate manner. The Bild-und-Filmamt is responsible for helping to accomplish these tasks."

12. Quoted in *Weimarer Republik,* ed. Kunstamt Kreuzberg and the Institut für Theaterwissenschaft der Universität Köln, 433.

2. 1919–1923: THE "GOLDEN YEARS"

1. For more detailed information about the development of factions that led to the formation of a majority SPD (MSPD), see Hans Manfred Bock, *Geschichte des 'linken Radikalismus' in Deutschland. Ein Versuch,* 74−97.

2. For more detailed information, see Bächlin, 34−54.

3. The Deutsches Lichtspiel Syndikat was the most powerful organization within a single branch. It was a distribution company formed by a number of important cinema owners who agreed to show their films under preferential conditions. By 1927 it controlled over five hundred theaters. The most impressive cartel between branches was Ufa. Its activity in all branches was ensured when

the government allowed it to subsume Nordisk, Messter, and PAGU at its inception. By 1921 it had also acquired Decla and Bioscop, two companies that had merged just a year earlier.

4. The best sources of information about the Phöbus affair are the detailed trade journal reports of late 1927. See, for example, "Die Phoebus dementiert" ("Phoebus Denies"), *L.B.B.*, 10 August 1927; "Um die Phoebus" ("About Phoebus"), *L.B.B.*, 12 November 1927; and "Skandalfilm der Reichswehr" ("Film Scandal of the Army"), *Die Welt am Abend*, 21 October 1927. A little later Otto Nebelthau wrote a novel based on the scandal; see his *Kapitän Thiele. Ein geschichtlicher Roman aus unseren Tagen.* See also Otto Gessler, "Affäre Lohmann—Ein Kapitel für sich," in *Reichswehrpolitik in der Weimarer Zeit,* ed. Kurt Sendtner, 443–457.

5. See his "Bedeutung des Films" ("The Meaning of Film"), *Moderne Kinematographie,* 1920, 26–32. Cited in Kracauer, 47.

6. For information about expressionism in German film, see Rudolf Kurtz, *Expressionismus und Film*; Eisner, *The Haunted Screen;* Huaco, 27–84; and Marc Silberman, "Industry, Text and Ideology in Expressionist Film," in *Passion and Rebellion: The Expressionist Heritage,* ed. Eric Bromer and Douglas Kellner, 374–383. From the perspective of audiences who experienced daily the contested transition from authoritarian monarchy to parliamentary democracy, the suggested readings of the cited films seem very plausible. Of course, other readings also are possible. For information about psychoanalytic approaches, see, among others, Thomas Elsaesser, "Cinema—the Irresponsible Signifier, or 'The Gamble with History': Film Theory or Cinema Theory?" *New German Critique* 40 (1987): 65–89; and Patrice Petro, "Modernity and Mass Culture in Weimar: Contours of a Discourse on Sexuality in Early Theories of Perception and Representation," *New German Critique* 40 (1987): 115–146.

7. In September 1919, when *The Cabinet of Dr. Caligari* had its premiere at the Marmorhaus in Berlin, moviegoers demonstrated against it, demanding refunds. After two showings the theater dropped the film from its program, and no other theater would show it. In response Pommer decided to launch a sophisticated publicity campaign, covering Berlin with posters depicting Conrad Veidt and captions such as "You must see *Caligari!*" "Have you seen *Caligari?*" etc. After six months of publicity, the same theater took the film again, and it played for three months. See Huaco, 34.

8. Moreck, 122–144. Here Moreck discusses a number of films in which the rules of conventional morality are broken. The transgressor suffers, and a father or some other representative of the patriarchal order plays the role of the savior. I would suggest that the perceived recipient for most of these films was the petty-bourgeois male. Some of the films certainly were pitched to the perceived interests of female audiences; however, I would argue that in those cases the female spectator was perceived first as petty-bourgeois and secondly as female. For a detailed consideration of this issue and the possibility for discerning patterns of female

spectatorship within this framework, see Patrice Petro, *Joyless Streets: Women and Melodramatic Representation in Weimar Germany.*

9. The censorship board's close scrutiny of the German left's film activity gained notoriety when Münzenberg submitted *Battleship Potemkin* at the beginning of 1926. The scrutiny intensified after 1929. While rejecting Prometheus films, such as *Falschmünzer* (*Counterfeiters,* 1928), SPD films, such as *Ins Dritte Reich* (*Into the Third Reich,* 1931), and even the commercial *Im Westen Nichts Neues* (*All Quiet on the Western Front,* 1930), the board accepted *Der alte Fritz* (*Old Fritz,* 1927), *Die letzte Kompagnie* (*The Last Company,* 1930), and *Berge in Flammen* (*Mountains in Flames,* 1931). For more information on censorship laws and practice, see Peter A. Hagemann, *Reichsfilmgesetze von 1895–1945,* and Wolfgang Petzet, *Verbotene Filme. Eine Streitschrift.*

3. THE SPD AND FILM: FROM CALLS FOR REFORM TO AFFIRMATION OF CINEMATIC ENTERTAINMENT AND EDIFICATION

1. For more detailed information, see "Die Veredelung des Films" ("The Refinement of Film"), *Vorwärts,* 7 February 1920; Kracauer, 46; and Moreck, 37–39. The National Assembly rejected the proposals and, instead, passed the Motion Picture Law. When viewed from this perspective, censorship was the lesser of two evils for individuals who held positions of leadership in the industry. Censorship boards could influence their decision-making process, but that was certainly preferable to losing control of the process completely.

2. The articles were A. Knoll, "Die Theater- und Filmgewerkschaft der Zukunft" ("The Theater and Film Union of the Future"), an article supporting the trade union movement; Joseph Frank, "Der Film von heute" ("The Film of Today"), which bemoans low artistic and moral quality of popular entertainment films, advocates censorship, and promotes educational films; and Hedwig Wachenheim, "Filmkunst- und -leid" ("Film Art and Suffering"), a short history of cinema that criticizes commercial film, remains skeptical about nationalization, and encourages the party to become more active in cinema.

4. FILM AND THE COMMUNIST LEFT: LEFTIST RADICALISM VERSUS DEMOCRATIC CENTRALISM AND THE CONSEQUENCES FOR A COMMUNIST FILM PROGRAM

1. For a detailed account of the revolutionary left's development during the period, see Ossip K. Fletchheim, *Die KPD in der Weimarer Republik,* 118–190;

Hans Manfred Bock, 74–132; and Ben Fowkes, *Communism in Germany under the Weimar Republic*, 19–109.

2. For a more detailed account of the revolutionary left's approach to cultural activity during the crisis years, see *Literaturdebatten in der Weimarer Republik*, ed. Manfred Nössig et al., 9–222; and Walter Fähnders and Martin Rector, *Literatur im Klassenkampf. Zur proletarisch-revolutionären Literaturtheorie 1919–1923*.

3. Bock, 89–92; Flechtheim, 126–128; and Fowkes, 19–23, offer more detailed accounts.

4. See Bock, 76–89; Flechtheim, 77–117; and Fowkes, 19–23.

5. For a more detailed discussion of this, see Bock, 105–115; Flechtheim, 133–137; and Fowkes, 24–73.

6. For example, after the Spartacists and the leftist radicals split at the Second Party Congress, the Comintern exerted pressure on the KPD to reconcile with those who had founded the Kommunistische Arbeiterpartei Deutschlands (KAPD). As a result, Paul Levi, Clara Zetkin, Ernst Däumig, Adolf Hoffman, and Otto Brass relinquished their Central Committee positions in the KPD. That paved the way for the left-leaning Soviet faction under the leadership of Heinrich Brandler and August Thalheimer to initiate the unsuccessful March uprisings of 1921. When the uprisings failed, the Comintern refused to recall Levi, who had criticized Soviet influence, but easily convinced Brandler that the revolutionary phase had ended.

7. There has been no comprehensive study of the *Proletkult*'s reception in Germany. For a Soviet perspective on the *Proletkult*, see, among others, Wladimir Gorbunow, *Lenin und der Proletkult*, trans. Ullrich Kuhirt and Ruth Czichon. Gorbunow's work includes an introductory chapter in which he evaluates Soviet research on the *Proletkult*. For the contemporary East German perspective, see *Literaturdebatten*, 197–222. For the West German perspective, see Walter Fähnders and Martin Rector, *Linksradikalismus und Literatur*, 2 vols., 1: 129–145. See also *Proletarische Kulturrevolution Sowjetrußland. 1917–1924*, ed. Richard Lorenz; Friedrich Wolfgang Knelleson, *Agitation auf der Bühne*, 256–270; and Peter Gorson and Eberhard Knödler-Bunte, *Proletkult*. See also Garland Eugene Crouch, *The Theory and Practice of A. A. Bogdanov's Proletcult*, and John H. Zammito, *The Great Debate: 'Bolshevism' and the Literary Left in Germany, 1917–1930*, 57–80.

8. For a more detailed account of this, see Fähnders and Rector, *Literatur im Klassenkampf*, 22–26.

9. For more information, see Fähnders and Rector, *Literatur im Klassenkampf*, 26–29.

10. The psychoanalytical work of Otto Gross and the vitalism and anarchism of Erich Mühsam's Gruppe Tat had influenced Jung as he developed concepts of collective rhythm, pleasure, and work. For more general information about

Franz Jung, see his autobiography, *Der Weg nach unten*. Fähnders and Rector discuss Jung's Proletkult experiments in *Literatur im Klassenkampf*, 29–31, and in *Linksradikalismus und Literatur* 1: 160–219. See also *Literaturdebatten*, 214–220.

11. Quoted in Fähnders and Rector, *Linksradikalismus und Literatur* 1: 180.

12. In *Literaturdebatten*, Nössig et al. explain this in greater detail; see 139–144.

13. See, for example, Clara Zetkin's comments in "Gegen das Kinowesen" ("In Opposition to Cinema").

14. For more information on Balázs, see Joseph Zsuffa, *Béla Balázs: The Man and the Artist*. See also Béla Balázs, *Essay, Kritik 1922–1932*, ed. Gertraude Kühn et al.

15. For more detailed information, see Lüdecke, 30–31, and Yvonne Leonard, "Die verdoppelte Illusion" ("The Doubled Illusion"), in *Erobert den Film!* 51.

16. Alexander Gorbunow provides the most detailed account, 98–189.

17. Gorbunow, 191–192. The conflict with the *Proletkult* occurred during a period in which Lenin and other Bolshevist leaders strove to develop Soviet society on the principles of democratic centralism. The Bolsheviks generally favored the centralist element in their approach to political and cultural organization. The threat of counterrevolution and the radically differing political and cultural viewpoints within the Soviet Union motivated Bolshevik leaders to emphasize an approach to culture that would allow them to promote the concepts that helped them to gain political power and to control the spread of dissenting opinions. They perceived film, theater, literature, and other art forms as educational tools to be used by the party's vanguard to illustrate what they perceived as the laws of natural and social development.

18. Kerschenzev's proposal resembled those of Dr. Wagner and others who had sought to use film to manipulate public opinion and win support for Germany's efforts in World War I.

19. Toni Stooss outlines this in more detail. See his "Erobert den Film!" ("Conquer Film!"), in *Erobert den Film!* 18–19. For more detailed information on the birth and early development of the IAH, see Rolf Surmann's *Die Münzenberg-Legende. Zur Publizistik der revolutionären deutschen Arbeiterbewegung 1921–1933*.

PART TWO: THE YEARS OF RELATIVE STABILITY: 1924–1928

1. For an introduction to the political, economic, and social history of the period, see, among others, Arthur Rosenberg, *Geschichte der Weimarer Repub-*

lik, ed. Kurt Kersten, 125–155; Helmut Heiber, *Die Republik von Weimar,* 115–151; A. J. Ryder, *Twentieth-Century Germany: From Bismarck to Brandt,* 245–282; and Craig, 469–533. I have based my introduction to Part Two to a large extent on information derived from these sources.

2. For more detailed information on the role of Hugo Stinnes and other speculators in Germany's economy during the crisis years, see Curt Geyer, *Drei Verderber Deutschlands,* especially the chapter on Stinnes, 27–55.

3. Most Weimar histories focus almost exclusively on the German public's antibolshevism and fascination with the United States. Yet, as the following chapter will demonstrate, both right- and left-wing political leaders, newspaper journalists, and to some extent the German people also criticized the constantly growing economic and cultural presence of the United States in Germany, while expressing a fair amount of fascination with the new Soviet society and its cultural products.

5. HOLLYWOOD, MOSCOW, AND THE CRISIS OF GERMAN FILM

1. Kracauer, *Caligari,* 131. For more detailed information about the petty-bourgeois mentality in Germany during the period, see Siegfried Kracauer, *Die Angestellten,* in *Schriften,* ed. Karsten Witte, 1: 205–281. For information about the similarities and differences between working-class and petty-bourgeois attitudes, see Erich Fromm, *The Working Class in Weimar Germany,* trans. Barbara Weinberger, ed. Wolfgang Bonss.

2. Lion Feuchtwanger succinctly described the proportional relationship between monarchists and republicans in *Erfolg.* In "Einige historische Daten" ("Some Historical Facts"), Book II, Chapter 14, 228, he notes: "In democratic Germany the advocates of feudal authority, the parties of the right, were slightly superior in numbers to the advocates of a more socially oriented government, the parties of the left. The materially less endowed belonged for the most part to the parties of the left, and the intellectually less endowed to the parties of the right." For an English translation, see Lion Feuchtwanger, *Success,* trans. Willa and Edwin Muir. I have used my own translation.

3. As a result of their efforts, Ufa received a loan of seventeen million marks, and its Hollywood partners agreed to distribute ten Ufa films of their choice yearly in their U.S. theaters. In return, Ufa was obliged to distribute ten Universal films and to join Paramount and MGM in organizing the Parufamet distribution company. Parufamet would distribute twenty films from each participating company. Paramount and MGM could choose their films for Parufamet distribution without consulting Ufa, and they stipulated that Ufa fill 75 percent of the screen-

ing time capacity in its theaters with Parufamet films. The *Lichtbild-Bühne* *(L.B.B.)* described the agreement succinctly in "Amerikanisierung der Ufa?" ("Americanization of Ufa?"), 9 January 1926.

4. According to a summary of government import control, which accompanied the published explanation of the 1930 law, as of 13 January 1925 a specific number of foreign films to be imported was no longer set. Instead, the government permitted distributors to import one foreign film for each German film they distributed. See Fritz Olimsky's dissertation, "Tendenzen der Filmwirtschaft und deren Auswirkung auf die Filmpresse," 55. Olimsky has thoroughly explained the contingency system and its abuse by commercial companies.

5. For a full account, see "Die Terra-Generalversammlung" ("The Terra Plenary Session"), *L.B.B.*, 15 September 1927.

6. For example, the *L.B.B.* reported on 4 June 1926, in an article entitled "Ludovicus Rex und seine Hintermänner" ("Ludovicus Rex and His Cohorts"), that a group of wealthy Bavarians had organized to finance films with a reactionary ideological orientation. Hilde Kramer, in "Die neue Film-Saison" ("The New Film Season"), *Die Rote Fahne*, 29 June 1926, claimed that the group included representatives of the German aristocracy, major industrial concerns, and the landed gentry. They financed films that were produced by the Deutscher Film GmbH in Munich.

7. See Ludwig Bernhard, *Der Hugenberg-Konzern*, 91–93; and "Scherl soll die Ufa finanzieren!" ("Scherl to Finance Ufa!"), *L.B.B.*, 21 February 1927.

8. "Aus dem Ufa-Konzern" ("From the Ufa Concern"), *Die Rote Fahne*, 28 December 1926.

9. "Die Filmzentrale des Filmkapitals" ("The Film Center of Film Capital"), *Die Rote Fahne*, 23 April 1927.

10. "Die Ufa Auslieferung an Hugenberg perfekt" ("Ufa's Delivery to Hugenberg Complete"), *Die Rote Fahne*, 1 April 1927.

11. John A. Leopold has outlined in great detail the emergence and development of the association. See *Alfred Hugenberg: The Radical National Campaign against the Weimar Republic*.

12. For a detailed description of Hugenberg's political program, see Leopold, 27–54.

13. *Jahrbuch der Filmindustrie* (Berlin, 1928), 181, quoted in *Weimarer Republik*, 464.

14. See, among others, Kracauer, *Caligari*, 134.

15. For a list of board members, see "Die Filmzentrale des Filmkapitals" ("The Film Center of Film Capital"), *Die Rote Fahne*, 23 April 1927. For a list of directors in 1928, see "Der neue Ufa-Vorstand" ("The New Ufa Executives"), *L.B.B.*, 24 January 1928. All subsequent references to Ufa executive committee meetings derive from the Ufa *Vorstandsprotokolle* located in the Bundesarchiv Koblenz. Numbers refer to package numbers.

16. See, for example, "Filmgeschäft mit Rußland" ("Film Deal with Russia"), *L.B.B.*, 1 May 1926.

6. THE DEVELOPING RELATIONSHIP BETWEEN POLITICS, ECONOMICS, AND COMMERCIAL FILM AESTHETICS

1. The *L.B.B.* filed a succinct report in "Der neue Kurs der Ufa" ("Ufa's New Course"), 15 September 1927.

2. The law was established in 1921, and *Fridericus Rex* was the first film to enjoy the tax advantage. See the review of *Fridericus Rex* in *Kinematograph*, 23 April 1922.

3. For a description of the *Lustbarkeitssteuer*, see Olimsky, 54–58; or Monaco, 46–47.

4. See *FurAbiD* 1: 266. The only films associated with the political left to receive the Lampe Committee's approval were the 1929 Soviet documentary *Pamir* (see the review of *Pamir* in *Film-Kurier*, 7 June 1929) and Pudovkin's *Sturm über Asien* (see Monaco, 58).

5. Information derived from personal interviews with Carl Junghans (August 1978), Erne Beier (Meseke) (November 1981), and Ilse Trautschold (May 1982).

6. As Lary May asserts in his book, *Screening out the Past: The Birth of Mass Culture and the Motion Picture Industry*, 233: "Rarely was the star portrayed as born into . . . status or wealth. Rather, he was an average, unknown . . . who used his talent for expressing charisma, charm, and sex appeal. Rising from anonymity, he acquired fame, which rested not on the domination of others, but on the ability to entertain and make people happy. This could indeed bring a kind of nobility. . . . Yet at all times, the stars were ordinary folks whose lavish life styles could be democratized." Although May refers here to male Hollywood stars of the 1920s, many of the same stars dominated the German screen too. And the German star system was similar to Hollywood's in many regards.

7. See Olimsky, 49. Ufa's activity provides a good example of what Jürgen Habermas describes as public relations (*öffentliche Arbeit*) in his *Strukturwandel der Öffentlichkeit*, 228–233.

8. The commercial film industry was even prepared to respond to the success of Soviet films with its own films about the Russian revolution. Pabst's film is a good example, demonstrating the industry's ability to adopt the theme but diffuse and even reverse the ideological thrust. For a discussion of *The Love of Jeanne Ney*, see Kracauer, *Caligari*, 172–178, or Toeplitz, 1: 434. Both describe well how the film neutralized the revolutionary quality of Ehrenburg's novel.

7. THE PAST AS METAPHOR FOR THE PRESENT AND *DER ALTE FRITZ (OLD FRITZ)* AS AN EXAMPLE

1. See Gerhard Schoenberner, "Das Preußenbild im deutschen Film. Geschichte und Ideologie" ("The Image of Prussia in German Film: History and Ideology"), in *Preussen im Film,* ed. Axel Marquardt and Heinz Rathsack, 12. *Preussen im Film* is an excellent collection of essays that provides both a wealth of information about and thought-provoking analyses of the Hohenzollern monarchy in commercial film. Despite the in-depth studies of ideological orientation in contributions such as Jan-Christopher Horak's "Liebe, Pflicht und die Erotik des Todes" ("Love, Duty, and the Eroticism of Death"), 205–218; and Gertrud Koch's "Der höhere Befehl der Frau ist ihr niederer Instinkt. Frauenhaß und Männer-Mythos in Filmen über Preussen" ("The Higher Order of Woman is Her Lovelier Instinct: Hatred of Woman and Male-Myth in Films about Prussia"), 219–233, there is a relative lack of attention paid to the use of filmic language and its influence on reception.

2. Helmut Regel, "Die Fridericus-Filme der Weimarer Republik" ("The Fridericus Films in the Weimar Republic"), in *Preussen im Film,* 124.

3. Eberhard Mertens, *Die großen Preussenfilme. I: Produktion 1921–1932,* vol. 5, *Filmprogramme,* x. According to Mertens, the films offered German audiences an opportunity to escape from everyday problems.

4. At the height of his popularity a joke even made its way through Berlin claiming that the star was in the process of completing his memoirs under the title: "Wie ich den Siebenjährigen Krieg gewann" ("How I Won the Seven Years' War"). See Hans Feld, "Potsdam gegen Weimar oder Wie Otto Gebühr den Siebenjährigen Krieg gewann" ("Potsdam versus Weimar or How Otto Gebühr Won the Seven Years' War"), in *Preussen im Film,* 72.

5. Regel, in *Preussen im Film,* 126. Regel asserts: "With long, epic breath Lamprecht lines up episode after episode in a sparse and-then-and-then manner. The result is that they often turn into mere genre images of a lovingly portrayed cultural history."

6. I use the terms *authentic* and *authenticity* consistently to refer to what I perceive as an effort to suggest that cinematic fiction corresponds to fact or reality, that it conforms to an original so as to reproduce essential features.

7. Hans Wollenberg (see "Der Alte Fritz"—"Old Fritz," *L.B.B.,* 23 January 1928) and Helmut Regel (in *Preussen im Film,* 127) suggest that Lamprecht included enough negative information about Friedrich II to inhibit the spectator's temptation to perceive him as a mythical hero. Wollenberg emphasizes Lamprecht's inclusion of the monarch's *greises Despotentum* (senile despotism), and Regel refers to the portrayal of his *Menschenverachtung* (misanthropy). What these writers perceived as Lamprecht's attempt to create a differentiated, real character may have increased viewer sympathy for the aging king, who struggled to serve his people, met with unwarranted opposition, and expressed his dissat-

isfaction. Lamprecht motivated the king's senile despotism sufficiently so that the viewer could perceive him as a hero and support his asceticism.

8. Commercial filmmakers produced very few major films that overtly criticized the Prussian heritage. *Der letzte Mann* (*The Last Laugh*, 1924), *Der Hauptmann von Köpenick* (*The Captain of Köpenick*, 1926), and *Die Hose* (*The Trousers*, 1927) thematized the Prussian obsession with authority, more specifically the fetishism of the uniform. Only two were unequivocally critical of the obsession. *The Last Laugh* allowed the audience to decide whether the hotel porter's tragedy rested more in his absolute identity with his uniform or in a cruel urban society that robbed him of his identity when it pragmatically decided that he was no longer productive. It seems likely that all three films did more to diffuse potential criticism of pro-Prussian films, i.e., they legitimized their ideological orientation more than they challenged it.

8. THE QUESTION OF SOCIAL MOBILITY AND A CLOSE LOOK AT *DIE VERRUFENEN (THE NOTORIOUS)*

1. The trend toward "New Objectivity" provided a context for the change. Many artists who had gained notoriety as expressionists became disappointed by what they perceived as less than adequate social innovations during the early years of the Weimar Republic. Some resigned themselves to the existing reality. Others renewed their search for artistic and political models with greater sobriety. Among other things, the cultures of the Soviet Union and the United States influenced those artists who continued to search. In both nations rational approaches to social planning and an artistic celebration of technology contributed significantly to the cultural image. German artists, including filmmakers, observed these apparently progressive cultures and borrowed from them in developing new, more objective modes of artistic expression. For more detailed accounts of New Objectivity, see, among others, John Willett, *Art and Politics in the Weimar Period.*

2. See *Der staatlich geförderte Propaganda und Lehrfilm im Auslande. Aufgaben unserer Regierung* (*State-Supported Propaganda and Educational Films Abroad: Tasks for Our Government*).

3. See Kracauer, *Caligari*, 157–160. Kracauer was among the first to distinguish Weimar film genres, such as the street films and Zille films. Whereas he described the evolution of genres as manifestations of the collective mind, the following discussion will demonstrate that they both reflected and generated ideological viewpoints in a process far more dialectical than Kracauer indicated.

4. For a more detailed account of the street film portrayal of the urban milieu, see Thomas Plummer et al., "Conservative and Revolutionary Trends in Weimar Film," in *Germany in the Twenties: The Artist as Social Critic*, ed. Frank D. Hirschbach et al., 77. In her *Joyless Streets: Women and Melodramatic Represen-*

tation in Weimar Germany, Patrice Petro argues that Weimar's street films provide the opportunity for female audiences to read them in ways that deviate from the dominant discourse of "male crisis." It is true that street film narratives frequently included central female figures, but such figures often appeared foremost as petty-bourgeois figures with corresponding aspirations. I would suggest that such figures appeared firstly as petty-bourgeois and secondly as women. The crisis portrayed in films such as *The Joyless Street* and *Tragedy of a Prostitute* appears more as the crisis of a social class than that of one or the other gender. Of course, it remains possible that female audiences would perceive the portrayed crisis as uniquely female. This seems most likely for those female spectators who already possessed a feminist perspective.

5. Although the middle-class engineer, Robert Kramer, is the only one to succeed in *The Notorious,* two working-class children find their way into healthy middle- to upper-class families in *The Illegitimate,* and the virtuous, hardworking wife of an alcoholic streetcar conductor begins a new life with a compassionate poet after her husband dies in *The Fallen.*

6. See, for example, Kracauer, *Caligari,* 165–189; Toeplitz, 1: 420–445; and Helmut Korte, ed., *Film und Realität in der Weimarer Republik,* 43–50.

7. Kracauer alludes to this with his reference to a "pictorial narrative of complete fluidity" (105).

8. A few filmmakers risked the public's criticism by abandoning standard narration and experimenting with less clearly organized forms of cinematic presentation. Walter Ruttman's *Berlin, Symfonie einer Großstadt (Berlin, Symphony of a Metropolis,* 1927) exemplified the tendency. However, projects like Ruttman's remained exceptions to the rule and normally failed to attract the financial backing of major producers. Ruttman's film, for example, was produced by Fox Europe as a contingency film.

9. THE SPD AND FILM: AMBIVALENCE TOWARD MAINSTREAM CINEMA AND THE INITIATION OF AN INDEPENDENT FILM PROGRAM

1. For an introduction to the role of the SPD during the years of relative stability, see Richard Breitman, *German Socialism and Weimar Democracy,* 114–143; and Michael Stürmer, *Koalition und Opposition in der Weimarer Republik 1924–1928.*

2. See Breitman, 114–130. In this section Breitman succinctly describes the SPD's continuing transition from a revolutionary to a reformist political party, using Rudolf Hilferding's development as an example. See also Wolfgang Abendroth, *Aufstieg und Krise der deutschen Sozialdemokratie. Das Problem der Zweckentfremdung einer politischen Partei durch die Anpassungstendenz von*

Institutionen an vorgegebene Machtverhältnisse, 59–66; and Dietmar Klenke, *Die SPD-Linke in der Weimarer Republik* 1: 72–84.

3. For a more detailed discussion, see Johanna Rosenberg, "Kunst und Kulturauffassungen in Umkreis der SPD—Karl Kautsky, Alfred Kleinberg, Anna Siemsen" ("Art and Concepts of Art in the SPD—Karl Kautsky, Alfred Kleinberg, Anna Siemsen"), in *Literaturdebatten,* 279–286.

4. For Anna Siemsen's perception of art, see her *Politische Kunst und Kunstpolitik* (*Political Art and Art Politics*). For her perception of party politics, see her *Parteidisziplin und sozialistische Überzeugung* (*Party Discipline and Socialist Conviction*). For an account of Anna Siemsen's life and work, see August Siemsen, *Anna Siemsen.*

5. Erwin Piscator's struggle with the Volksbühne provides a good example of the parameters for SPD cultural activity during the period. Piscator, as the Volksbühne director from 1924 to 1927, continually strove to institute elements of a *Proletkult* theater. In 1927 he finally resigned in the wake of a controversy over his production of Ehm Welk's *Gewitter über Gottland* (*Storm over Gottland*). For more detailed accounts, see Heinrich Goetz, *Erwin Piscator in Selbstzeugnissen und Bilddokumenten,* 34–54; and Heinrich Braulich, *Die Volksbühne,* 108–129.

6. See Wilhelm L. Guttsman, *The German Social Democratic Party, 1875–1933,* especially Chapter 5, "The elective fatherland: Socialist subculture from ghetto to republic," 167–218. Here, 189.

7. There were, of course, isolated exceptions to the general trend. See Guttsman, 189–191, for information about attempts by the Neue Richtung (a group that sympathized with the SPD) to deconstruct authoritarian relationships in education, albeit prior to 1924, and the organization of political courses for the rank and file in Munich in 1924. One possible reason for the limited success of these programs might have been that the SPD for such a long time had encouraged its members to assimilate bourgeois standards of education and art. Social Democratic workers were perhaps more inclined to integrate themselves into the existing social structure than to actively participate in changing it.

8. Guttsman, 196. As he indicates, "artistic events" attracted the largest audiences in 1927–1928.

9. Guttsman, 195. Here Guttsman explains the perceived tasks of the SPD's *Kulturkartelle* and their limited influence.

10. Such articles as "Der Film in Naturfarben" ("Film in Natural Colors"), 13 February 1924, and "Film und Volkserziehung" ("Film and People's Education"), 16 July 1924, again emphasized both a fascination with the film medium's mimetic capacity and its suitability for educational purposes.

11. One of the films, a Phöbus production, *Im Namen des Kaisers* (*In the Kaiser's Name*), used elements of the Wilhelminian myth to bolster the image of the kaiser as a benevolent patriarch.

12. Journalists, such as Herman Lücke, prescribed the same self-criticism for the national organization of theater owners. In his report of a theater owners' national convention, "Kriegsfilme" ("War Films"), 21 January 1927, Lücke admonished them for criticizing French, English, and American films about World War I. Using a degree of sarcasm, he accused them of their own special brand of nationalism.

13. Only one article, "Die Technik des Glücks" ("The Technology of Happiness"), 5 September 1928, in which a *Vorwärts* reporter described a typical day of production in the Berlin-Staaken studios, had any encouragement for a grassroots movement by workers to develop their own alternative to mainstream cinema.

14. Peter Schumann discusses the cooperative effort in "'Aus der Waffenschmiede der SPD.' Zur sozialdemokratischen Filmarbeit in der Weimarer Republik," in *Erobert den Film!* 80–81. See also *FurAbiD* 2: 443.

15. Film-Oberprüfstelle No. 201 (Berlin, 18 March 1926), quoted in *FurAbiD* 2: 439–442.

16. See "Bericht von der Tonfilm-Propaganda-Autofahrt in den Bezirken Brandenburg, Halle, Pommern und Mecklenburg" ("Report from the Sound Film Propaganda Automobile Trip in the Districts of Brandenburg, Halle, Pommerania, and Mecklenburg"), *Monatliche Mitteilungen,* October/December 1930, 10, quoted in Schumann, 84.

17. For an evaluation of this scene, see the *Vorwärts* review (11 December 1928), quoted in Schumann, 81.

10. THE KPD AND FILM: THE DEFEAT OF LEFTIST RADICALISM, THE THEORY OF THE "SCHEMING" CAPITALIST FILM INDUSTRY, AND THE COMMUNIST RESPONSE FROM *PANZERKREUZER POTEMKIN* (*BATTLESHIP POTEMKIN*) TO PROMETHEUS

1. Ossip K. Flechtheim provides an excellent description of KPD policy and programs in *Die KPD in der Weimarer Republik;* see especially 191–247. See also Hermann Weber, *Die Wandlung des deutschen Kommunismus. Die Stalinisierung der KPD in der Weimarer Republik,* vol. 1; Günter Hortzschansky et al., *Ernst Thälmann. Eine Biographie,* 255–426; and Fowkes, 110–144. In 1928 the KPD shifted to the left again. I will discuss that shift in Chapter 15.

2. See Fähnders and Rector, *Linksradikalismus und Literatur,* vol. 2; Zammito, 81–112; and Johanna Rosenberg, "Die Linke und das Ende der revolutionären Nachkriegskrise," in *Literaturdebatten,* 234–235.

3. The Verlag für Literatur und Politik in Berlin published Frida Rubiner's translation of Trotsky's essays and distributed it in Germany later in 1924. It soon became the topic of many articles and public discussions.

4. See Leon Trotsky, *Literature and Revolution,* trans. Rose Strunsky, 197.

5. See Trotsky, 185. Here Trotsky contradicts himself. His definition of culture as a phenomenon that "embraces and penetrates all fields of human work" (202) implies that the proletariat's military, political, and economic work, etc., should be considered elements of its culture. Trotsky admits this at one point by asserting: "our proletariat has a political culture, within limits sufficient to secure its dictatorship, but it has no artistic culture" (203). His claim evokes the suspicion that when Trotsky refers to cultural construction, in contrast to securing power and accumulating a surplus, he actually means artistic culture. At least during the stage of proletarian transition, Trotsky seemed content to uphold the separation of art and everyday life, despite his claim that a primary goal of the proletarian revolution should be to overcome the separation (see 11).

6. The series included three parts, "Ueber proletarische Kultur" ("On Proletarian Culture"), 31 May 1925, "Proletarische Kampfkultur" ("Proletarian Cultural Struggle"), 7 June 1925, and "Im Kampf mit welchen Elementen entwickelt sich eine proletarische Kultur?" ("In Conflict with Which Forces Does Proletarian Culture Develop?"), 21 June 1925. As outlined in Chapter 4, when Heinrich Lauffenberg, Karl Schröder, etc., founded the KAPD early in 1922, many radical intellectuals who supported and experimented with *Proletkult* concepts turned their attention away from the KPD and aligned themselves with the new party. Although the number of *Proletkult* proponents diminished after 1922, a few individuals, including Wittfogel and Karl Korsch, persisted with efforts to establish a theoretical foundation for a radically democratic proletarian culture.

7. While Wittfogel attacked Trotsky in *Die Rote Fahne,* a similar debate developed in the KAPD journal *Proletarier.* See Fähnders and Rector, *Linksradikalismus und Literatur* 2: 54–62; and Johanna Rosenberg, in *Literaturdebatten,* 267–271.

8. For a more detailed account, see Johanna Rosenberg, in *Literaturdebatten,* 362–378.

9. Willi Münzenberg in *Thesen und Resolutionen des XI. Parteitages der KPD in Essen,* quoted in Surmann, *Die Münzenberg-Legende,* 87.

10. Surmann has produced the most detailed account of the IAH and its media activity in *Die Münzenberg-Legende.* See also Helmut Gruber, "Willi Münzenberg's German Communist Propaganda Empire 1921–1933," *Journal of Modern History* 38.3 (1966): 278–297.

11. Cited by Johanna Rosenberg in *Literaturdebatten,* 393.

12. See *Blätter für Alle* 12 (1927), quoted in Surmann, 99.

13. *Die Rote Fahne* also accepted advertisements for a variety of films with no apparent restrictions. In addition to announcements about the success of *The Forge* (31 October 1924) and *Liberated People* (26 November 1925), an advertisement for Cecil B. De Mille's *The Volga Boatman,* distributed by Ufa, appeared on 25 September 1926.

14. See Alfred Durus, "Ein 'pazifisitischer' Film des französischen Imperialis-

mus. *Verdun"* ("A 'Pacifist' Film of French Imperialism: *Verdun"*), *Die Rote Fahne,* 7 July 1929.

15. *Die Welt am Abend,* which appeared for the first time in Berlin in 1926, grew to become one of the most widely distributed evening newspapers in Germany, with a circulation of almost 175,000 in 1928. It was so successful that the IAH experimented temporarily with a regional edition in the *Ruhrgebeit* and started a corresponding morning edition, *Berlin am Morgen,* in 1929.

16. See Heinz Willmann, *Geschichte der Arbeiter-Illustrierte-Zeitung 1921– 1938,* 34. The coverage of film in the *AIZ* was by no means as consistent or extensive as in *Die Rote Fahne, Die Welt am Abend,* and *Berlin am Morgen.* The occasional articles were usually one page in length, advertising a new Soviet or Prometheus film, and included more space for illustrations than for text. Only a handful of articles criticized the commercial film industry, and none of them did so in more detail than contributions to the other newspapers of the Communist press. See, for example, the excellent cartoon parody of commercial film genres in *AIZ* 9 (1929).

17. IAH newspapers also uncritically praised IAH films, but apparently with no reservations.

18. Sarcasm and blunt criticism were far more prevalent in *Die Rote Fahne.* Its critics apparently perceived their readers as committed opponents of the existing social order and likely to accept and even draw encouragement from biting critiques. The IAH newspapers displayed greater caution. However, they, too, paid little attention to the filmic techniques for influencing audience reception when criticizing mainstream historical films.

19. For a brief introduction to Eisenstein, Pudovkin, and their aesthetic differences, see Toeplitz, 1: 299–341.

20. For a thought-provoking philosophical and historical explanation of the KPD's strategy during the years of relative stability and its position in the development of Comintern policy between 1918 and 1934, see Russel Jacoby, *The Dialectic of Defeat.* Jacoby argues that orthodox Marxists in the Weimar Republic uncritically embraced enlightenment concepts of science and progress. As a result, he asserts, they developed a cult of success, exaggerating their victories, drawing attention away from mistakes, and, in the process, inhibiting the development of a radically democratic Marxism which would have nurtured critical skills.

21. For an excellent example, see "Sturm über Asien" ("Storm over Asia"), *Die Rote Fahne,* 8 January 1929.

22. Reprinted in Lüdecke, 75–105. Here, 105.

23. See "Rundschreiben von Herbst 1928 . . ." ("Flyer from Fall 1928 . . ."), cited in *FurAbiD* 2: 227–228.

24. For a detailed history of Prometheus, see Meier, "Materialien zur Geschichte der Prometheus Film-Verleih und Vertriebs-GmbH. 1926–1932" ("In-

formation on the History of the Prometheus Film-Verleih und Vertriebs-GmbH: 1926–1932"), *Deutsche Filmkunst.*

25. See Reichskommissar für Überwachung der öffentlichen Ordnung, 3543/ 26A, Berlin, 28 April 1926 (DZA Potsdam, Reichsministerium des Innern, No. 13511).

26. For more detailed information on the initial reception of the film in the Soviet Union, see Yon Barna, *Eisenstein*, 102–104.

27. According to a report in *Der Film* (23 May 1926, 16), 210 theaters—in Berlin alone—had booked the film!

28. According to Kurt Grimm, who represented Ufa in Leipzig and joined Prometheus in October 1926, Pfeiffer and Unfried had made costly mistakes in distributing *Battleship Potemkin*. He determined that their inadequate organization had enabled theater owners to cheat Prometheus out of tens of thousands of marks. See Kurt Grimm, "Zur Geschichte der Prometheus Film-Verleih und Vertriebs-GmbH" ("On the History of the Prometheus Film-Verleih und Vertriebs-GmbH").

29. Because Prometheus owned none of its own equipment and facilities, it depended completely on the willingness of commercial producers to rent it what was needed to produce films. In the case of *Superfluous People* it seems likely that the Phönix film company granted Prometheus access to its studios in exchange for the right to distribute the film. This is corroborated by Axel Eggebrecht in "Deutsch-russische Filmgemeinschaft" ("German-Russian Film Cooperative"), *AIZ* 21: 1926.

30. See letter from Prometheus (Emil Unfried) to Eisenstein dated 1 June 1926. Letter available in the holdings of the Stiftung Deutsche Kinemathek in West Berlin.

31. See Axel Eggebrecht, "German-Russian Film Cooperative." Eggebrecht asserted that difficulties with the censorship of *Battleship Potemkin* had motivated Prometheus to choose less provocative material. A letter from Prometheus to Sowkino dated 16 April 1926 indicates that Eggebrecht was correct. After describing the censorship difficulties, the letter states: "Above all it is necessary for us to acquire an equally good artistic film without a blatant political tendency."

32. For more detailed production information, see Grimm.

33. See letter from Edmund Meisel to Sergei Eisenstein date 5 July 1928. Letter available in holdings of the Stiftung Deutsche Kinemathek in West Berlin.

34. See, for example, Béla Balázs, "Der revolutionäre Film" ("The Revolutionary Film"), *Die Rote Fahne*, 10 October 1922; "Nur Stars!" ("Only Stars!"), *Filmtechnik* (Halle/Saale) 7, 1926; "Die Film-Krisis" ("The Film Crisis"), *Das Tagebuch* 18, 1928; and "Zur Kulturphilosophie des Films" ("On the Cultural Philosophy of Film"), *Das Wort* (Moscow) 3, 1938. All have been reprinted in Béla Balázs, *Essay, Kritik 1922–1932*, 71–74, 83–86, 105–109, and 148–177.

35. See Rudolf Schwarzkopf's account in "Abenteuer um Abenteuer" ("Adventure after Adventure"), *Film und Volk*, April 1928, 11.

36. See Meier, 2: 57, for an expression of this argument.

37. The review of *Eins + Eins = Drei* in *Der Film,* 10 December 1927, also suggests that the film is a parody.

38. At this point the Prometheus assimilation of commercial marketing techniques also included advertisements that incorporated excerpts from reviews and distributors' telegrams to interest theater owners and spectators.

39. See *Der Film,* 1 August 1927, for a descriptive review of *The Red Front Marches.*

40. Gerd Meier has outlined the history of Derussa in an unpublished article, "Notizen zur Geschichte der 'Derussa,' Deutsch-Russische Film-Allianz A.G. 1927–1929" ("Notes on the History of 'Derussa,' Deutsch-Russische Film-Alliance A.G. 1927–1929"). In addition to the Derussa agreement, the Soviet Trade Bureau negotiated an agreement between National Film und Wufku in 1928. See *Film-Kurier,* 2 February 1928.

41. For information about the historical figure and the developing legend, see *Schinderhannes,* ed. Manfred Franke.

42. See, for example, Clara Viebig, *Unter dem Freiheitsbaum* (1922) and Curt Elwenspoek, *Schinderhannes—ein rheinischer Rebell* (1925).

43. See reviews in *L.B.B.,* 2 February 1928, and in *Film-Kurier,* 2 February 1928.

44. For detailed information on reorganization and consequences for Prometheus, see "Prometheus-Meschrabpom-Rus," *L.B.B.,* 12 May 1928; and "Prometheus-Meschrapbom Kino?" *Film-Kurier,* 23 May 1928.

45. See *Filmblätter* of the Staatliches Filmarchiv der DDR, 23, quoted in *Film im Klassenkampf,* 13.

46. See Meier, "Notes on the History of 'Derussa,'" 5; and "Das Derussa Programm" ("The Derussa Program"), *L.B.B.,* 7 July 1928.

47. Prometheus also announced plans to produce an adaptation of Émile Zola's *Germinal,* but the film never appeared. See *Film-Kurier,* 2 August 1928; and the *L.B.B.,* 3 August 1928.

48. I will discuss the tendency in further detail in Chapter 15. Once again it seems appropriate to refer to Russel Jacoby and his focus on orthodox Marxism's preoccupation with science.

II. THE BIRTH OF THE VOLKSFILMVERBAND: PARTISAN NONPARTISANSHIP AND GRASS-ROOTS ORGANIZATION FROM ABOVE?

1. For more detailed information about the VFV, see Karl Tümmler, "Film und Volk," *Diplomarbeit im Fernstudium Geschichte* (1961), and "Zur Geschichte des Volksfilmverbandes," *Filmwissenschaftliche Mitteilungen* 5 (1964):

1224; and Richard Weber's introductions in *Film und Volk*, 5–27, and *Arbeiter-bühne und Film*, 5–23.

2. See "Rudolf Schwarzkopf . . . ," in *FurAbiD* 2: 244–248.

3. There was another possible reason for the VFV's interest in soliciting the involvement of artists and intellectuals: it wanted to maintain a nonpartisan image. Whatever the reason or reasons, the effect was the same.

4. See "Protokoll . . . ," in *FurAbiD* 2: 249–256.

5. A production team consisting of personnel from Sowkino and Prometheus filmed the second documentary, *Das Dokument von Shanghai* (*The Document from Shanghai*) during an expedition to China in 1927. Coincidentally, the team was in Shanghai at the time of the revolutionary uprisings in March 1927. In addition to documenting the terrible living conditions in that city, the members also had an opportunity to film the uprising. The film premiered in the Tauentzienpalast on 30 October 1928 and was significant also as the first film associated directly with the Volksfilmverband.

PART THREE: THE END OF THE WEIMAR REPUBLIC: 1929–1933

1. For an introduction to the political, economic, and social history of the period, see, among others, Arthur Rosenberg, *Geschichte der Weimarer Republik*, 183–211; Heiber, 196–276; Ryder, 252–282; and Craig, 524–568.

12. THE GREAT COALITION AND THE DISINTEGRATION OF PARLIAMENTARY DEMOCRACY

1. The SPD attempted to adjust to decreasing tax revenue and the loss of loan assistance from the United States. Its efforts focused on reallocating money from defense spending to social programs, renegotiating the terms of the Versailles Treaty, and increasing taxes. For a detailed account, see Breitman, 148–153.

2. For detailed descriptions of the relationship between the powerful interest groups of the right and the rise of National Socialism, see, among others, Karl Dietrich Bracher, *Die Auflösung der Weimarer Republik*, esp. 198–228 and 407–442; and David Abraham, *The Collapse of the Weimar Republic: Political Economy and Crisis*. Abraham's book has stimulated a heated controversy. See, for example, *American Historical Review* 88 (1983): 1143–1149. Despite the controversy, his perspective warrants serious consideration. In addition to criticizing the capitalist elite for its contribution to the unstable economy, many Germans, including members of the old agrarian sector, the artisan class, the small merchant class, as well as members of these groups who had become petty-

bourgeois bureaucrats or blue-collar workers, harbored at least a latent skepticism about capitalism, industrialization, urbanization. For a detailed account of Weimar Germany's dissatisfaction with "modern" society, see George L. Mosse, *The Crisis of German Ideology*, 237–317.

3. As Henry Turner has asserted, while most heavy industrialists and other members of the capitalist elite turned their backs on parliamentary democracy between 1928 and 1930, only some of them aligned themselves directly with the NSDAP and contributed financially. And many of those who did support the NSDAP directly, including Alfred Hugenberg, did so in the hope that they could use the National Socialists to defeat their republican and Marxist opponents. They hoped that the NSDAP would eventually falter and that they would be able to assume power. See Henry Turner, "Big Business and the Rise of Hitler," in *Nazism and the Third Reich*, 89–108.

4. For information about the KPD's political development between 1928 and 1933, see, among others, Flechtheim, 52–61 and 248–288; Hermann Weber, 1: 186–247; Hortzschansky et al., 427–644; and Fowkes, 145–171.

5. See, for example, the KPD's cooperation with the National Opposition in organizing a plebiscite to depose the Social Democratic coalition in Prussia in 1931, as outlined in Flechtheim, 277–278.

6. The National Socialists were able to attract large numbers of constituents from all social classes except from the ranks of the blue-collar workers. As George Mosse has noted: "Except for those who joined the Nazis at an early date (and these came largely from among the unemployed), the industrial workers were not attracted to the *Völkisch* movement, for it had little to offer them that was not at variance with a smooth functioning industrial society. A reversion to the idyllic estate system had little appeal for them" (*The Crisis of German Ideology*, 262–263).

7. Flechtheim notes that as the KPD under the leadership of Ernst Thälmann, Hermann Remmele, and Heinz Neumann intensified its allegiance to Stalin and the Comintern, it intensified the campaign to defend the Soviet Union and to present Soviet society as a model for development. See Flechtheim, 262–263.

8. For a more detailed account of this phenomenon, see Mosse, *Crisis*, 280–293.

9. George Mosse, *Masses and Man: Nationalist and Fascist Perceptions of Reality*, 2. Here Mosse describes a more general nationalism that influenced social development significantly throughout Europe beginning at the turn of the century. His comments apply extremely well also to the specific type of nationalism promoted by the NSDAP during the final years of the Weimar Republic.

10. This does not imply that Germany would abandon industrialization, urbanization, modernization. As Mosse asserts: "Nationalization did not seek to destroy the process of industrialization; on the contrary, it deliberately furthered it in order to increase the country's might and prosperity. But industrialization was kept subordinate to an anti-industrial ideology, treated as a technological

advance rather than as leading to a new perception of the world" (*Masses and Man*, 3). For more on this, see also Jeffrey Herf, *Reactionary Modernism: Technology, Culture, and Politics in Weimar and the Third Reich.*

11. Mosse discusses the fear of the "other," concentrating on anti-Semitism in *The Crisis of German Ideology*, 88–107 and 294–311. For a psychoanalytical discussion that traces the fear of the other to a specifically Wilhelminian variation of a pre-Oedipal complex, see Klaus Theweleit, *Männerphantasien*, esp. 1: 253–286 and 521–547.

13. SOUND, THE ECONOMIC CRISIS, AND COMMERCIAL FILM'S IMAGES OF THE PAST, PRESENT, AND FUTURE

1. Many film historians have outlined the development of sound film in Germany. Among others, see Olimsky, 162–168; Bächlin, 54–82; and Kalbus, 2: 8–16.

2. See, for example, Bundesarchiv Koblenz document R109, 1026a, 12 April 1927; and R109, 1026a, 2 September 1927.

3. For Ludwig Klitzsch's account of the process, see "Deutschland, das kommende Produktionszentrum Europas" ("Germany, the Future Production Center of Europe"), *L.B.B.*, 29 July 1930. Between 1926 and 1929 Warner Brothers had purchased rights from Western Electric to produce sound films, marketed a number of commercially successful films, including *Don Juan* (1926) and *The Jazz Singer* (1927), and recovered from near bankruptcy to become one of the leading film producers in the United States. By 1929 there was no market for silent films in the United States.

4. In 1930 the Dutch Küchenmeister concern controlled approximately 68 percent of Tobis, and a German bank consortium under the leadership of the Commerz- und Privatbank controlled about 30 percent. See Bächlin, 61.

5. Bächlin, 64–65. The Küchenmeister-Tobis-Klangfilm group attained control of the sound film markets in Germany, Holland, Austria, Hungary, Switzerland, Denmark, Sweden, Norway, Finland, Czechoslovakia, Yugoslavia, Bulgaria, Rumania, and Dutch India.

6. See Olimsky, 65; and Bächlin, 62–63.

7. Olimsky outlines the process in greater detail.

8. Bächlin estimates an increase of 25–33 percent. According to Bächlin (63), although the demand for silent films decreased rapidly after 1929, sound films accounted for only 32 percent of German film production as late as 1931, and the major German companies produced most of these. In contrast, 75 percent of all imported films (primarily from the United States) were sound films by 1931. The figures indicate that although a number of German companies continued to produce films, most of them concentrated on less expensive silent films. As the market changed, silent films generated a diminishing return and forced ever-

increasing numbers of German producers into dormancy or out of business. Olimsky suggests a similar development for the period of relative stability (12).

9. See Toeplitz, 2: 193.

10. See "Deutschland, das kommende Produktionszentrum Europas," *L.B.B.*, 29 July 1930.

11. See "Neue geistige Inhalte" ("New Spiritual Contents"), *L.B.B.*, 20 July 1932.

12. For a more detailed discussion of the effect the transition to sound and the economic crisis had on commercial film production in general, and specifically in Germany, see Bächlin, 54–82. A good example of a company's autocratic control over production during the period is the frequently cited case of *Der blaue Engel* (*The Blue Angel*, 1930). See Werner Sudendorf, *Marlene Dietrich*, 1: 69.

13. See Olimsky, 74–80, for a discussion of the struggle for journalistic independence between 1929 and 1931.

14. Conference report of the Spitzenorganisation der Deutschen Filmindustrie from 23 October 1930, quoted in Olimsky, 75.

15. "Auf dem Wege zum Ufa-Monopol" ("On the Way to an Ufa Monopoly"), *L.B.B.*, 14 September 1929. The *Arbeiterbühne und Film* outlined Emelka's development from an independent company to a part of the Hugenberg Concern in "Neuer Filmskandal in Deutschland" ("New Film Scandal in Germany"), 11 (1930): 21–23.

16. Articles, such as "Politisierung des Kinos" ("Politicizing Cinema"), *L.B.B.*, 26 October 1931; and "Das Kino: Ein Asyl Jenseits der Politik!" ("Cinema: A Refuge beyond Politics!"), *L.B.B.*, 25 April 1932, indicate that many critics persisted in their reliance on a modified concept of autonomous art. They favored entertainment and rejected any serious focus on current issues.

17. See the following representative articles for information about the film industry's requests for government assistance: "Steuersenkung um 50 percent gefordert" ("50 Percent Tax Decrease Demanded"), *L.B.B.*, 23 March 1931; "Film im Währungs-Chaos" ("Film in Currency Chaos"), *L.B.B.*, 10 October 1931; and "Deutsche Filmpolitik nach deutschen Interessen" ("German Film Policy According to German Interests"), *L.B.B.*, 9 May 1932. The German government responded to the request for production assistance, but not until 1933 when the National Socialist dictatorship had emerged and moved to control all forms of mass media. See Bächlin, 80.

18. For information about the censorship of the mentioned films, see "Der Fall Seeger" ("The Seeger Case"), *L.B.B.*, 23 March 1931, on *All Quiet on the Western Front* and *Into the Third Reich;* "Warum *Kuhle Wampe* verboten wurde" ("Why *Kuhle Wampe* Was Forbidden"), *L.B.B.*, 11 April 1932; and "Warum *Enthusiasmus* nicht-mehr zugelassen wird" ("Why *Enthusiasm* Is No Longer Permitted"), *L.B.B.*, 9 October 1931.

19. See Kracauer, *Caligari*, 216.

20. See Kalbus, 2: 25–32 and 79–84; and Kracauer, *Caligari*, 203–272. Additional genres included military farces, mountain films, and films about mysterious, often upper-class or even aristocratic criminals. They receive no special attention here because they have been treated adequately by film historians such as Kracauer and Toeplitz and promoted many of the same values present in the genres treated here.

21. The *Rowohlt Filmlexikon*, ed. Liz-Anne Bawden, 2: 449–450, provides information about the birth and development of Nero-Film. To the best of my knowledge, no one has published a study of Nero's unique contribution to Weimar cinema.

22. Kracauer, *Caligari*, 203–272, and Toeplitz, 2: 192–223, have outlined the ideological orientation of representative films from each of the most popular genres. The following discussion functions, therefore, only as the introduction which is necessary to provide a context for an analysis of the German left's responses to commercial film production during the period.

23. Kracauer has noted the emphasis (*Caligari*, 263), but he does not position the Prussian history films within the context of an ongoing ideological struggle between opposing economic and political interest groups. Instead of characterizing the films as products of interest groups associated with the most wealthy and influential members of the National Front—men who consciously used film to influence public opinion—Kracauer persists with his claim that commercial film only reflected the psychological dispositions of the collective mind.

24. For more detail, see Kracauer, *Caligari*, 269–270. The concept of the Frontsoldat as a model for the *Volksgemeinschaft* and its role in prefascistic culture have been investigated more in relationship to literature. See, for example, Karl Prümm, "Das Erbe der Front. Der antidemokratische Kriegsroman der Weimarer Republik und seine nationalsozialistische Fortsetzung," in *Die deutsche Literatur im Dritten Reich*, 138–164. A comprehensive study of World War I in the films of the Weimar Republic would be very valuable.

25. For more detailed analysis of this film, see, among others, B. Ruby Rich, "*Mädchen in Uniform:* From Repressive Tolerance to Erotic Liberation," *Jump Cut* 24/25 (March 1981): 44–50.

26. See Kracauer, *Caligari*, 227. *Maidens in Uniform*, as a critique of Prussian pedagogical techniques, suggests an interesting counterbalance to *The Blue Angel*. A comparison of the films and an investigation of the possible cause-and-effect relationship between them might be fruitful.

27. For plot summaries and interpretations, see Kracauer, *Caligari*, 232–235 and 239–242.

28. See Anthony Munson, "*Niemandsland*," in *Film and Politics in the Weimar Republic*, ed. Thomas Plummer et al., 75.

29. For a more detailed account, see Toeplitz, 2: 62–64.

30. Kracauer does not differentiate further. In reality the street films and Zille

films of the stable period upheld the myth only for those who had not yet become entrapped in the lumpen-proletarian quagmire of the street. Prodigal sons of middle-class families might be rescued, and philanthropic matrons might save unblemished children, but there was no hope for the majority of people who inhabited the dangerous street.

31. Wolfgang Gersch has provided the most detailed account of the film's production history. See *Film bei Brecht*, 48–97, esp. 58–71.

32. Jan Knopf succinctly describes Brecht's critique of traditional dramatic aesthetics and his concept of epic theater as an alternative in *Brecht Handbuch*, 378–424. Gersch discusses the adaptation of the epic theater concept to Brecht's work on the *Threepenny Opera* filmscript.

33. The company accused Brecht of failing to submit a segment of the script punctually and of intensifying the socially critical quality of the stage version. Brecht had been working on the script through the spring and summer of 1930, and he had made a number of changes that, among other things, more clearly identified Macheath's gangsters as members of the dominant classes in the twentieth-century capitalist societies and more directly suggested the need for social revolution. He had also integrated new songs, captions, and camera techniques to disrupt the film's illusion of reality and stimulate critical reception.

34. For an excellent and extremely detailed account of the experimentation with sound and the theoretical discussion about sound's effect on the film medium between 1929 and 1933, see Toeplitz, 2: 27–100. Toeplitz discusses the introduction of sound generally, but he also provides useful information about the specific development in Germany. Kalbus's discussion, although it concentrates specifically on German film, is by comparison somewhat superficial. See Kalbus, 2: 10–16.

35. A good example was Richard Oswald's adaptation of Zola's *Dreyfus* (1930), which had been successful as a drama in Berlin.

36. For a general discussion of the development toward what Toeplitz refers to as the audiovisual unit, see Toeplitz, 2: 83–100.

37. Wilhelm Thiele began to challenge the principles of authenticity in *The Three from the Gas Station* (1930), in which he integrated music into everyday situations without requiring an accompanying orchestra. See Toeplitz, 2: 61–62.

38. Toeplitz, 2: 98. Pabst's attitude demonstrates the continued influence of New Objectivity on German art. For a discussion of the role New Objectivity played in the artistic production of Weimar's final period, see John Willett, *Art and Politics in the Weimar Period*, 177–200, esp. 193–200.

39. For general information about *Comradeship*, see Toeplitz, 2: 211–213; and Kracauer, *Caligari*, 239–242.

40. Fritz Lang, M. *Cinemathek-Ausgewählte Filmtexte*, 18, quoted in Toeplitz, 2: 215.

14. THE SPD AND FILM: THE INTENSIFYING CRITIQUE OF POLITICAL REACTION IN COMMERCIAL FILM AND THE PARTY'S PROGRAM OF CINEMATIC PROPAGANDA

1. For general information about the SPD's developing film program, see Peter B. Schumann, "Aus der Waffenschmiede der SPD. Zur sozialdemokratischen Filmarbeit in der Weimarer Republik," in *Erobert den Film!* 81–85; and Hans-Michael Bock, "'Brüder zum Licht!' Kino, Film und Arbeiterbewegung," in *Arbeiterkultur in Hamburg: 1929–1933,* 298–316.

2. Heinrich Schulz, the president of the Sozialistischer Kulturbund, expressed the SPD's dedication to enlightenment progress and to the use of film for that purpose in an address to the national convention of the Sozialistischer Kulturbund in 1929. In the address "Film und Funk und ihre Bedeutung für die Arbeiterschaft" ("The Significance of Film and Radio for the Workers"), *Film und Funk. Sozialistischer Kulturtag in Frankfurt a.M. 28–29. Sept. 1929,* 9–14, Schulz explained: "Is it necessary to explain . . . the significance of film for the working class, now and in the future? The workers' movement wishes to conquer . . . the world. Not for the sake of order, rather to free itself from economic and intellectual subservience" (11).

3. See, for example, "Ein Volksroman wird Film" ("A People's Novel Becomes a Film"), *Vorwärts,* 9 October 1932. The review of *Gilgi, eine von uns,* an adaptation of Irmgard Keuner's novel about a stenographer, proclaims, "In the book as in the film, a remarkable document about the working girl of today— just as humane as it is realistic."

4. The *Vorwärts* reaction to Fridericus films such as *Das Flötenkonzert von Sanssouci* is a good example. In their attempt to discredit the films, *Vorwärts* editors published a number of articles, including "Das wahre Bild Friedrichs II" ("The True Image of Friedrich II"), 29 December 1930, in which renowned historians called into question the authenticity of the cinematic portrayal. Such critiques challenged the authority of the Fridericus films to supply a correct account of Prussian history, but they reinforced the belief in historical objectivity and the authority of experts to write history, i.e., to ascribe ideological meaning to the past for the masses.

5. See also "Hurra, das Wanderkino! Ein Bild von der Wahlpropaganda unserer Partei" ("Hurrah, the Traveling Movie Theater! A Depiction of Our Party's Election Propaganda"), *Vorwärts,* 26 July 1930.

6. See Hans Manfred Bock, 140. In October 1931 Anna Siemsen, August Siemsen, and other left-wing Social Democrats abandoned their efforts to challenge the party leadership and founded their own Sozialistische Arbeiterpartei Deutschlands. See also Hanno Drechsler, *Die Sozialistische Arbeiterpartei Deutschlands (SAPD). Ein Beitrag zur Geschichte der deutschen Arbeiterbewegung am Ende der Weimarer Republik,* 21–119.

7. The SPD published a report on the convention. See *Film und Funk.*

8. See Leo Kestenberg, "Tonfilm" ("Sound Film"), *Film und Funk,* 30–33; and Klaus Pringheim, "Filmmusik" ("Film Music"), *Film und Funk,* 34–38. Kestenberg described the development of sound reproduction very generally and indicated that it was too early to determine what effect sound would have on cinema. The guiding principle for an evaluation of the effect, he argued, should be the intellectual and sensual refinement of the German people. Kestenberg's orientation revealed his allegiance to an older generation of Social Democrats who promoted artistic autonomy and viewed interaction with art as an aesthetic activity. Klaus Pringheim criticized the film industry's inadequate attention to music. Without explaining precisely how film music should function, Pringheim demanded high standards of performance and implied that music could enhance the artistic quality of the medium.

9. In the final presentation, "Das neue Lichtspielgesetz" ("The New Film Censorship Law"), 39–45, Klara Bohm-Schuch outlined in detail the development of film censorship in the Weimar Republic and argued that ideologically conservative tendencies had grown even more prevalent in recent years. Bohm-Schuch supported Nestriepke's position, arguing that the SPD should participate more actively in shaping censorship policy to ensure that it could defend republican interests. Heinrich Schulz reinforced her proposal in the ensuing discussion.

10. The only other cultural activist in the SPD who approached Nestriepke's level of sophistication in the understanding of the existing cinematic codes was Alexander Gidoni. See "Wege zum proletarischen Film" ("Ways to Proletarian Film"), *Die Gesellschaft* 7 (1930): 54–68. Gidoni's essay was the only contribution on film to the SPD's theoretical journal during the final years of the Weimar Republic. Gidoni, like Nestriepke, described film's uniquely optical language and affirmed its use by filmmakers to influence audience reception. Gidoni looked to Soviet film for examples of proletarian film art and implied that similar developments in German film art would occur after a social revolution.

11. Schumann derives much of his information about the SPD's film program from the *Monatliche Mitteilungen* and suggests that the journal stimulated local activity. While Schumann's assertion seems correct, it only partially explains the journal's orientation and its methods.

12. As Schumann has noted (*Erobert den Film!* 84), only 15 percent of the almost 220 films distributed by the FuL in 1931 were SPD films.

13. Other animated campaign films included *Ins dritte Reich* (*Into the Third Reich*) and *Ritter von Kiekebusch kämpft um Preussen* (*Knight Kiekebusch Fights for Prussia*). Schumann suggests that the FuL produced animated films to criticize the SPD's political opponents without naming or portraying specific individuals and thus minimized the likelihood of censorship. The censors did prohibit *Into the Third Reich.* See "Zensur gegen Trickfilm" ("Censorship against Animated Film"), *Monatliche Mitteilungen,* April/May 1931. Their decision suggests either that the intended abstraction was inadequate or perhaps

that the SPD had succeeded in exposing the connections between National Socialism and heavy industry. In 1931 the governing parties attempted to conceal such connections.

14. See Schumann, in *Erobert den Film!* 85. Schumann uses the relatively neutral verb *erleichtern*, implying that the films made the SPD's analysis easier to understand for average German voters.

15. For more detailed information about the production and reception of *Brothers*, see Hans-Michael Bock, 308–309.

16. See Hans-Michael Bock, 308, for background information on Werner Hochbaum and his film production.

17. See Schumann, *Erobert den Film!* 83. The Rote Gewerkschafts-Opposition (RGO) emerged in November 1929 in opposition to what many KPD union members felt was a counterproductive and conciliatory approach to labor problems in the Allgemeiner Deutscher Gewerkschaftsbund (ADGB). Although *Brothers* appeared months before the RGO was founded, Schumann's account is very plausible. Long before they organized, the KPD opposition began to voice its discontent with the ADGB leadership.

18. It seems likely that Hochbaum used natural settings and nonprofessional actors to minimize production costs as well. The orientation of advertising and the narrative perspective suggest that his primary concern was to establish the authenticity of the filmic portrayal.

19. Plummer makes this point in his analysis of *Brothers*. See Plummer et al., *Film and Politics in the Weimar Republic*, 83.

15. THE KPD AND FILM: FROM STUBBORN PERSEVERANCE TO ELEVENTH-HOUR EXPERIMENTS WITH ALTERNATIVE FORMS OF PRODUCTION AND RECEPTION

1. For a detailed description of the BPRS and its activities, see Helga Gallas, *Marxistische Literaturtheorie*.

2. See *Literaturdebatten*, Nössig et al., 587.

3. Rolf Surmann has outlined very precisely the continued activities of the IAH between 1929 and 1933 (128–223). See also Gruber.

4. See, for an example, Thalheimer's preface to the Universum Bücherei edition of Franz Mehring's works from 1929. Thalheimer praised Mehring's materialist revision of the idealist components in Kant's aesthetics, foregrounded Mehring's concept of dialectical interdependence between aesthetic and socio-historical development, and asserted that the working class could produce no great works of art as long as a dominant imperialistic class exploited it. K. A. Wittfogel responded to such claims by renewing his campaign to demonstrate

that workers not only could, but already had begun to, develop their own culture in the process of class struggle.

5. For a comprehensive discussion of the debate within the KPD about a Marxist aesthetics during the final years of the Weimar Republic, see Manfred Nössig, "Das Ringen um Proletarisch-Revolutionäre Kunstkonzeptionen," in *Literaturdebatten*, 469–709. Nössig perpetuates the traditional images of Karl Korsch and K. A. Wittfogel as *Renegaten*, but he also criticizes the early fanaticism of Johannes R. Becher, favors Brecht's position in his debate with Lukács, and generally portrays socialist-realist and radically democratic tendencies in the development of Marxist aesthetics at the end of the Weimar era as equally useful (706). See also Fähnders and Rector, *Linksradikalismus und Literatur* 2: 207–223; and Zammito, 113–168.

6. See Nössig in *Literaturdebatten*, 518. In the preceding chapter Johanna Rosenberg outlines Becher's development to the beginning of Weimar's final phase; see 414–424.

7. See, for example, Becher's critique of Alfred Döblin's *Berlin Alexanderplatz*, "Einen Schritt weiter," printed in Johannes R. Becher, *Publizistik I. 1912–1938*, 224.

8. Nössig describes the orientation succinctly by outlining Lukács's position on literary forms of expression. See *Literaturdebatten*, 647–648.

9. For a more detailed analysis of Brecht's aesthetic models during the final years of the Weimar Republic, see Heinz Brüggemann, *Literarische Technik und soziale Revolution;* Reiner Steinweg, *Das Lehrstück;* and Jan Knopf, *Brecht Handbuch.*

10. It is interesting to note that instead of advocating stricter censorship of the films that they opposed, the Communist film journalists more often demanded the abolition of censorship.

11. See *FurAbiD* 2: 347–389 for a collection of Weltfilm memos and film lists. The documents provide an informative overview of the organization's approach to film distribution and its model for film events.

12. Dudow came to Berlin in 1922 and studied dramaturgy and filmmaking. In Berlin he aligned himself with the KPD and then spent a year studying in Moscow. Upon his return, he began directing documentary films before collaborating with Brecht on the *Kuhle Wampe* project in 1931–32. For more information about Dudow, see Hermann Herlinghaus, *Slatan Dudow.*

13. Gerd Meier, "Notizen zur Geschichte der 'Derussa,' Deutsch-Russische Film-Allianz A. G. 1927–1929."

14. See the report on Giltmann in *Der Film*, 9 November 1929.

15. For more detail on the difference between the stage and film versions, see Herbert Ihering's review in *Der Börsen-Courier*, 16 February 1929.

16. See the *Münchener Kommentar zum Bürgerlichen Gesetzbuch,* ed. Kurt Rebmann, 5: 604–606. I would like to thank Richter Hermann Noack of West Berlin for drawing my attention to this source.

17. Michael Hanisch has provided a foundation for my treatment of *Jenseits der Strasse*. See *Filmblätter*.

18. In her recent study of melodrama in Weimar cinema, *Joyless Streets,* Patrice Petro suggests that bourgeois men are not the sole focus of films such as *Tragedy of the Prostitute*. While it is true that an aging prostitute, Auguste, figures very prominently in that film, one might argue that her prominence is associated with her desire to become at least a lower-middle-class woman. I would argue that in many Weimar melodramas class difference and allegiance distinguish female figures at least as clearly as does gender.

19. As Thomas Plummer has noted, the montage sequence again recalls Eisenstein's narrative style in *Battleship Potemkin*. See Plummer et al., *Film and Politics in the Weimar Republic,* 65.

20. Willi Döll describes Tuscherer's management in a letter to Mr. Gero Gandert of the Stiftung Deutsche Kinemathek. I would like to thank Mr. Gandert for granting me access to the correspondence.

21. For more detailed information about the plot, see Margot Michaelis, "*Mutter Krausens Fahrt ins Glück*. Eine exemplarische Analyse," in Helmut Korte, ed., *Film und Realität in der Weimarer Republik,* 103–168; and *Mutter Krausens Fahrt ins Glück. Filmprotokoll und Materialien,* ed. Freund and Hanisch. See also Jan Christopher Horak, "*Mother Krause's Trip to Happiness,* Kino Culture in Weimar Germany, Part 2, 'Tenements Kill Like an Ax.'" *Jump Cut* 27 (July 1982): 55–56.

22. As Patrice Petro has noted (*Joyless Streets,* 150–152) the narrative makes a further distinction between the empowered Max and the relatively helpless Erna. The film valorizes patriarchal positions by associating social progress with Max's ability to assist Erna and her family.

23. For descriptions of the films, see Meier, "Materialien zur Geschichte der Prometheus Film-Verleih und Vertriebs-GmbH 1926–1932," *Deutsche Filmkunst* 5 (1962): 179–180 and 6 (1962): 221–222.

24. Meier discusses the reception of the films in *Deutsche Filmkunst* 7 (1962): 276–277 and 8 (1962): 310–311.

25. Erna (Meseke) Beier discussed her employment with Prometheus in a private interview with me in November 1981.

26. See the following *L.B.B.* reports: "Gerichtlicher Vergleich bei Prometheus" ("Bankruptcy Proceeding for Prometheus"), 17 December 1931; "Stürmischer Prometheus Versammlung" ("Stormy Prometheus Meeting"), 20 January 1932; and "Prometheus beantragt Konkurs" ("Prometheus Files for Bankruptcy"), 8 February 1932.

27. Taken from the interview with Erna (Meseke) Beier. She reported that, during one of their conversations, Dudow asked her to explain her activity with the Communist-led Fichte Sport Club.

28. For a concise discussion of Brecht's *Lehrstücktheorie,* see Knopf, 422–424.

29. For a more detailed outline of the production history of *Kuhle Wampe,* see

Bertolt Brecht, *Kuhle Wampe. Protokoll des Films und Materialien,* ed. Wolfgang Gersch and Werner Hecht, 171–179; and Gersch, 101–139. See also Reinhold Happel's analysis of the film in *Film und Realität in der Weimarer Republik,* 169–212.

30. "We grew increasingly certain that the process of organizing the production was an essential component of the aesthetic work. That was only possible because the process in its totality was political" (Bertolt Brecht, *Schriften zum Theater,* 243).

31. See, for example, Brecht's description of the relationship to Tobis-Melofilm in Brecht, *Kuhle Wampe,* 89–91.

32. Hanns Eisler, "Funktion und Dramaturgie (der Filmkunst)," in Brecht, *Kuhle Wampe,* 97–99.

16. THE INEVITABLE DECLINE OF THE VFV

1. Leo Lania, "Hunger im Kohlenrevier" ("Hunger in the Coaling Region"), *Film und Volk,* April 1929, 2. His references to the film as the unifying of documentary and feature indicated a desire to convince audiences that the portrayal was authentic and more trustworthy than those of the commercial films. Although he solicited the active participation of workers, Lania's primary intention was to increase the film's authenticity.

2. See, for example, *L.B.B.,* 3 May 1929.

3. For two differing accounts of the transition, see *Film und Volk,* 16–18; and Tümmler, "Film und Volk," *Diplomarbeit,* 81–114.

4. For a substantial collection of documents explaining the goals of IfA's film department, see *FurAbiD* 2: 390–407.

5. It is interesting to note how a patriarchal perspective is valorized here by a female critic. Sand suggests that the relationship between the husband and wife is similar to that between the parent and child. The juxtapositions also suggest that the male perspective, in contrast to those of the wife and child, is that from which sensory experience can be organized intellectually. For more information about the degree to which Weimar culture generally valorized intellectual activity and associated it with the male perspective, see Petro.

6. For information about the agitprop movement, see, among others, Friedrich Wolfgang Knellesen, *Agitation auf der Bühne,* 271–292.

CONCLUSION

1. Max Horkheimer and Theodor Adorno, "The Culture Industry: Enlightenment as Mass Deception," in *Dialectic of Enlightenment,* trans. John Cumming, 120–167.

2. Their emphasis on capitalism's influence on the quality of cinema is evident from the outset: "Yet city housing projects designed to perpetuate the individual as a supposedly independent unit in a small hygienic dwelling make him all the more subservient to his adversary—the absolute power of capitalism" (120).

3. Horkheimer and Adorno, 124–136. It is interesting that Horkheimer and Adorno introduced their concept of standardization at approximately the same time Bächlin employed the concept in his description of cinema's quality as a commodity. There are many similarities between Horkheimer and Adorno's assessment and Bächlin's.

4. See, for example, their assessment of consumer needs: "The stronger the positions of the culture industry become, the more summarily it can deal with consumers' needs, producing them, controlling them, disciplining them, and even withdrawing amusement" (144). Horkheimer and Adorno did posit the concept of autonomous art as a progressive alternative to the culture industry's activity, and Adorno, especially, vacillated between skepticism and moderate optimism about the possibilities for subversive cultural activity, but their positions remained for the most part pessimistic.

5. My investigation to a large extent corroborates the claims of Oskar Negt and Alexander Kluge about the Communist left's attempts to establish a proletarian public sphere. See their *Öffentlichkeit und Erfahrung: Zur Organisationsanalyse von bürgerlicher und proletarischer Öffentlichkeit*, especially 341–355 and 384–405.

BIBLIOGRAPHY

OFFICIAL DOCUMENTS

Bericht über die Verhandlungen des XI. Parteitages der Kommunistischen Partei Deutschlands (Sektion der Kommunistischen Internationale). Essen, vom 2.– 7. März 1927. Berlin, 1927.

Das Jahrbuch der Sozialdemokratie. Berlin, 1927.

Records and correspondence of the Reichsministerium des Innern, "Reichskommissar zur Überwachung der öffentlichen Ordnung," selected by and in the possession of the Staatliches Filmarchiv der DDR, Berlin.

Sozialdemokratischer Parteitag 1925 in Heidelberg. Protokoll mit dem Bericht der Frauenkonferenz. Berlin, 1925.

Thesen und Resolutionen des XI. Parteitages der Kommunistischen Partei Deutschlands (Sektion der Kommunistischen Internationale). Essen, vom 2.– 7. März 1927. Berlin, 1927.

Vorstandsprotokolle. Records and correspondence of the Universum Film A.G. (Ufa) package number R109 (Bundesarchiv Koblenz). Records of the business operations of Ufa during the 1920s.

PERSONAL SOURCES

Correspondence between Willi Döll and Gero Gandert. Stiftung Deutsche Kinemathek, West Berlin.

Correspondence between Prometheus and Sergei Eisenstein. Staatliches Filmarchiv der DDR, Berlin, GDR.

Correspondence between Edmund Meisel and Sergei Eisenstein, 1926–1928. Stiftung Deutsche Kinemathek, West Berlin.

Interview with Erne (Meseke) Beier (Prometheus executive secretary) in Berlin, GDR, November 1981.
Interview with Gerhard Bienert (actor) in West Berlin, May 1982.
Interview with Babette Gross (Willi Münzenberg's closest friend) in Munich, August 1978.
Interview with Carl Junghans (editor and director) in Munich, August 1978.
Interview with Hertha Thiele (actress) in Berlin, GDR, March 1982.
Interview with Ilse Trautschold in West Berlin, May 1982.

NEWSPAPERS, MAGAZINES, AND JOURNALS

Arbeiterbühne und Film (1930–1931).
Arbeiter-Illustrierte-Zeitung (1925–1933).
Berlin am Morgen (1929–1933).
Berliner Lokal-Anzeiger (1926–1933).
Blätter für Alle (1926–1929; in 1929 the name changed to *Magazin für Alle*).
Der Börsen-Courier (1929).
8-Uhr Abendblatt (1926–1933).
Eulenspiegel (1928–1931).
Der Film (1926–1933).
Film-Kurier (1925–1933).
Film Journal (1927).
Filmtechnik (1926).
Film und Volk (1929–1930).
Die Film-Welt (1929–1933).
Die deutsche Filmzeitung (1929).
Die Gesellschaft (1924–1933).
Die Glocke (1924).
Die Hamburger Volkszeitung (1929).
Illustrierter Film-Kurier (1925–1933).
Internationale Presse-Korrespondenz (1923).
Jungsozialistische Blätter (1926).
Kinematograph (1918–1933).
Lichtbild-Bühne (1918–1933; in 1926 the name changed to *Licht Bild Bühne*).
Die Linkskurve (1929–1933).
Magazin für Alle (1929–1933).
Moderne Kinematographie (1920).
Monatliche Mitteilungen (1929–1933).
Die Neue Zeit (1895–1924; beginning in 1924, *Die Gesellschaft*, 1924–1933).
Proletarier (1924–1927).
Das Reichsfilmblatt (1929–1933).
Die Rote Fahne (1918–1933).

Der Sozialdemokrat (1919).
Sozialistische Bildung (1929).
Die Sozialistische Film-Kritik (1930–1931).
Das Tagebuch (1928).
Ufa-Wochenmagazin (1929–1933).
Vorwärts (1918–1933).
Die Welt am Abend (1926–1933).

BOOKS AND ARTICLES

There are a number of good, although somewhat outdated, sources for information about studies on Weimar cinema. See, especially: Hans Traub, *Das deutsche Filmschrifttum,* ed. Lehrschau der Ufa (Leipzig: K. W. Hiersemann, 1940); Siegfried Kracauer, *From Caligari to Hitler* (Princeton: Princeton University Press, 1947); Dieter Prokop, *Soziologie des Films* (Neuwied and Berlin: Luchterhand, 1970); and Paul Monaco, *Cinema and Society* (New York: Elsevier, 1976).

Abendroth, Wolfgang. *Aufstieg und Krise der deutschen Sozialdemokratie.* 4th expanded ed. Köln: Pahl-Rugenstein, 1978.
Abraham, David. *The Collapse of the Weimar Republic: Political Economy and Crisis.* Princeton: Princeton University Press, 1981.
Altenloh, Emilie. *Zur Soziologie des Kinos: Die Kino-Unternehmung und die sozialen Schichten ihrer Besucher.* Jena: Eugen Diedrichs, 1914. Reprinted in facsimile by Medienladen, Hamburg, 1977.
American Historical Review 88 (1983): 1143–1149.
Angress, Werner. *Stillborn Revolution: The Communist Bid for Power in Germany, 1921–1923.* Princeton: Princeton University Press, 1963.
Arbeiterbühne und Film. 1930–1931. Reprinted with an introduction by Richard Weber. Köln: Verlag Gaehme Henke, 1974.
Atwell, Lee. *G. W. Pabst.* Boston: Twayne, 1977.
Bächlin, Peter. *Der Film als Ware.* Frankfurt a.M.: Fischer, 1975.
Balázs, Béla. *Essay, Kritik 1922–1932.* Edited by Gertraude Kühn, Manfred Lichtenstein, Eckart Jahnke. Berlin, GDR: Staatliches Filmarchiv der DDR, 1973.
Barna, Yon. *Eisenstein.* Bloomington: Indiana University Press, 1966.
Bathrick, David, et al., eds. Special Issue on Weimar Film Theory. *New German Critique* 40 (Winter 1987).
Becher, Johannes R. *Publizistik I. 1912–1938.* Berlin, GDR: Aufbau, 1977.
Beiträge zur deutschen Filmgeschichte. Edited by Horst Schneider, Hans Lohmann, and Heinz Baumert. Berlin, GDR: Deutsche Hochschule für Film und Fernsehen, 1964.

Berlau, Joseph. *The German Social Democratic Party 1914–1921.* New York: Columbia University Press, 1949.

Bernhard, Ludwig. *Der Hugenberg-Konzern. Psychologie und Technik einer Großorganisation der Presse.* Berlin: Julius Springer, 1928.

Bock, Hans Manfred. *Geschichte des 'linken Radikalismus' in Deutschland. Ein Versuch.* Frankfurt a.M.: Suhrkamp, 1976.

Bock, Hans-Michael. "'Brüder zum Licht!' Kino, Film und Arbeiterbewegung." In *Arbeiterkultur in Hamburg: 1929–1933,* 298–316. Hamburg, 1981–1982.

Bogdanov, A. A. *Die Kunst und das Proletariat.* Translated by Gr. Jarcho. Leipzig: Wolgast, 1919.

Bracher, Karl Dietrich. *Die Auflösung der Weimarer Republik.* Stuttgart and Düsseldorf: Ring, 1957.

Braulich, Heinrich. *Die Volksbühne.* Berlin, GDR: Henschel, 1974.

Brauneck, Manfred. *Die Rote Fahne.* Munich: Wilhelm Fink, 1973.

Brecht, Bertolt. *Kuhle Wampe. Protokoll des Films und Materialien.* Edited by Wolfgang Gersch and Werner Hecht. Frankfurt a.M.: Suhrkamp, 1969.

———. *Schriften zum Theater.* Edited by Werner Hecht. Berlin, GDR: Henschel, 1964.

Breitman, Richard. *German Socialism and Weimar Democracy.* Chapel Hill: University of North Carolina Press, 1981.

Brennicke, Ilona, and Joe Hembus, eds. *Klassiker des deutschen Stummfilms. 1910–1930.* Munich: Goldman, 1983.

Brüggemann, Heinz. *Literarische Technik und soziale Revolution.* Reinbeck bei Hamburg: Rowoholt, 1973.

Bürger, Peter. "Institution Literatur und Modernisierungsprozeß." In *Zum Funktionswandel der Literatur,* edited by Peter Bürger, 9–32. Frankfurt a.M.: Suhrkamp, 1983.

Conradt, Walter. *Kirche und Kinematograph.* Berlin, 1910.

Craig, Gordon. *Germany 1865–1945.* New York: Oxford University Press, 1978.

Crouch, Garland Eugene. *The Theory and Practice of A. A. Bogdanov's Proletcult.* Ann Arbor, Mich.: University Microfilms, 1974.

Drechsler, Hanno. *Die Sozialistische Arbeiterpartei Deutschlands (SAPD). Ein Beitrag zur Geschichte der deutschen Arbeiterbewegung am Ende der Weimarer Republik.* Meisenheim am Glan: Hain, 1965.

Drucker, Samuel. "Das Kinoproblem und unsere politischen Gegner." *Die Neue Zeit,* 6 March 1914: 867–872 and 13 March 1914: 907–912.

Ehrenburg, Ilja. *Die Traumfabrik.* Translated by Rudolf Selke. Berlin: Malik, 1931.

Eisner, Lotte. *L'Ecran demoniaque.* Paris: Collection Encyclopédie du Cinéma, Editions André Bonne, 1952; *Die dämonische Leinwand. Die Blütezeit des deutschen Films.* Wiesbaden-Biebrich: Verlagsgesellschaft Feldt & Co., 1965;

The Haunted Screen: Expressionism in German Cinema and the Influence of Max Reinhardt. Translated by Roger Greaves. Berkeley and Los Angeles: University of California Press, 1969.

Elsaesser, Thomas. "Cinema—the Irresponsible Signifier, or 'The Gamble with History': Film Theory or Cinema Theory?" *New German Critique* 40 (1987): 65–89.

Elwenspoek, Curt. *Schinderhannes—ein rheinischer Rebell.* Stuttgart: Süddeutsches Verlagshaus, 1925.

Engels, Sybille. "Der Film im Propagandaverständnis deutscher Parteien in der Weimarer Republik." *Magisterarbeit,* Ludwigs-Maximilian-Universität, Munich, 1983.

Erobert den Film! Proletariat und Film in der Weimarer Republik. Edited by Die Neue Gesellschaft für Bildende Künste (NGBK) and Die Freunde der deutschen Kinemathek e.V. West Berlin: NGBK, 1977.

Evans, Richard. *The Politics of Everyday Life.* Totowa, N.J.: Barnes & Noble, 1982.

Fähnders, Walter, and Martin Rector. *Linksradikalismus und Literatur.* 2 vols. Reinbeck bei Hamburg: Rowohlt, 1974.

———. *Literatur im Klassenkampf. Zur proletarisch-revolutionären Literaturtheorie 1919–1923.* Munich: Hanser, 1971.

Feuchtwanger, Lion. *Erfolg.* Berlin: Keipenheuer, 1930. For an English translation, see *Success.* Translated by Willa and Edwin Muir. New York: Literary Guild, 1930.

Filmblätter. Berlin, GDR: Staatliches Filmarchiv der DDR, 1971.

Film im Klassenkampf—zu den Traditionen proletarischer Filmbewegung in Deutschland vor 1933. Berlin, GDR: Staatliches Filmarchiv der DDR, 1973.

Film und Funk. Sozialistischer Kulturtag in Frankfurt a.M. 28.–29. Sept. 1929. Berlin: Sozialistischer Kulturbund, 1929.

Film und revolutionäre Arbeiterbewegung in Deutschland 1918–1932 (FurAbiD). Edited by Gertraude Kühn, Karl Tümmler, and Walter Wimmer. 2 vols. Berlin, GDR: Henschel, 1975.

Film und Volk. 1928–1930. Reprinted with an introduction by Richard Weber. Köln: Verlag Gaehme Henke, 1975.

Flechtheim, Ossip K. *Die KPD in der Weimarer Republik.* 2d ed. Frankfurt a.M.: Europäische Verlagsanstalt, 1976.

Förster, Franz. "Das Kinoproblem und die Arbeiter." *Die Neue Zeit,* 26 December 1913: 483–487.

Fowkes, Ben. *Communism in Germany under the Weimar Republic.* New York: St. Martin's, 1984.

Frank, Joseph. "Der Film von heute." *Die Neue Zeit,* 10 October 1919: 40–44.

Fromm, Erich. *The Working Class in Weimar Germany.* Translated by Barbara Weinberger. Edited by Wolfgang Bonss. Cambridge, Mass.: Harvard University Press, 1984.

Fülberth, Georg. *Proletarische Partei und bürgerliche Literatur. Auseinandersetzungen in der deutschen Sozialdemokratie der II. Internationale über Möglichkeiten und Grenzen einer sozialistischen Literaturpolitik.* Neuwied and Berlin: Luchterhand, 1972.

Furian, Heinz J. "Zwischen 'Caligarismus' und Realismus. Ein Beitrag zur kritischen Darstellung der deutschen Filmgeschichte." *Deutsche Filmkunst* 1–4 (1957): 9–13, 41–45, 81–84,107–109; and 1–3 (1958): 14–19, 50–53, 79.

Gallas, Helga. *Marxistische Literaturtheorie.* Neuwied and Berlin: Luchterhand, 1971.

Germany in the Twenties: The Artist as Social Critic. Edited by Frank Hirschbach et al. New York: Holmes and Meier, 1982.

Gersch, Wolfgang. *Film bei Brecht.* Berlin, GDR: Henschel, 1975.

Gessler, Otto. "Affäre Lohmann—Ein Kapitel für sich." In *Reichswehrpolitik in der Weimarer Zeit,* edited by Kurt Sendtner, 443–457. Stuttgart: Deutsche Verlagsanstalt, 1958.

Geyer, Curt. *Drei Verderber Deutschlands.* Berlin: JHW Dietz, 1924.

Gidoni, Alexander. "Wege zum proletarischen Film." *Die Gesellschaft* 7 (1930): 54–68.

Goertz, Heinrich. *Erwin Piscator in Selbstzeugnissen und Bilddokumenten.* Reinbeck bei Hamburg: Rowohlt, 1974.

Gorbunow, Wladimir. *Lenin und der Proletkult.* Translated by Ullrich Kuhirt and Ruth Czichon. Berlin, GDR: Dietz, 1979.

Gorson, Peter, and Eberhard Knödler-Bunte. *Proletkult.* Stuttgart-Bad Cannstadt: Frohmann-Holzboog, 1974.

Grebing, Helga. *Geschichte der deutschen Arbeiterbewegung.* Munich: Nymphenburger, 1966.

Grimm, Kurt. "Zur Geschichte der Prometheus Film-Verleih und Vertriebs-GmbH." Manuscript. Staatliches Filmarchiv der DDR.

Gruber, Helmut. "Willi Münzenberg's German Communist Propaganda Empire 1921–1933." *Journal of Modern History* 38.3 (1966): 278–297.

Guttsman, Wilhelm L. *The German Social Democratic Party, 1875–1933.* London and Boston: Allen & Unwin, 1981.

Habermas, Jürgen. *Strukturwandel der Öffentlichkeit.* Neuwied and Berlin: Luchterhand, 1962.

Hagemann, Peter A. *Reichsfilmgesetze von 1895–1945.* West Berlin, 1967.

Hansen, Miriam. "Early Silent Cinema: Whose Public Sphere?" *New German Critique* 29 (Spring/Summer 1983): 147–184.

Heiber, Helmut. *Die Republik von Weimar.* Munich: Deutscher Taschenbuch Verlag, 1966.

Herf, Jeffrey. *Reactionary Modernism: Technology, Culture, and Politics in Weimar and the Third Reich.* New York: Cambridge University Press, 1984.

Herlinghaus, Hermann. *Slatan Dudow.* Berlin, GDR: Henschel, 1965.

Hoffman, Ludwig, and Daniel Hoffmann Ostwald. *Deutsches Arbeitertheater 1918–1933.* 2 vols. Berlin, GDR: Henschel, 1977.

Horak, Jan Christopher. "*Mother Krause's Trip to Happiness,* Kino Culture in Weimar Germany, Part 2, 'Tenements Kill Like an Ax.'" *Jump Cut* 27 (July 1982): 55–56.

Horkheimer, Max, and Theodor Adorno. *Dialectic of Enlightenment.* Translated by John Cumming. New York: Herder and Herder, 1972.

Hortzschansky, Günter, et al. *Ernst Thälmann. Eine Biographie.* Berlin, GDR: Dietz, 1979.

Huaco, George. *The Sociology of Film Art.* New York: Basic Books, 1965.

Jacoby, Russel. *The Dialectic of Defeat.* Cambridge: Cambridge University Press, 1981.

Jansen, Peter, and Wolfram Schütte, eds. *Film in der DDR.* Munich: Hanser, 1977.

Jason, Alexander. *Jahrbuch der Filmindustrie.* Berlin, 1928.

Joachin, Hans. "Romane aus Amerika." *Die Neue Rundschau* 2 (1930): 398.

Jung, Franz. *Der Weg nach Unten.* Neuwied and Berlin: Luchterhand, 1961.

Kaes, Anton. "The Debate about German Cinema: Charting a Controversy (1919–1929)." Translated by David J. Levin. *New German Critique* 40 (Winter 1987): 7–33.

———. *Kino-Debatte. Texte zum Verhältnis von Literatur und Film 1909– 1929.* Tübingen: Niemeyer, 1978.

Kalbus, Oskar. *Vom Werden deutscher Filmkunst.* 2 vols. Altona-Bahrenfeld: Cigaretten-bilderdienst, 1935.

Kautsky, Karl. *Die materialistische Geschichtsauffassung.* 2 vols. Berlin: JHW Dietz, 1927.

Kerschenzev, Platon M. *Das schöpferische Theater.* Hamburg: C. Hoym, 1922.

Keun, Irmgard. *Gilgi, eine von uns.* Berlin: Universitas, 1931.

Kleinberg, Alfred. *Die deutsche Dichtung in ihren sozialen, zeitlichen und geistesgeschichtlichen Bedingungen.* Berlin: JHW Dietz, 1927.

Klenke, Dietmar. *Die SPD-Linke in der Weimarer Republik.* Münster: Litverlag, 1983.

Kleye, Herbert. "Film und Lichtbild im Dienste der deutschen Arbeiterbewegung 1919–1933." *Deutsche Filmkunst* 1 (1956): 148–152.

Knelleson, Friedrich Wolfgang. *Agitation auf der Bühne.* Edited by Carl Niessen. Emsdetten: Lechte, 1970.

Knoll, A. "Die Theater- und Filmgewerkschaft der Zukunft." *Die Neue Zeit,* 28 February 1919: 521–525.

Knopf, Jan. *Brecht Handbuch.* Stuttgart: Metzler, 1980.

Korte, Helmut, ed. *Film und Realität in der Weimarer Republik.* Munich: Hanser, 1978.

Kracauer, Siegfried. *Die Angestellten.* In *Schriften,* edited by Karsten Witte, 1: 205–281. Frankfurt a.M.: Suhrkamp, 1971.

————. *From Caligari to Hitler: A Psychological History of German Film*. Princeton: Princeton University Press, 1947. For an unabridged German version, see *Von Caligari zu Hitler*. Vol. 2 of *Schriften*, edited by Karsten Witte. Frankfurt a.M.: Suhrkamp, 1979.

Kresse, Helmut. "Die Rolle des sowjetischen Films in der ideologischen Arbeit der KPD von 1922 bis 1933." Dissertation. Alexander von Humboldt Universität, Berlin, GDR, 1974.

Krieger, Ernst. *Der staatlich geförderte Propaganda- und Lehrfilm im Auslande. Aufgaben unserer Regierung*. Berlin: Ufa, 1919.

Kurtz, Rudolf. *Expressionismus und Film*. Berlin: Lichtbildbühne, 1926.

Lang, Fritz. *M. Cinemathek-Ausgewählte Filmtexte*. Edited by Enno Patalas. Hamburg: Marion von Schröder, 1963.

Lavallée, Monique. "Ideologievermittlung im Film—untersucht am Beispiel des deutschen expressionistischen Films der Weimarer Republik." Magisterarbeit. Freie Universität, West Berlin, 1983–84.

Lenin, V. I. *Collected Works*. Translated by Bernard Isaacs and Joe Feinberg. Edited by Julius Katzer. 23 vols. Moscow: Progress, 1964.

Leopold, John A. *Alfred Hugenberg: The Radical National Campaign against the Weimar Republic*. New Haven: Yale University Press, 1977.

Lidtke, Vernon. *The Alternative Culture: Socialist Labor in Imperial Germany*. New York: Oxford University Press, 1985.

Literaturdebatten in der Weimarer Republik. Edited by Manfred Nössig et al. Berlin, GDR: Aufbau, 1980.

Lüdecke, Willi. *Der Film in Agitation und Propaganda der revolutionären deutschen Arbeiterbewegung (1919–1933)*. West Berlin: Oberbaum, 1973.

Maehl, William. *The German Socialist Party: Champion of the First Republic, 1918–1933*. Philadelphia: American Philosophical Society, 1986.

Manvell, Roger, and Hermann Fraenkel. *The German Cinema*. New York: Praeger, 1971.

May, Lary. *Screening out the Past: The Birth of Mass Culture and the Motion Picture Industry*. New York: Oxford University Press, 1980.

Mehring, Franz. *Gesammelte Schriften und Aufsätze in Einzelausgaben*. Edited by Eduard Fuchs. 12 vols. Berlin: Soziologische Verlagsanstalt, 1929.

Meier, Gerd. "Materialien zur Geschichte der Prometheus Film-Verleih und Vertriebs-GmbH 1926–1932." *Deutsche Filmkunst* 1–8 (1962): 12–16, 57–60, 97–99, 137–140, 177–180, 221–224, 275–277, and 310–312.

————. "Notizen zur Geschichte der 'Derussa,' Deutsch-Russische Film-Allianz A.G. 1927–1929." Manuscript. Staatliches Filmarchiv der DDR.

Mertens, Eberhard. *Die großen Preußenfilme I: Produktion 1921–1932*. Vol. 5 of *Filmprogramme*. Hildesheim and New York: Olms, 1981.

Monaco, Paul. *Cinema and Society: France and Germany during the Twenties*. New York: Elsevier, 1976.

Moreck, Curt. *Sittengeschichte des Kinos*. Dresden: Paul Aretz, 1926.

Mosse, George. *Masses and Man: Nationalist and Fascist Perceptions of Reality.* New York: Howard Fertig, 1980.

———. *The Crisis of German Ideology.* New York: Grosset & Dunlap, 1964.

Münchener Kommentar zum Bürgerlichen Gesetzbuch. Edited by Kurt Rebmann. Munich: C. Beck'sche, 1978.

Münzenberg, Willi. *Erobert den Film, Winke aus der Praxis für die Praxis proletarischer Filmpropaganda.* Berlin, 1925.

Mutter Krausens Fahrt ins Glück. Filmprotokoll und Materialien. Edited by Rudolf Freund and Michael Hanisch. Berlin, GDR: Henschel, 1976.

Nebelthau, Otto. *Kapitän Thiele. Ein geschichtlicher Roman aus unseren Tagen.* Hamburg: Hanseatische Verlagsanstalt, 1929.

Negt, Oskar, and Alexander Kluge. *Öffentlichkeit und Erfahrung: Zur Organisationsanalyse von bürgerlicher und proletarischer Öffentlichkeit.* Frankfurt a.M.: Suhrkamp, 1972.

Olimsky, Fritz. "Tendenzen der Filmwirtschaft und deren Auswirkung auf die Filmpresse." Inaugural dissertation. Friedrich Wilhelm Universität, Berlin, 1931.

Pabst, Rudolf. "Die Bedeutung des Films als Wirtschafts- und Propaganda-Mittel." *Moderne Kinematographie* 1 (1920): 25–32.

Pannekoek, Anton. *Weltrevolution und Kommunistische Taktik.* Vienna: Abeiterbuchhandlung, 1920.

Petro, Patrice. *Joyless Streets: Women and Melodramatic Representation in Weimar Germany.* Princeton: Princeton University Press, 1989.

———. "Modernity and Mass Culture in Weimar: Contours of a Discourse on Sexuality in Early Theories of Perception and Representation." *New German Critique* 40 (1987): 115–146.

Petzet, Wolfgang. *Verbotene Filme. Eine Streitschrift.* Frankfurt a.M.: Societäts-verlag, 1931.

Plummer, Thomas, et al. "Conservative and Revolutionary Trends in Weimar Film." In *Germany in the Twenties: The Artist as Social Critic,* edited by Frank D. Hirschbach et al., 74–85. New York: Holmes and Meier, 1980.

———. *Film and Politics in the Weimar Republic.* New York: Holmes and Meier, 1982.

Preussen im Film. Edited by Axel Marquardt and Heinz Rathsack. Reinbeck bei Hamburg: Rowohlt, 1981.

Prokop, Dieter. *Soziologie des Films.* Neuwied and Berlin: Luchterhand, 1970.

———, ed. *Materialien zur Theorie des Films.* Frankfurt a.M.: Fischer, 1971.

Proletarische Kulturrevolution Sowjetrußland 1917–1921. Edited by Richard Lorenz. Munich: Deutscher Taschenbuch Verlag, 1969.

Prümm, Karl. "Das Erbe der Front. Der antidemokratische Kriegsroman der Weimarer Republik und seine nationalsozialistische Fortsetzung." In *Die deutsche Literatur im Dritten Reich,* edited by Horst Denkler and Karl Prümm, 138–164. Stuttgart: Reclam, 1976.

Rich, B. Ruby. "*Mädchen in Uniform:* From Repressive Tolerance to Erotic Liberation." *Jump Cut* 24/25 (March 1981): 44–50.

Rodenberg, Hans. *Hans Rodenberg—Protokoll eines Lebens.* Edited by Rolf Richter et al. Berlin, GDR: Henschel, 1980.

Rosenberg, Arthur. *Geschichte der Weimarer Republik.* Edited by Kurt Kersten. Frankfurt a.M.: Europäische Verlagsanstalt, 1961.

———. *Imperial Germany: The Birth of the German Republic 1871–1918.* Translated by Ian F. D. Morrow. Boston: Beacon, 1964.

Rowohlt Filmlexikon. Edited by Liz-Anne Bawden. 6 vols. Reinbeck bei Hamburg: Rowohlt, 1978.

Ryder, A. J. *Twentieth-Century Germany: From Bismarck to Brandt.* New York: Columbia University Press, 1973.

Schinderhannes. Edited by Manfred Franke. West Berlin: Klaus Wagenbach, 1977.

Schröder, Karl. *Vom Werden der neuen Gesellschaft.* Berlin: Verlag der KAPD, 1920.

Schweigert, Rudolf. "Proletarischer Film und bürgerliche Reaktion. Klassenkämpferische Auseinandersetzungen um die Zensur der Filme *Panzerkreuzer Potemkin* (1926) und *Kuhle Wampe* (1932)." Magisterarbeit. Freie Universität, West Berlin, 1975–76.

Seidl, Claudius. *Der deutsche Film der fünfziger Jahre.* Munich: Heyne, 1987.

Siemsen, Anna. *Parteidisziplin und sozialistische Überzeugung.* Berlin: Laubsche, 1931.

———. *Politische Kunst und Kunstpolitik.* Berlin: Laubsche, 1927.

Siemsen, August. *Anna Siemsen.* Frankfurt a.M.: Europäische Verlagsanstalt, 1951.

Silberman, Marc. "Industry, Text and Ideology in Expressionist Film." In *Passion and Rebellion: The Expressionist Heritage,* edited by Eric Bromer and Douglas Kellner, 374–383. New York: Universe Books, 1983.

Sowjetischer Dokumentarfilm. Edited by Wolfgang Klaue and Manfred Lichtenstein. Berlin, GDR: Staatliches Filmarchiv der DDR, 1967.

Steinweg, Reiner. *Das Lehrstück.* Stuttgart: Metzler, 1972.

Studien zur ideologischen Entwicklung der KPD 1919–1923. Edited by Werner Imig and Walter Kissljakow. Berlin, GDR: Dietz, 1981.

Stürmer, Michael. *Koalition und Opposition in der Weimarer Republik 1924–1928.* Düsseldorf: Droste, 1967.

Sudendorf, Werner. *Marlene Dietrich.* 2 vols. Munich: Hanser, 1978.

Surmann, Rolf. *Die Münzenberg-Legende. Zur Publizistik der revolutionären deutschen Arbeiterbewegung 1921–1933.* Köln: Prometh, 1982.

Swoboda, Stefan. "Zur theoretischen und praktischen Aneignung des Mediums Film durch die revolutionäre deutsche Arbeiterbewegung bis 1933 unter besonderer Berücksichtigung von *Mutter Krausens Fahrt ins Glück* (1929) und

'*Kuhle Wampe*' *oder Wem gehört die Welt* (1932)." Diplomarbeit. Johann Wolfgang von Goethe Universität, Frankfurt a.M., 1976.

Theweleit, Klaus. *Männerphantasien*. 2 vols. Frankfurt a.M.: Roter Stern, 1977. For an English translation, see *Male Fantasies*. Translated by Stephen Conway et al. Minneapolis: University of Minnesota Press, 1987–1989.

Toeplitz, Jerzy. *Geschichte des Films*. Translated by Lilli Kaufmann and Christiane Mückenberger. 4 vols. Berlin, GDR: Henschel, 1975–1978.

Traub, Hans. *Das deutsche Filmschrifttum*. Edited by Lehrschau der Ufa. Leipzig: K. W. Hersemann, 1940.

Trotsky, Leon. *Literature and Revolution*. Translated by Rose Strunsky. New York: International Publishers, 1925.

Tümmler, Karl. "Deutsche Arbeiterbewegung und nationaler Film." *Deutsche Filmkunst* 10 (1962): 379–385.

———. "Film und Volk." Diplomarbeit im Fernstudium Geschichte. Alexander von Humboldt Universität, Berlin, GDR, 1961.

———. "Zur Geschichte des Volksfilmverbandes." *Filmwissenschaftliche Mitteilungen* 5 (1964): 1224.

Turner, Henry. "Big Business and the Rise of Hitler." In *Nazism and the Third Reich*, edited by Henry Turner, 89–108. New York: Quadrangle, 1972.

Viebig, Clara. *Unter dem Freiheitsbaum*. Stuttgart: Deutsche Verlagsanstalt, 1923.

Wachenheim, Hedwig. "Filmkunst- und leid." *Die Neue Zeit* 10 (March 1923): 447–451 and 16 (March 1923): 475–479.

Wagner, Dr. *Das Bild- und Film-Amt und seine Aufgaben*. Berlin: Kriegspresseamt, 1917.

Weber, Hermann. *Die Wandlung des deutschen Kommunismus. Die Stalinisierung der KPD in der Weimarer Republik*. 2 vols. Frankfurt a.M.: Europäische Verlagsanstalt, 1969.

Weimarer Republik. Edited by Kunstamt Kreuzberg and the Institut für Theaterwissenschaft der Universität Köln. West Berlin and Hamburg: Elefanten, 1977.

Weinberg, H. G. *The Lubitsch Touch: A Critical Study*. New York: E. P. Dutton, 1968.

Willett, John. *Art and Politics in the Weimar Period*. New York: Pantheon, 1978.

Willmann, Heinz. *Geschichte der Arbeiter-Illustrierten Zeitung 1921–1938*. Berlin, GDR: Dietz, 1975.

Wollenberg, Hans H. *Fifty Years of German Film*. Translated by Ernst Sigler. London: Falcon, 1948.

Zaddach, Gerhard. "Der literarische Film. Ein Beitrag zur Geschichte der Lichtspielkunst." Inaugural dissertation. Breslau, Berlin: Druck von P. Funk, 1929.

Zamitto, John H. *The Great Debate: 'Bolshevism' and the Literary Left in Germany, 1917–1930*. New York: Peter Lang, 1984.

Zetkin, Clara. "Gegen das Kinowesen." *Der Sozialdemokrat*. Stuttgart, 11 December 1919.

Zimmerman, Karl. "Von Caligari bis heute." *Neue Deutsche Hefte* 53 (1958): 825.

Zsuffa, Joseph. *Béla Balázs: The Man and the Artist.* Berkeley and Los Angeles: University of California Press, 1987.

Zuckmayer, Carl. *Schinderhannes.* Berlin: Arcadia, 1927. Frankfurt a.M.: Fischer, 1981.

INDEX